Electrifying Europe

Foundation for the History of Technology & Aksant Academic Publishers
Technology and European History Series

Ruth Oldenziel and Johan Schot
(Eindhoven University of Technology)
Series Editors

The Technology and European History series seeks to present scholarship about the role of technology in European history in the nineteenth and twentieth centuries. The series focuses on how technical communities, nation-states, businesses, social groups, and other actors have contested, projected, performed, and reproduced multiple representations of Europe while constructing and using a range of technologies. The series understands Europe both as an intellectual construct and material practice in relation to spaces inside as well as outside Europe. In particular, the series invites studies focusing on Europe's (former) colonies and on the two new superpowers of the twentieth century: the United States of America and the Soviet Union. Interdisciplinary work is welcomed. The series will offer a platform for scholarly works associated with the Tensions of Europe Network to find their way to a broader audience. For more information on the network and the series, see: www.tensionsofeurope.eu

Books in series
1. Judith Schueler, *Materialising identity. The co-construction of the Gotthard Railway and Swiss national identity* (Amsterdam, June 2008)
2. Vincent Lagendijk, *Electrifying Europe. The power of Europe in the construction of electricity networks* (Amsterdam, August 2008)
3. Frank Schipper, *Driving Europe. Building Europe on roads in the twentieth century* (Amsterdam, September 2008)
4. Adri Albert de la Bruhèze and Ruth Oldenziel (editors), *Manufacturing technology: manufacturing consumers. The making of Dutch consumer society* (Amsterdam, Autumn 2008)

Foundation for the History of Technology
The Foundation for the History of Technology (SHT) aims to develop and communicate knowledge that increases our understanding of the critical role of technology in the history of the Western world. Since 1988 the foundation has been supporting scholarly research in the history of technology. This has included large-scale national and international research programs and numerous individual projects, many in collaboration with Eindhoven University of Technology. The SHT also coordinates the international research network Tensions of Europe: Technology and the Making of Europe. For more information see: www.histech.nl

Electrifying Europe

The power of Europe in the construction of electricity networks

Vincent Lagendijk

aksant
Amsterdam 2008

ISBN 978-90-5260-309-4
© 2008, Vincent Lagendijk

This publication is made possible by:
Fondation Électricité de France
Stichting Unger-Van Brerofonds
Foundation for the History of Technology

Design and typesetting: Ellen Bouma, Alkmaar, the Netherlands
Cover image: Copyright NASA, collection Visible Earth (http://visibleearth.nasa.gov/).

Aksant Academic Publishers, P.O. Box 2169, NL-1000 CD Amsterdam, The Netherlands, www.aksant.nl

Printed and bound by CPI Group (UK) Ltd, Croydon, CR0 4YY

Acknowledgements

Writing a Ph.D, dissertation is commonly viewed as a long and lonely activity. Indeed, I occasionally had troubles explaining to friends and family that spending six to eight hours a day poring over old papers, often several days in succession and away from home, can be interesting and entertaining. Yet on a daily basis I was hardly lonely. I had fruitful interactions with colleagues, as my dissertation project was a part of the research program *Transnational Infrastructures and the Rise of Contemporary Europe* (www.tie-project.nl). Conversations with Irene Anastasiadou, Sorinela Ciobica, and Suzanne Lommers have formed my thinking about my topic and source material. I particularly share many good memories with Frank Schipper; ranging from testing all the different cakes in the UN restaurant, and smelly cheeses in French freezers, to trying to finish our manuscripts in the New York Public Library. In Eindhoven our paths finally crossed, after living and studying in close proximity for quite some time. Alec Badenoch not only deserves credit for his editing work, but also for making me more aware of the importance of media in history.

My two supervisors, Johan Schot and Geert Verbong, were influential as well. Geert was in particular important for getting the project on the track in the first year, and has been a critical reader of draft chapters. Johan introduced me to history of technology, and inspired me about the TIE project. He was a great motivator towards the end of the writing process. Both deserve credit for giving me relative liberty in doing research, and for taking that back at the right moment. Erik van der Vleuten has been something of a shadow supervisor, and provided valuable opinions and feedback. My other colleagues of the Eindhoven University of Technology and the Foundation for the History of Technology made up an inspiring working environment. Lidwien Hollanders-Kuipers and Roeslan Leontjevas were indispensable for their practical assistance. I thank Thomas Lindblad and Jeroen Touwen for showing me the job advertisement, which I would otherwise have missed.

In 2004 the *Fondation Électricité de France* awarded me with a research grant, enabling me to expand the scope of my study. I thank them for their generous support, and in particular Yves Bouvier for his assistance on practical matters. I am

Image drawn by Alec Badenoch for the TIE project website.

grateful to the Society for the History of Technology (SHOT) for their financial support to visit annual meetings, and for naming me International Scholar for 2005-2007. SHOT as well as the *Tensions of Europe* network have been important places of interaction, where I could – so to speak – meet the people I read. I profited in particular from discussions with Arne Kaijser from practically the beginning of my project. At the *Tensions* summer school in Bordeaux, the enthusiasm of Christophe Bouneau gave me the indication that the book was progressing along. Tom Misa gave useful advice in a writing masterclass. I also benefited from the Ph.D, course of the Dutch N.W. Posthumus Institute, and my fellow participants. At the ESTER seminar in Brescia I received useful comments by Ben Gales and Peter Scholiers.

My research was done in a number of archives and libraries, and I am grateful to the helpful staff I encountered. I in particular wish to thank the following: Joceline Collonval of the Historical Archives of the European Commission, Françoise Peemans of the Belgian Diplomatic Archive, Anne-Marie Smith and Johannes Geurts at NATO Archives, and Frantisek Cahyna, Olivier Feix and Marcel Bial at UCTE. Special thanks go out to Bernhardine Pejovic (League of Nations Archives),

Esther Trippel-Ngai, Sylvie Carlon-Riera, and Maria Sanchez (all United Nations Geneva Archives). They made long stays in Geneva comfortable and entertaining. Several people were helpful in helping me to locate sources, including Waqar Zaidi, Liane Ranieri, Yves Berthelot, Jan-Anno Schuur, E. A. Tyurina, Stellan Andersson, Petr Veselký, and Marian Rose-Heineman. Walter Fremuth filled many voids I could not found answered by other sources. I very much enjoyed his hospitality during a two-day interview on the outskirts of Vienna, in close proximity to former East-West transmission lines.

My research has brought me to many places over the last years, but it always brought me home as well. Here, parents, parents-in-law, my brother, and my friends have always been supportive and helpful. But "home" was not only a comfortable place to work. It also was a place where science hardly mattered. Irma, later joined by Sander, are my connection to contemporary life, and brought me love and joy.

At home, history did not so much matter; only the future did. And it continues to do so.

Oss, June 30, 2008

Table of contents

List of illustrations

Tables

Figures

Abbreviations

AC	alternating current
AEG	Allgemeine Elektrizitäts-Gesellschaft
BBC	Brown Boveri & Cie
CDO	Central Dispatch Organisation
CEEC	Committee of European Economic Co-operation
CEEU	Commission for Enquiry on European Union
CEQ	Committee on Electric Questions
CIGRE	Conférence Internationale des Grands Réseaux de Transport d'Énergie Électriques à Très Haute Tension
CMEA	Council of Mutual Economic Assistance
COCOM	Coordinating Committee for Multilateral Export Controls
CoEP	Committee on Electric Power
CPTE	Coordination de la Production et du Transport de l'Énergie électrique
CSCE	Conference on Co-operation and Security in Europe
DC	direct current
ECA	Economic Cooperation Administration
ECONAD	Committee of Economic Advisers
ECOSOC	Economic and Social Council
EECE	Emergency Economic Committee for Europe
ERP	European Recovery Programme
EU	European Union
EUROPEL	Compagnie Européenne pour Entreprises d'Electricité et d'Utilité Publique
FRG	Federal Republic of Germany
GDR	German Democratic Republic
GNP	gross national product
GWh	gigawatt per hour
HV	high voltage
HVDC	high voltage direct current
Hz	Hertz
IBRD	International Bank for Reconstruction and Development
ICC	International Chamber of Commerce

IEC	International Electrotechnical Commission
ILO	International Labour Organisation
IMI	International Management Institute
IPS	Interconnected Power Systems
kV	kilovolt
KWh	kilowatt per hour
LoN	League of Nations
LTS	Large Technical Systems
MW	megawatt
NATO	North Atlantic Treaty Organisation
OAPEC	Organisation of Arab Petroleum Exporting Countries
OCT	Organisation for Communications and Transit
OECD	Organisation for Economic Cooperation and Development
OEEC	Organisation for European Economic Cooperation
OSR	Office of the U.S. Special Representative in Europe
PNJ	Pennsylvania-New Jersey Interconnection
PUP	Public Utilities Panel
RWE	Rheinisch-Westfälischen Elektrizitätswerks AG
SHAEF	Supreme Headquarters of the Allied Expeditionary Force
SOFINA	Société Financière de Transports et d'Entreprises Industrielles
SSR	Socialistic Soviet Republic
TECAID	Technical Assistance
TSO	transmission network operator
UCPTE	Union pour la Coordination de la Production et du Transport de l'Électricité
UCTE	Union for the Coordination of Transportation of Electricity
UFIPTE	Union Franco-Ibérique pour la Coordination de la Production et du Transport d'Électricité
UN	United Nations
UNDP	United Nations Development Programme
UNECE	United Nations Economic Commission for Europe
UNIPEDE	Union Internationale des Producteurs et Distributeurs d'Énergie Électrique
UNRRA	United Nations Reconstruction and Rehabilitation Administration
WEC	World Energy Council
WEWA	Wasserkraft- und Elektrizitätswirtschafts Amtes
WPC	World Power Conference

Chapter 1 Introduction
In search of European roots

Gales blazed across the Alpine region as usual during autumn. In the early morning of September 28, 2003 a severe storm forced a tree to sway near the Italian-Swiss border. Unfortunately, the branches tripped a power line. The load of the disturbed line is automatically divided among other cables. These transmission lines were already utilized close to their full capacity. To relieve them from excessive load, the Italian *transmission network operator* (TSO) decided to cut down electricity imports by 300 MW. Twenty-four minutes later another tree hit a high voltage line. This second incident overloaded remaining transmission lines between Italy and Switzerland. In order to contain the problem, Italy was isolated from the European grid of the *Union for Coordination of Transportation of Electricity* (UCTE) – encompassing the cooperation between 23 European TSOs.

This separation from the UCTE network caused a frequency instability in Italy, which eventually led to the collapse of the domestic system.[1] Less than two minutes after Italy's isolation from the European interconnected network the entire Italian peninsula was deprived of electrical power. The largest blackout in Italian history was a fact. All over the country trains came to a halt and traffic lights went off. In Rome, where the annual all-night festival *Notte Bianca* was taking place, plunged into darkness. The Roman subway system came to halt, trapping thousands of passengers. The Vatican put backup generators into action, enabling the pope to proclaim new cardinals on early Sunday morning. An ongoing liver transplant had to be aborted and postponed in a Trieste hospital. Only after half a day the whole of Italy was once again supplied. The blackout not only disrupted Italian society, but also led to the death of at least four people.[2]

The UCTE immediately appointed a committee to evaluate the blackout. Not awaiting the report, various actors began to search for the roots of the blackout, and initially pointed fingers at each other across the Alps. An Italian newspaper

---

1 This account is based upon the UCTE reports concerning the blackout. UCTE, *Final Report of the Investigation Committee on the 28 September 2003 Blackout in Italy* (Brussels: UCTE, 2004), http://www.ucte.org/_library/otherreports/20040427_UCTE_IC_Final_report.pdf.
2 "Blackout, tre morti in Puglia, Sicilia ancora al buio," *La Repubblica*, September 28, 2003, http://www.repubblica.it/2003/i/sezioni/cronaca/blackitalia/citta/citta.html.

Figure 1.1 – Lights out at the Colosseum in Rome. Source: AP / Reporters

reported how Swiss and French authorities blamed Italy for not handling the crisis properly.[3] In response, the Italian TSO claimed that their inability to restore control over the system was not the root of the blackout. Italy's TSO argued that the tree starting the chain of events was on Swiss soil.[4] The Swiss *Neue Zürcher Zeitung* printed the response of the Swiss TSO, which admitted that the blackout indeed originated on Swiss soil.[5] Yet it stressed that Italy's domestic handling of the situation was not their area of responsibility. Swiss authorities stressed that national TSOs themselves are "in the last place responsible for the supply within their own boundaries".[6]

Despite these conflicting opinions on the origins of the incident, a consensus seemed to exist on structural issues at the root of the blackout. These primarily concerned the Italian position within the European interconnected network. The

---

3 "Blackout, per Parigi e Berna la responsabilità è italiana," *La Repubblica*, September 28, 2003, http://www.repubblica.it/2003/i/sezioni/cronaca/blackitalia/cause/cause.html.

4 "Black out, Marzano apre inchiesta 'Troveremo presto i responsabili,'" *La Repubblica*, September 28, 2003, http://www.repubblica.it/2003/i/sezioni/cronaca/blackitalia/marzano/marzano.html.

5 H. Blattmann, "Zu früh für Schuldzuweisungen," *Neue Zürcher Zeitung*, September 28, 2003, 13.

6 Blattmann, "Hochspannung zwischen Schweiz und Italien. Bericht zur Ursache des Blackouts," *Neue Zürcher Zeitung*, September 28, 2003, 13. Original German text is "letztlich selber verantwortlich sein für Versorgung innerhalb der eigenen Grenzen".

director of the French TSO identified Italy's strong dependence on imported electricity as a key problem. In other words, Italian reliance upon electricity imports made it a weak link within the European electricity network.[7] The capacity of transmission lines between Italy and its neighboring countries thus urgently needed expansion. This view of a "risky" interdependence was shared by Italy's ministry of economic affairs.[8] The leading Italian employers' federation *Confindustria* not only resented the high electricity prices in Italy due to its external interdependence. It also saw the blackout as an upshot of a long-lacking clear national energy policy.[9]

Not just national TSOs and policies were subjected to criticism. A commentator in *Le Monde* regarded the creation of the European electricity market by the European Union (EU) as uneven and lacking sufficient regulation.[10] EU Energy Directives resulted in increasing international commercial electricity flows. Yet this was not matched by an increase in cross-border transmission capacity. In addition, Italian and French procedures for handling international flows were not harmonized. Switzerland, a key country for electricity transits in Europe, did not even have to comply with EU-regulation as a EU non-member.[11]

This negative view upon the formation of a European electricity market formation was not shared by the responsible EU Commissioner, however. In November 2003, Loyola de Palacio – EU Commissioner for Transport and Energy – stated in a speech that "recent blackout events in Europe cannot sensibly be blamed on the market opening process".[12] To her, the events in Switzerland and Italy were due to a lack of communication between TSOs which is "unacceptable whether or not the electricity market is open or not".[13]

In April 2004 UCTE released its final report. According to the report the blackout had both national and European roots. UCTE endorsed the view that Italian and Swiss TSOs responded without sufficient urgency. Similarly, Italy's inability to cope with the isolation from the UCTE-grid was acknowledged by the report. UCTE also placed the blackout within the context of the development

---

7 Pascal Galinier, "Les risques et faiblesses d'un réseau sature. La panne en Italie souligne la fragilité de l'Europe de l'électricité," *Le Monde*, September 30, 2003.

8 "Black out, Marzano."

9 "Confindustria: 'L'elettricità è emergenza nazionale'," *La Repubblica*, September 28, 2003, http://www.repubblica.it/2003/i/sezioni/cronaca/blackitalia/confind/confind.html.

10 Galinier, "Les risques."

11 Ibid.

12 Loyola de Palacio, "Challenges Towards a Unified European Energy Market" (presented at the Roundtable on energy, Nyenrode, The Netherlands, November 13, 2003), 3. She refers to *blackouts* in the plural as in the same year disruptions occurred in London (August 28) as well as in southern Sweden and eastern Denmark (September 23). Earlier that year, a lengthy blackout disrupted life in north-eastern United States and south-eastern Canada (August 14).

13 Ibid., 13

of a European electricity market, resulting in an increase of cross-border flows. According to UCTE, these were "out of the scope of the original system design". To them the interconnected system in Europe was built as a "backbone for the security of supply".[14] This point of view was endorsed by EURELECTRIC, an organization representing the European electricity industry. It equally recognized the large amounts of commercial flows as one of the main causes of the power failure.[15]

It is not my intention to make a detailed anatomy of this blackout. Rather, I want to use this example to shed light upon the structure of the electricity system in Europe. The various responses to the blackout suggest that national systems are the main building blocks of the European system. While there are three coordination centers in the UCTE area, there is no centrally controlled European network.[16] A EU policy directed towards an internal electricity market did not change this. Following the Italian blackout, *Le Monde* concluded that the European system remains governed by national regulators and managers, who often act according to national priorities.[17] On the other hand, the blackout also indicates that national TSOs do not have total control of the domestic electricity supply. Incidents outside Italy triggered a sequence of events which led to a breakdown of its electricity system. If the Italian network had not been isolated, electricity supply in other European countries could have been affected. This is to say that electricity networks in Europe are to a very large extent interwoven, technologically, institutionally and economically. Countries rely on their neighbors, not only in terms of import and export, but also to meet technical requirements in order not to jeopardize transnational system integrity.

With regard to the European electricity system – the subject of this inquiry –, one might be inclined to link its development to the formation of an internal electricity market under the aegis of the EU. This is nevertheless not the case. The real first step towards a common electricity market was a result of the Single European Act signed in 1985. Yet the development of the interconnected European network is the result of a development which already started in the 1920s, and is not directly connected to the history of the EU and its predecessors. In Interwar years the construction of a transnational electricity network was already conceived as a specific *European* project. European network-building gained further momentum after WWII, and came to include most European countries by 1995.

---

14 UCTE, *Final Report*, 3
15 Union of the Electricity Industry–EURELECTRIC, *Power Outages in 2003. Task Force Power Outages* (Brussels: EURELECTRIC, June 2004), 13.
16 The centers are in Braunweiler (Germany), Laufenburg (Switzerland), and Belgrade (Serbia). See http://www.ucte.org/aboutus/tsoworld/systemoperation/ (accessed November 1, 2007).
17 Galinier, "Les risques."

The process of network integration in Europe has largely escaped the eye of historians of European integration. Studies of European integration have primarily dealt with the development of the European Community since 1951, and more specifically with issues of political and economic cooperation. A few specialized studies of the development of a common energy policy – including electricity – are available, but their results are hardly included in the main textbooks on European integration.[18] These studies mainly focus on the role of the European Commission or the interplay between nation-states and Community bodies, and ignore the work of other international actors such as the UCPTE and engineering organizations. This neglect is remarkable because as historians Badenoch and Fickers have argued that technological infrastructures might well be perceived as the "essence of European integration". Not only do they provide the material basis for flows of goods, people, capital and services which the EU and its predecessors sought to create, but they have also been mobilized as symbols and metaphors of European integration.[19] European integration history, primarily centering upon the development of the EU and its predecessors, neglects the integrating effects of networks. Van der Vleuten and Kaijser have noted in their literature overview these histories "fail to analyze [the shaping and entanglement of infrastructures] with broader historical developments".[20] For the study of the neglected role of infrastructure, and more broadly technology, in the European integration process, Thomas Misa and Johan Schot proposed to use the concept of *hidden integration*.[21] In a more recent paper Schot explains that "hidden" not only refers to the neglect by historians, but also to the explicit strategy of engineers to "technify" discussions on European

---

18 This is the case in for example N.J.D. Lucas, *Energy and the European Communities* (London: Europa Publications, 1977); Stephen Padgett, "The Single European Energy Market: The Politics of Realization," *Journal of Common Market Studies* 30, no. 1 (1992): 53-75; Janne Haaland Matlary, *Energy Policy in the European Union* (London: Palgrave Macmillan, 1997); Susanne K. Schmidt, *Liberalisierung in Europa. Die Rolle der Europäischen Kommission* (Frankfurt: Campus Verlag, 1998); Padgett, "Between Synthesis and Emulation: EU Policy Transfer in the Power Sector," *Journal of European Public Policy* 10, no. 2 (2003): 227-245; and most recently Julie Cailleau, "Energy: from Synergies to Merger," in *The European Commission, 1958-1972. History and Memories*, ed. Michel Dumoulin (Brussels: Office for Official Publications of the European Communities, 2007), 471-490.
19 Alexander Badenoch and Andreas Fickers, "Introduction: Untangling Infrastructures and Europe: Mediations, Events, Scales," in *Europe Materializing? Transnational Infrastructures and the Project of Europe*, ed. Alexander Badenoch and Andreas Fickers (London: Palgrave, forthcoming).
20 Erik Van der Vleuten and Arne Kaijser, "Networking Europe," *History and Technology* 21, no. 1 (2005): 30. They made a similar point in their "Prologue and Introduction: Transnational Networks and the Shaping of Contemporary Europe," in *Networking Europe: Transnational Infrastructures and the Shaping of Europe, 1850-2000*, ed. Van der Vleuten and Kaijser (Sagamore Beach: Science History Publications, 2006), 7.
21 Thomas J. Misa and Johan Schot, "Inventing Europe: Technology and the hidden integration of Europe. Introduction," *History and technology* 21, no. 1 (2005): 1-22. The notion of hidden integration was first introduced by Johan Schot as a core concept in Johan Schot, "Transnational Infrastructures and the Rise of Contemporary Europe: Project proposal," Transnational Infrastructures of Europe Working Documents Series, no.1 (Eindhoven: Eindhoven University of Technology), http://www.tie-project.nl/publications/pdf/Proposal.pdf.

integration in order to reduce the influence of political and non-experts actors as much as possible.[22] This is not to imply that the aims and stakes of engineers were free of political content. In many instances they saw technological solutions as an alternative to a political path, or as a continuation of politics by technical means.

This study can thus be perceived as an inquiry into the hidden integration of the European electricity system. In addition to fill a gap in the literature, this book also sheds light on the intentions, ideas and strategies of engineers, various companies and their international organizations. The inquiry pursues the following questions: 1) How, when and why did the notion of a European electricity system take root? 2) How did it develop throughout the decades up to the end of the twentieth century, and how did it affect the actual transnational network construction? 3) Which actors played an influential role?

In the remainder of this introduction, I first present an overview of relevant approaches and findings present in the existing historiography on the development of electricity networks. This is followed by a section that discusses available findings specifically on the European electricity system. Subsequently, I discuss the approach I use to answer my main questions, and I elaborate on the sources used. Finally, in the last section I introduce the structure of the book.

Histories of electrification

In the scholarly field of history of technology there is a substantial literature about processes of electrification and network-building. This section surveys this field, and seeks to identify which insights and concepts are useful for this study. I will depart from Thomas Hughes' ground-breaking work, which inspired other scholars to write mainly national histories of electrification. In *Networks of Power*, Hughes compared electricity network development in Berlin, Chicago, and London.[23] His thoughts inspired a new field preoccupied with the study of so-called *Large*

---

22 Johan Schot, "Transnational Infrastructures and European Integration," in *Europe Materializing?*, ed. Badenoch and Fickers I profited from discussion on the implications of this concept for my thesis with Johan Schot. Also see the recent Johan Schot and Vincent Lagendijk, "Technocratic Internationalism in the Interwar Years: Building Europe on Motorways and Electricity Networks," *Journal of Modern European History* 7, no. 2 (forthcoming 2008), 196-217.
23 Thomas P. Hughes, *Networks of Power: Electrification in Western Society, 1880-1930* (Johns Hopkins University Press, 1983).

Technical Systems (LTS).[24] Hughes defined electricity networks as socio-technical systems including technological components, but also institutional and organizational ones, as well as natural resources, and legislation.[25] These systems were constructed by so-called *system builders*, which could be either people or institutions.[26] They were guided by a number of principles. Two important ones that also play a role in the building of international connections were *load factor* and *economic mix*. Since electricity cannot easily be stored, network operators sought to use generating capacity to a maximum at all time, and hence create a high load. A high load factor thus reflects high usage of the system's equipment and is a measure of efficiency.[27] Economic mix refers to the optimal use of a combination of various energy sources in the system in order to create economic advantages and increase the system reliability. For this reason system builders sought, for example, to use hydroelectric plants or mine-based lignite-fired plants, also when they were located in another country. [28]

Hughes attributes much importance to these two concepts. He noted in *Networks* that "[i]f a would-be Darwin of the technological world is looking for laws analogous to the environmental forces that operate in the world of natural selection, the economic principles of load factor and economic mix are likely candidates".[29] In *American Genesis* Hughes takes his argument about the importance of system-builders one step further.[30] He argues that large technical systems were central in the creation of the modern technological nation. Hughes articulates a 20th century history for the United States that logically follows the growth of systems. First, he

---

24 Following *Networks* more systematic inquiries into the theoretical meanings of LTS have been made, including by Hughes himself, as well as the application of LTS concepts on historical developments other than electrification. Most notable are Wiebe E. Bijker, Thomas Parke Hughes, and T.J. Pinch, eds., *The Social Construction of Technological Systems: New Directions in the Sociology and History of Technology* (Cambridge: MIT Press, 1987); Renate Mayntz and Thomas P. Hughes, eds., *The Development of Large Technological Systems* (Frankfurt am Mainz: Campus Verlag, 1988); and Olivier Coutard, ed., *The Governance of Large Technical Systems* (London: Routledge, 1999). For an overview of two decades of LTS research see Van der Vleuten, "Understanding Network Societies: Two Decades of Large Technical System studies," in *Networking Europe*, ed. Van der Vleuten and Kaijser, 279-314.

25 Hughes, "The Evolution of Large Technical Systems," in *The Social Construction*, ed. Bijker, Hughes, and Pinch.

26 Ibid., 51-52. System-builders, implementers of technological innovations within an institutional and cultural framework, are not necessarily people. Due to up-scaling and increasing complexity of systems since the First World War, the system-building process gradually shifted from inventor-entrepreneurs to organizations and governments. After WWII, European institutions played a significant role as well. Also see Hughes, *Rescuing Prometheus: Four Monumental Projects that Changed the Modern World* (New York: Pantheon Books, 1998).

27 Hughes, *Networks*, 218-221.

28 Ibid., 366-367.

29 Ibid., 462.

30 Hughes, *American Genesis: A Century of Invention and Technological Enthusiasm, 1870-1970* (London: Viking, 1989).

discusses the invention of systems, then the spread of large systems, and finally the emergence of reactions to the systems.

Over the last two decades, a wide variety of historical research on electrification has been inspired by the LTS approach. The majority of histories of electrification are from a national perspective.[31] Most attention has gone to developments in the United States, and northern and western parts of Europe. To my knowledge, hardly any systematic accounts of Central and Eastern Europe are available – either in English or native languages.[32] In both France and Italy large multi-volume historical accounts on electricity have been published.[33] The role of the French *Association pour l'histoire de l'électricité en France*, which has sponsored conferences starting in 1983, has been important. Since that year it also published the *Bulletin d'histoire de l'électricité*, which appears twice a year.[34] Thirteen colloquiums were organized between 1983 and 2002. Many focused primarily on French developments, but several conferences had explicit international perspectives.[35]

In general, most studies recognize and acknowledge the importance of the work of Hughes. Economic mix and load factor are regularly used to explain the

---

31 Examples of books based on dissertation research are Timo Myllyntaus, *Electrifying Finland : The Transfer of a New Technology into a Late Industrialising Economy* (London: ETLA, 1991); Jonathan Coopersmith, *The Electrification of Russia, 1880-1926* (Ithaca: Cornell University Press, 1992); and Van der Vleuten, "Electrifying Denmark: A Symmetrical History of Central and Decentral Electricity Supply until 1970" (PhD diss., University of Aarhus, 1998). A good example of a multi-author is Ana Cardoso de Matos et al., *A Electricidade em Portugal: Dos primórdios à 2ua Guerra Mundial* (Lisbon: Museu de Electricidade, 2004). For The Netherlands, see the chapters on Energy, edited by G.P.J. Verbong and other in: J.W. Schot, H.W. Lintsen, and A. Rip, eds., *Techniek in Nederland in de Twintigste Eeuw*, vol. 2, *Delfstoffen, Energie, Chemie* (Stichting Historie der Techniek, 2000).

32 One example is L'udovít Hallon, "Systematic Electrification in Germany and in Four Central Europe States in the Interwar Period," *ICON* 7 (2001): 135-147. Hallon's article sketches the main outlines of electrification in the region, with a strong emphasis on German developments. His sources on Central Europe concern contemporary sources. More general studies of the region do point to the importance of electrification, but without going into detail or referring to more comprehensive publications. See for example Iván T. Berend, *Decades of Crisis: Central and Eastern Europe Before World War II* (Berkeley: University of California Press, 1998), 219 and 229.

33 In Italy the *Storia dell'industria elettrica in Italia* has appeared in five volumes (volume three comprises two books) starting in 1992. In France the *Histoire générale de l'électricité en France* was published in three volumes between 1991 and 1996. They also published a research guide which gives detailed information about journals, historical studies, and useful archives concerning the history of electricity in France. See Arnaud Berthonnet, *Guide du chercheur en histoire de l'électricité*, Éditions La Mandragore (Paris, 2001).

34 In 2003 the name of the journal has been renamed *Annales historiques de l'électricité*, now published under the auspices of the *Fondation Électricité de France*.

35 Thirteen colloquiums were organised between 1983 and 2002. Many primarily focused on French developments, but several explicitly addressed international histories and perspectives. See for example Fabienne Cardot, ed., *1880-1980. Un siècle d'électricité dans le monde: Actes du Premier colloque international d'histoire de l'électricité* (Paris: Presses Universitaires de France, 1987); and Monique Trédé, ed., *Électricité et électrification dans le monde: Actes du deuxième colloque international d'histoire de l'électricité, organisé par l'Association pour l'histoire de l'électricité en France, Paris, 3-6 juillet 1990* (Association pour l'histoire de l'électricité en France, 1992).

growth of systems. Yet Hughes emphasis on "natural" system growth has been crit-
icized.[36] Van der Vleuten has argued convincingly that the presupposed economic
logic of an ever increasing scale cannot be upheld for the history of electrification
in Denmark.[37] Van der Vleuten showed that no Danish consensus existed on the
economic superiority of a large scale electricity system. Decentralized systems co-
existed with centralized systems for most of the 20th century.[38]

Complementary to Hughes' systems approach, another seminal work is
Electrifying America by David Nye. He introduced the user and cultural perspective in the history of electrification. Although users are not central in this book,
this branch of literature has led to useful conclusions that influenced my research.
First, because it stressed that electricity network development was not "a 'natural' or 'neutral' process; everywhere it was shaped by complex, political, technical,
ideological interaction".[39] Second, because it shows the salience of ideological and
cultural factors. Similar findings are put forward by various authors in the field
of *Alltagsgeschichte*, which focused on the cultural history of electricity and its
symbolism in daily life.[40] All point to the importance of ideas and expectations
that accompany and guide the construction of electricity systems. As we will see,
such ideas also played an important role in building international connections in
Europe.

Other historians of electricity networks have shown that nationalism provided
a stimulus for expanding networks and interconnecting systems. Often technological infrastructures were built to serve specific national socio-economic and political
aims. Gabrielle Hecht discussed the notion of *technopolitics* in her work on French
postwar identity in relation to nuclear technology, meaning "the strategic practice
of designing or using technology to constitute, embody or enact political goals".[41]

---

36 See for example Joachim Radkau, "Zum ewiger Wachstum verdammt? Jugend und Alter grosstechnischer Systeme," in *Technik ohne Grenzen*, ed. Ingo Braun and Bernward Joerges (Frankfurt am Mainz:
Surhkamp, 1994), 50-106.
37 Van der Vleuten, "Electrifying."
38 Ibid., 327. Also see the recent Erik van der Vleuten and Rob Raven, "Lock-In and Change: Distributed
Generation in Denmark in a Long-Term Perspective," *Energy Policy* 34, no. 18 (2006): 3739-3748.
39 Nye, *Electrifying America: Social Meanings of a New Technology, 1880-1940* (Cambridge: MIT Press,
1990), 138-139.
40 Notable works include Beate Binder, *Elektrifizierung als Vision: Zur Symbolgeschichte einer Technik im
Alltag* (Tübingen: Vereinigung für Volkskunde, 1999); and also Coutard, "Imaginaire et developpement des
reseaux techniques. Les apport de l'histoire de l'électrification rurale en France et aux Etats-Unis," *Réseaux*
5, no. 109 (2001): 76-94. Also Kline's work on rural electrification in the United States is noteworthy
in that respect. See Ronald R. Kline, *Consumers in the Country. Technology and Social Change in Rural
America* (Baltimore: The Johns Hopkins University Press, 2000).
41 Hecht, *The Radiance of France: Nuclear Power and National Identity After World War II* (Cambridge:
MIT Press, 1998); and Hecht, "Technology, Politics and National Identity in France," in *Technologies of
Power: Essays in Honor of Thomas Parke Hughes and Agatha Chipley Hughes*, ed. Gabrielle Hecht and
Michael Thad Allen (Cambridge/London: MIT Press, 2001), 256-257.

In an inspiring paper, Mats Fridlund and Helmut Maier introduced the term *engineering nationalism* as a process whereby network technologies became tools for nation-building and nationalistic objectives in the hands of engineers.[42] The authors indicate how electricity projects were pursued to support national industry and autonomy in Sweden and Germany. In the latter country military objectives played a central role in discourses on network-building between 1933 and 1945.

The state was often the central actor in promoting electrification, although stronger in some countries than in others. In his history of the electrification of Russia, Coopersmith claims that states do not utilize technologies in a vacuum, but "such actions occur within a pattern including prior state interest in the technology, a politically connected engineering or scientific entrepreneur, a ruling party facing a perceived challenge or crisis, and a political leader who promotes the technology for specific political goals".[43] Network development thus mattered to the actors involved in nation-state building. Historians for their part confirmed the integrating impact of infrastructures. Van der Vleuten for example claimed that in The Netherlands "networks increasingly tied together the entire country […] into a single artificial space", enabling complete utilization, industrialization and cultivation.[44]

This aspect is recognized by students of nationalism as well. Weber saw the geographical spreading of road and rail infrastructures as crucial agents of change in modernizing the country-side, creating markets, and making its inhabitants "French".[45] For reasons related to nation-building, rural electrification was often promoted by national authorities.[46] According to Oliver Coutard, it was part of governments' policy of modernization, carried by social modernizers and politicians.[47] It also aimed to provide the whole country "the means and symbols of

---

42 Mats Fridlund and Helmut Maier, "The Second Battle of the Currents" (working paper, Department of History of Science and Technology, Royal Institute of Technology, 1996), 3-4. A recent work on engineering national is S. Waqar H. Zaidi, "The Janus-face of Techno-Nationalism. Barnes Wallis and the 'Strength of England'," *Technology and Culture* 29, no. 1: 62-88.
43 Coopersmith, *The Electrification*, 152.
44 Van der Vleuten, "Introduction: Networking Technology, Networking Society, Networking Nature," *History and Technology* 20, no. 5 (2004): 195.
45 Eugen Joseph Weber, *Peasants into Frenchmen: The Modernization of Rural France, 1870-1914* (Stanford University Press, 1976), in particular chap. 12 on roads.
46 These processes have been well-documented for France, the United States, and the Soviet Union. See respectively T. Nadau, "L'Électrification rurale," in *l'Interconnexion et le marché, 1919-1946*, vol. 2 of *Histoire générale de l'Électricité en France*, ed. Maurice Lévy-Leboyer and Henri Morsel (Paris: Fayard, 1994), 1199-1232; Kline, *Consumers;* and Coopersmith, *The Electrification.*
47 Coutard, "Imaginaire," 79

modern civilization", including economic backward areas.[48] Often authorities (on various levels) took on the role of pioneer in an attempt to bring nature and society "to order" by using high-modernist ideology.[49] The building of electricity systems was thus presented as a stimulus to economic development, modernization, and national unification. As we will observe later in this book, similar arguments played a role at the international level.

Towards a history of the European system

The above mentioned examples mainly concerned national developments. Although international developments are by far less well-documented, processes of electrification and network-building are not confined to national borders. Histories dealing with specifically European system-building are even rarer. In this section, I review that which has been written, how it is useful for this book, and which perspectives are missing.

Several publications compare various national paths of developments, like the unpublished *habilitation* of Denis Varaschin.[50] He emphasizes the national style of electrification in western European countries, without saying much about cooperation between countries. Robert Millward wrote a national comparison between transport, energy and telecommunications infrastructures, and their respective governance forms.[51] As he emphasizes similarities and contrasts between national developments, little to no attention is spent on international network-building. Within business history a substantial amount of work has analyzed the activities

---

48 Nadau, "L'Électrification," 1200 Original French text is "des outils et des symboles de la civilisation moderne". A related chapter about how infrastructures transform rural places is Kaijser, "Nature's Periphery: Rural Transformation by the Advent of Infrasystems," in *Taking Place: The Spatial Contexts of Science, Technology and Business* (Sagamore Beach: Science History Publications, 2006), 151-186.
49 James C. Scott, *Seeing Like a State: How Certain Schemes to Improve the Human Condition Have Failed* (New Haven: Yale University Press, 1998), 4.
50 Varaschin, "Etats et électricité en Europe occidentale. Habilitation à diriger des recherches" (Habilitation, Université Pierre-Mendes-France: Grenoble III , 1997). I have used a copy held by the *Fondation Electricité de France* in Paris.
51 Millward, *Private and Public Enterprise in Europe: Energy, Telecommunications and Transport, 1830-1990* (Cambridge: Cambridge University Press, 2005).

of international engineering firms.[52] Here again, international network-building is not part of the narrative.

Arne Kaijser's work on network-building in Scandinavia mainly consisted of a national comparison between countries. He nevertheless pays attention to international developments. According to Kaijser, interconnections between regional systems were sought to gain economies of substitution (improving economic mix) by combining different hydropower resources in Finland, Norway, and Sweden.[53] In addition, collaboration between Denmark and Sweden in the form of a submarine cable had a catalytic effect upon the interconnection process, especially within Denmark. This specific cable, intended to transmit the Swedish summer surplus of hydropower to Denmark, was later also used for flows in the opposite direction.[54] Here Kaijser points to the difference between *planned* and *evolving* systems, or how linkages built for a particular intention can be used for other purposes as well.[55] In a 1997 publication, Kaijser explicitly speaks of transnational connections and argues their construction was strongly influenced by the socio-economic and political context, and should be placed within the according institutional setting.[56]

A limited number of studies have shed some light on the development of a European electricity system. Although they lack an adequate empirical basis, they do provide a general outline of the process. One of these is authored by Henri Persoz.[57] He uses a framework analogous to Hughes to explain the development of a European system. Before WWI, electricity producers improved their load factor by expanding their clientele, also across borders if these plants happen to be

---

52 See for example Luciano Segreto, "Financing the Electric Industry Worldwide: Strategy and Structure of the Swiss Electric Holding Companies, 1895-1945," *Business and Economic History* 23, no. 1 (1994): 162-175; and Peter Hertner, "Les sociétés financières suisses et le développement de l'industrie électrique jusqu'à la première guerre mondiale," in *1880-1980*, ed. Cardot, 341-356. A substantial business history of electrification just appeared; William Hausman, Mira Wilkins, and Peter Hertner, *Global Electrification: Multinational Enterprise and International Finance in the History of Light and Power* (Cambridge: Cambridge University Press, 2008). A preview has been published as William J. Hausman, Mira Wilkins, and John L. Neufeld, "Multinational Enterprise and International Finance in the History of Light and Power, 1880s-1914," *Revue économique* 58, no. 1 (2007): 175-190.
53 Kaijser, "Controlling the Grids: The Development of High-Tension Power Lines in the Nordic Countries," in *Nordic Energy Systems: Historical Perspectives and Current Issues*, ed. Arne Kaijser and Marika Hedin (Chicago: Science History Publications, 1995), 33.
54 Ibid., 37-38.
55 Ibid., 52.
56 Kaijser, "Trans-Border Integration of Electricity and Gas in the Nordic Countries, 1915-1992," *Polhem* 15 (1997): 4-43. A similar point is made in Lars Thue, "Electricity Rules: The Formation and Development of the Nordic Electricity Regimes," in *Nordic Energy*, ed. Kaijser and Hedin, 11-30.
57 Henri Persoz, "Les grands réseaux modernes," in *Une oeuvre nationale: L'Équipement, la croissance de la demande, le nucléaire (1946-1987)*, vol 3, of *Histoire générale de l'électricité en France*, ed. Henri Morsel (Paris: Fayard, 1996), 783.

located at the border. In addition, engineers tried to create an economic mix by interconnecting hydroelectric and thermal electricity plants, again also across national boundaries. The main rationale was to use waterpower as optimal as possible, and to avoid spilling of hydroelectricity and fuel. Interconnected operation brought more efficiency. It enabled the transmission of electricity from one power station to the other in cases of emergencies. Therefore utilities could decrease their additional generation capacity, which they kept in reserve to cover demand in exceptional situations. Persoz's explanation for the progress towards a European system is thus located in system dynamics using Hughsian concepts such as economic mix and load factor.

A report by Verbong et al confirms the role of "system dynamics" behind the growth of a European network.[58] The authors distilled three general phases of European collaboration; accidental cooperation (1915-1950), a European network within national institutional boundaries (1950-1990s), and crossing institutional boundaries (since 1990s).[59] Georg Boll showed a similar story for the development from local German systems, to Germany being part of a European *Verbundswirtschaft*.[60] An unpublished French master's thesis by Julian Barrère added more detail to these stages.[61] Barrère observed the formation of international non-governmental organizations in the first phase, which represented the interests of the electricity industry. These organizations contributed to the exchange of ideas on network development. After WWII, Barrère underlines the role of the *Organization for European Economic Cooperation* (OEEC, 1948), and also the UCPTE (1951) as important platforms for international collaboration.[62] He regards the liberalization of energy markets by the EU since the 1990s as a new phase.[63] Persoz added that in this period the connection of Eastern and Western

58 G. Verbong, E.van der Vleuten, and M.J.J. Scheepers, *Long-Term Electricity Supply Systems Dynamics: A Historical Analysis* (Eindhoven: SUSTELNET, 2002).
59 Ibid., 20-24.
60 See Georg Boll, *Entstehung und Entwicklung des Verbundbetriebs in der deutschen Elektrizitätswirtschaft bis zum europäischen Verbund. Ein rückblick zum 20-jährgen Besiehen der Deutschen Verbundsgesellschaft e.V., Heidelberg* (Frankfurt: Verlags- u. Wirtschaftges, d. Elektrizitätswerke m.b.H., 1969), 126-129. This history of Germany's electricity system from 1969 did spend a mere three pages to describe cooperation within a European framework. Throughout the rest of the text, however, related international events are mentioned.
61 Julien Barrère, "La genèse de l'Europe électrique: Les logiques de l'interconnexion transnationale (début des années 1920-fin des années 1950)" (PhD diss., Université de Bordeaux-III, 2002). The thesis was supervised by Christophe Bouneau. It was written on the basis of conference reports and documents published by various international organisations. A solid account by any means– especially for a master's thesis –, Barrère often uses France as a starting point and focuses mainly on technical reasons to create a European system. I have used a copy held by the *Fondation Electricité de France* in Paris.
62 The *Union for the Production and Coordination of Transportation of Electricity* (UCPTE) is the same as the current-day UCTE. The 'P' of production was dropped in 1998 as a response to EU policy.
63 This is the case with Verbong, Vleuten, and Scheepers, *Long-Term*, 23ff.

European networks was also a crucial new development for Europe's electricity industry.[64]

Several other historians recognize the crucial role of international organizations and networks of people, usually made up of engineers. Christophe Bouneau places the birth of a transnational network of engineers in the Interwar period. He discerns a technical "International" with a technocratic world view, which grew by means of international congresses and associations.[65] For the period after WWII, Bouneau recognizes the importance of engineers in organizations like OEEC and UCPTE. Barjot and Kurgan made a comparable argument, while also indicating the involvement of financial institutions and engineering firms for the period up to WWII.[66] They suggest a number of general consequences of growth of this expert community. First, this community fostered the growth of interconnections. Second, engineering associations stimulated a scientific spirit and an exchange of knowledge, aimed at rationalizing electricity systems. Third, it stimulated new modes of operation whereby not only entrepreneurs played a crucial role, but also various nation-states.[67]

These findings provided useful starting points for my research. Still, I consider the explanation for the proliferation of a European system as incomplete, for two main reasons. First of all, these historical accounts all stress technical-economic attributes as determinants of growth, and thus cannot explain why actors tried to built European networks as a "regional" optimum. The technical-economic "logics" of continuous scale increase are never questioned. Hence, Henri Persoz places the history of the European interconnected system in the light of an implacable principle – "a movement without ending" – within the electricity industry, recognizing the need to connect electricity networks with others until the whole planet is interconnected.[68] He thereby admits that his interpretation is not a suitable explanation for the question why explicitly a European system came about.[69]

My second objection is that the peculiarity of the drive towards a *European* system is not sufficiently taken into account. It is essential to understand why en-

---

64 Persoz, "Les grands," 812ff.
65 Christophe Bouneau, "Les réseaux de transport d'électricité en Europe occidentale depuis a fin du XIXe siècle: De la diversité des modèles nationaux à la recherche de la convergence européenne," *Annales historiques de l'électricité* 2 (2004): 31-33. This edition of *Annales historiques* is a special issue commemorating the 20th anniversary of the publication of Hughes' *Networks of Power*.
66 Dominique Barjot and Ginette Kurgan, "Les réseaux humains dans l'industrie électrique," *Annales historiques de l'électricité* 2, (2004): 69-88.
67 Ibid., 80-81.
68 Persoz, "Les grands," 783.
69 Ibid., 784.

gineers speak of a *European* system, and not any other international or regional system. Whereas historians sought to explain the growth of national networks by pointing at national(istic) discourses and ideological inspiration, these factors are neglected by historians who study the growth of a European system. Yet at the same time, there are indications that such motives played a role. Barrère briefly touches upon two interwar grand schemes for a European grid, and Boll describes one as well.[70] Both, however, do not contextualize the plans, nor analyze the underlying ideas other than technical ones. Others have shown in limited cases that ideas about Europe influenced the design of power plants and network. A good example is the work done by Alexander Gall on the so-called *Atlantropa* project.[71] German engineer Herman Sörgel, the architect of the project, proposed to lower the Mediterranean by building a dam between Gibraltar and Tangiers.[72] In the 1930s he added a European electricity network, fed by the hydroelectric plant planned at the dam. Sörgel legitimated his bold plan by claiming that a physical bond between nations was a better warranty for peace than paper treaties.[73]

Persoz, too, hints at engineers' idealistic inspiration for interconnecting countries. He briefly mentions that ideas of solidarity and the hope of avoiding past tragedies inspired discussions on European interconnections in the 1950s. He observed similar notions in the political vision of the EU with regard to international interconnections, in particular in the case of connections between Western, and Central and Eastern Europe.[74] It is perhaps Persoz personal background as an electrical engineer, who was deeply engaged in international collaboration, which prevented him from further questioning these assumptions and their meaning for the European integration of electricity networks.[75]

---

70 Barrère, "La genèse," 134-136; and Boll, *Enstehung*, 62-64.

71 Gall, *Das Atlantropa-Projekt: Die Geschichte einer gescheiterten Vision. Herman Sörgel und die Absenkung des Mittelmeers* (Frankfurt: Campus Verlag, 1998); and more recently his "Atlantropa: A Technological Vision of a United Europe," in *Networking Europe*, ed. Van der Vleuten and Kaijser, 99-128.

72 See Sörgel, *Atlantropa* (München: Piloty & Loehle , 1932).

73 He wrote that "[d]ie Verkettung Europas durch Kraftleitungen ist eine bessere Friedensgarantie als Pakte auf dem Papier; denn mit der Zerstörung der Leitungen würde sich jedes Volk selbst vernichten." Ibid., 118-119.

74 Persoz, "Les grands," 788-789.

75 Before his retirement, Persoz has worked for *Électricité de France* as well as being a member of UNIPEDE and CIGRE, and mainly devoted his time to international collaboration and network-building.

Unpacking the European system

Besides providing a general periodization, the existing literature leads to three ob-
servations. First, international network-building has a dynamic of its own worth
studying. The development should not be taken for grant. Second, ideological
convictions played a role in thinking about and planning a European system and
the socio-economic and political context clearly affected network-building. And
third, international organizations and engineering communities can be perceived
as crucial agents for international network-building. These attempts to infrastruc-
tural integration were not picked up by historians of European integration, likely
since these developments took place outside of the political sphere. This is what I
have labeled hidden integration above. This section reviews ways to "unpack" this
hidden integration.

To analyze processes of hidden integration I use the particular concept of
European system-builders as recently developed by Van der Vleuten et al.[76] These
authors have adapted Hughes' notion of system-builders in order to "study actors in the international arena working simultaneously on transnational infrastructures *and* taking 'Europe', however defined, as their sphere of activity".[77] Thus
the objects of focus in this study are international organizations and engineering
communities that acted explicitly as European system-builders. I preserve Hughes'
emphasis on the socio-technical nature of these systems, enabling me to look beyond technological elements, and to equally take political and economic aspects of
system-building into account. It also implies that socio-technical system-building
is not seen as a straightforward and rational activity, but an often contested and
negotiated process, affected by contextual factors.[78] Different from Hughes is the
focus on transnational system-builders. To some extent this is a methodological
move. Dealing with each European country individually is impossible to research.
Looking at transnational system-builders enables to focus on an arena where all
these countries met.

The word "transnational" has been around for quite a while but gained significance within political science in the 1960s.[79] Robert Keohane and Joseph Nye used

---

76 Van der Vleuten et al., "Europe's System Builders: The Contested Shaping of Transnational Road, Electricity and Rail Networks," *Contemporary European History* 16, no. 3 (2007): 321-348.

77 Ibid., 326.

78 Van der Vleuten and Kaijser, "Networking Europe," 24.

79 Two recent articles delve deeper into the origins of transnational history. See Pierre-Yves Saunier,
"Learning by Doing: Notes About the Making of the 'Palgrave Dictionary of Transnational History,'" *Journal of Modern European History* 6, no. 2 (2008): 159-179; and Van der Vleuten, "Towards a Transnational
History of Technology. Meanings, Promises, Pitfalls," *Technology and Culture* 49, no. 4 (2008, forthcoming).

"transnational" to depict forms of interaction between non-state actors over national boundaries.[80] They pled to study not only intergovernmental organizations, but also non-governmental organizations. This does not imply that the importance of nation-states and borders is underestimated. On the contrary, some have even argued that transnational ties should be conceived as strengthening rather than weakening the power of nation-states.[81] While some barriers are dissolved, others are created or reinforced.

Applied in historical studies, the transnational turn also represented a break with nation-state centered history. This has resulted in a focus upon actors who lack clear nation-state loyalties or whose agendas supersede national interests. Much emphasis remains on the study of international organizations. They represent a valuable research site to examine ideological and European agendas. Though initially a domain of study of political scientists, the work of international organizations has recently become an object of study for transnational history.[82] According to Akira Iriye, international organizations testify to the awareness of people and nations that "they shared certain interests and objectives across national boundaries and they could best solve their problems by pooling their resources and effecting transnational cooperation".[83] In addition, examining international organizations enables to look beyond national objectives only. It helps to unveil a specific transnational European agenda, and to show that the history of the European interconnected network is more than the sum of all national histories alone.[84]

Another element of transnational history is useful to help identify systembuilders. According to Patricia Clavin, transnationalism is not only about international organizations, but also about people and "the social space that they inhabit, the networks they form and the ideas they exchange".[85] An exemplary study is Evangelista's *Unarmed Forces*, as he described how a transnational movement of

---

80 Kiran Klaus Patel, "Überlegungen zu einer transnationalen Geschichte," *Zeitschrift für Geschichtswissenschaft* 52, no. 7 (2004): 629.

81 Clavin, "Introduction: Defining Transnationalism," *Contemporary European History* 14, no. 4 (2005): 431.

82 The relation between transnational history and international organisations has recently been explored in Iriye, *Global Community: The Role of International Organizations in the Making of the Contemporary World* (Berkeley: University of California Press, 2002).

83 Ibid., 9.

84 A similar point is made in Michael Gehler and Wolfram Kaiser, "Transnationalism and Early European Integration: The Nouvelles Equipes Internationales and the Geneva Circles, 1947-1957," *The Historical Journal* 44, no. 3 (2001): 773-798.

85 Clavin, "Introduction," 422.

scientists opposed the nuclear arms race during the Cold War.[86] His book clearly shows how international human networks of engineers pursued a common aim. Evangelista's book also highlights the role of a specific group of people, namely communities of experts.[87] For this study, a transnational approach thus enables a view on human networks of engineers, and an assessment of their ideas of Europe connected to their system-building.

What these system-builders saw as "European" needs further specification. Although nowadays "Europe" almost seems to correspond with the EU, its historical definition is all but clear-cut.[88] Most scholars agree that "Europe" is more than a geographical space, but also an idea. The building blocks of this supposed European idea or identity are formed by what some regard as the European legacy or European experience.[89] Historian Pim den Boer divides this European legacy into three notions: one of a Christian Europe, a shared European civilization, and a European notion of freedom.[90] Despite this scholarly attention for a supposed common European past, others tried to refute this proposition. Shore and Black for example argued that the view of a single European past makes a too sharp distinction between who is and who is not "European", and may "add to the tide

86 Matthew Evangelista, *Unarmed Forces: The Transnational Movement to End the Cold War* (Ithaca: Cornell University Press, 1999).

87 Their role is also stressed by Clavin, "Introduction," 427. Clavin's expert communities border on what has been described elsewhere as epistemic communities. See Peter M. Haas, "Introduction: Epistemic Communities and International Policy Coordination," *International Organization* 46, no. 1 (1992): 1-35. He defines an epistemic community as "a network of professionals with recognised expertise and competence in a particular domain and an authoritative claim to policy-relevant knowledge within that domain or issue-area".

88 Historical studies of the idea of Europe are abundant and include Denys Hay, *Europe: The Emergence of an Idea* (New York: Harper & Row, 1966); Carl H. Pegg, *Evolution of the European Idea, 1914-1932* (Chapel Hill/London: University of North Carolina Press, 1983); Kevin Wilson and Jan van der Dussen, *The History of the Idea of Europe* (London: Routledge, 1995); Gerard Delanty, *Inventing Europe: Idea, Identity, Reality* (New York: St. Martin's Press, 1995); Brian Nelson, David Roberts, and Walter Veit, eds., *The Idea of Europe: Problems of National and Transnational Identity* (Providence: Berg, 1992); Elisabeth du Réau, *L'Idée d'Europe au XXe siècle: Des mythes aux réalités* (Brussels: Editions Complexe, 1996); Anthony Pagden, ed., *The Idea of Europe: From Antiquity to the European Union* (Cambridge University Press, 2001); and Menno Spiering and Michael Wintle, eds., *Ideas of Europe Since 1914: The Legacy of the First World War* (New York: Palgrave, 2002).

89 For a discussion see Wintle, "Cultural Identity in Europe: Shared Experience," in *Culture and Identity in Europe: Perceptions of Divergence and Unity in Past and Presence*, ed. Wintle (Aldershot: Avebury, 1996), 12-14.

90 See amongst others his "Europe to 1914: The Making of an Idea," in *The History*, ed. Wilson and Van der Dussen, 13-82. For more on a Europe of Christianity see Hay, *Europe*. Agnes Heller's view on Europe is in some way comparable with Ernest Gellner's loose equalisation of nationalism and modernisation with her insistence that "European culture *is* modernity". See Heller, "Europe: An Epilogue?," in *The Idea of Europe*, ed. Nelson, Roberts, and Veit, 22; and Ernest Gellner, *Nations and Nationalism* (Ithaca: Cornell University Press, 1983).

of xenophobia and racism".[91] Others contend that the historical foundations of Europe as a delineated entity is weak. Anthony Smith sees this as "Europe's true dilemma"; a choice between unacceptable historical myths and memories on the one hand, and on the other hand a patchwork, a memory-less scientific "culture" held together solely by the political will and economic interest that are so often subject to change.[92]

The latter point of Smith is crucial; the idea of Europe is historically subjected to change. In analogy to Borneman and Fowler, this book will threat Europe not as a "stable, sovereign, autonomous object", but rather as existing only in historical relations.[93] According to them, historical actors have related to Europe as a strategy of representing themselves and as a device of power. I too do not work with a fixed and predetermined definition of Europe, neither from a geographical nor a cultural point of view. My actors, the system-builders, determine what is European and what is not. This implies that "Europe" was neither a logical, uncontested or a single grand project. Rather, building an electrical Europe was a layered process, hardly undisputed and natural. Visions of a European system also reflected different geographies of Europe, including some countries while excluding others. These geographies not only varied among engineers and politicians involved, but were also reflected – and caused – by membership of international organizations, both governmental and non-governmental.

Sources and limitations

In the case of national electrification, the primary system-builders often include the state, along with national utilities and national engineering associations. For the development of a European interconnected network, the system-building process was fragmented over a number of international organizations. The organizations that were involved in European system-building are the primary focus of this study. Different types of organizations have been the object of study.

First of all, I looked at a number of intergovernmental organizations, including

---

91 Cris Shore and Annabel Black, "The European Communities and the Construction of Europe," *Anthropology Today* 8, no. 3 (1992): 11. Another article making a case for this argument is Jan Nederveen Pieterse, "Fictions of Europe," *Race and Class* 32, no. 3 (1991): 3-10.
92 Anthony D. Smith, "National Identity and the Idea of European Unity," *International Affairs* 68, no. 1 (1992): 73-74.
93 John Borneman and Nick Fowler, "Europeanization," *Annual Review of Anthropology* 26 (1997): 489. Others have suggested a similar approach. See for example Hayden White, "The Discourse of Europe and the Search for a European Identity," in *Europe and the Other and Europe as the Other*, ed. Bo Stråth (Brussels: Peter Lang, 2000), 67.

the League of Nations (LoN, 1920-1946), the International Labor Organization (ILO, 1919), the Organization for European Economic Cooperation (OEEC, 1948-1961), the United Nations Economic Commission for Europe (UNECE, 1947) and several institutions of the (now) European Union. Since little to none secondary literature exists on their activities with regard to electricity, I primarily relied on archival sources and official documents.

Second of all, another focus was on international non-governmental organizations directly dealing with electricity. This includes associations of electrical engineers, utility managers and network operators, like UNIPEDE and the World Power Conference (now World Energy Council, WEC). In general, these organizations did not receive wide historical attention. Incidentally an academic publication appeared, and in some instances commemorative overviews were commissioned – as was the case for UNIPEDE/EURELECTRIC and WEC.[94] These however primarily focus on the more recent period. Unfortunately their voluminous congress reports are not widely available in libraries, and series are often incomplete. I therefore chose to focus mainly on UNIPEDE, the organization most closely related to network-building, and examine all their proceedings starting in 1926. Within the same category is the UCPTE, which comprises a personal union between network operators. Their activities also had to bear historical scrutiny. I made a thorough study of their private archives as well as their official documentation.

These two categories contain the most important European system-building organizations with regard to electricity. In addition, several additional archives have been used, either to fill blank spots or to cross-check other archival pieces and perspectives. I made extensive use of the National Archives of the United States to describe the role of the Marshall Plan on electricity network-building in Europe. I further used additional archives, including the national archives of Austria, Belgium, Switzerland, and the archives of the North Atlantic Treaty Organization (NATO, 1949). Furthermore, I incidentally relied on journals and newspapers, and also conducted one interview. Besides qualitative sources I also used quantitative data to illustrate the development of international collaboration in Europe.

I am aware that a strong focus on international actors and use of mainly archival research has several limitations. Although archives are regarded a primary re-

---

94 See respectively Paul K. Lyons, *75 Years of Cooperation in the Electricity Industry* (Brussels: Union of the Electricity Industry/EURELECTRIC, 2000); and Ian Fells, *World Energy 1923-1998 and Beyond: A Commemoration of the World Energy Council on its 75th Anniversary* (London: Atalink Projects / World Energy Council , 1998).

source, their content is always selective. What is eventually kept, and how it is filed, represents a choice of the archivist. For this selection, historians in turn make their own assessments. Despite the fact that I did extensive research in most key archives, I too made a selection of what I found most valuable for this study. One other drawback of archival research could be the lack of recent material. Researchers are often restricted by archival laws, restricting access to material younger than 30 years. In my case, this was not an issue for at least a number of archives. For several key archives, including that of UNECE and UCPTE, I was allowed access to recent documents as well. Restrictions do not apply to the archive of the League of Nations, and the policy with regard to documents of EU institutions is rather liberal. The only two archives which likely hold more relevant material that I did not see are the National Archives in Washington D.C and NATO.

In considering secondary literature and archival sources, the main void in this study is a lack of knowledge on Central and Eastern European developments. Not only is there little written on national or regional histories of electrification, archival sources are rare and difficult to access. One obvious source would have been the Central and Eastern European equivalent of the UCPTE, the Central Dispatch Organization. This organization ceased to exist in 2005, and their private archive remained closed to historians.[95] The current state and location of the archive is unknown. The archives of the Council for Mutual Economic Assistance (CMEA, 1949), located in Moscow, are open to researchers but as of yet highly unorganized.[96]

With regard to transnational history, there have been complaints that the field is too absorbed with studying international organizations. In defense, Clavin asserted that many of these institutions have seen little study by historians. She notes that "archival research has drawn out their complex relationship to national and supranational power with a subtlety and depth that has eluded the writing of some international political scientists on the subject".[97] I cannot but agree with her.

One pitfall of a transnational approach is less attention for national perspectives. This does not imply that national developments are ignored completely. In various instances I refer to national developments. Yet most of my examples are drawn from countries whose history with regard to electricity has been well documented. Two other countries that I regularly describe, namely Austria and Yugoslavia, played exceptional roles in European network-building. Although I

---

95 Petr Veselký (Secretary of CDO), letters to author, June 3, 2004 and December 8, 2004.
96 E. A. Tyurina (Director of the Russian State Archive of the Economy), e-mail message to author, January 16, 2006. The archives are open, but not very organised, and lack a decent inventory. At that moment, no funds were available to improve that situation.
97 Clavin, "Introduction," 424.

believe that a historical survey of international collaboration from a national perspective would almost certainly result in another perspective of the past, I strongly
believe that transnational and national histories complement rather than conflict
with each other.

Another drawback of a focus on transnational actors and organizations is that
it excludes ideas and visions that were not brought forward to these international
forums. A good example can be taken from existing historiography. The above-
mentioned *Atlantropa* project was not picked up by any of the system-builders I
studied, and thus not features in this book. In other words, there may have been
other more nationally or locally confined plans for a European system that I did
not take into account.

One other consequence of the approach is that I did not deal substantially with
the Nazi era. That period is relatively short, and already quite well-documented
in terms of secondary literature. Although historian Bernhard Stier has argued
that the Nazi influence on network-building in Europe is underestimated, he also
points to the fact that German archives are not complete on this matter.[98] Other
related material on Nazi network-building is scattered over various national archives, and often incomplete. My own experiences in the Bundesarchiv in Vienna
confirm this, as Nazi period files were very incomplete. I therefore relied on secondary literature to sketch the main developments of that distinct period.

Structure

The book has a chronological perspective of the development of a European system. Chapter 2 charts the electricity sector in Europe in the beginning of the 20th
century. By then the electricity industry already had an international character as
transmission lines and entrepreneurs operated across borders. In this period the
first international engineering associations related to electricity were founded. At
the same time, national governments sought to steer the development of networks
and increasingly safeguarded electricity as a national resource.

The 1920s and 1930s are the focal point of Chapter 3. It answers my first research question by describing how an agenda for a European electricity system
originated, within the context of the emerging European movement. Not only engineering associations, but also intergovernmental organizations like the League

---

98 Bernhard Stier, "Expansion, réforme de structure et interconnexion européenne: Développement et
difficultés de l'électricité sous le nazisme, 1939-1945," in *Les entreprises du secteur de l'énergie sous l'Occupation*, ed. Varashin (Arras: Artois Presses Université, 2006), 289-290.

of Nations and International Labor Organization played an instrumental role. Important actors in this period are electrical engineers, but also include policy-makers, entrepreneurs, and economists. Most of them were somehow connected to the European movement. Ideas on Europe were inspired by political stalemate and economic distress. The notion of a European network fed on these problems.

The war and subsequent period is covered by Chapter 4. The main topic of this chapter is the institutionalization of cross-border cooperation. This was solidified in the form of regional power pools, starting in Western Europe with UCPTE. That region also experienced profound American influences through the European Recovery Program (ERP), which also sought to stimulate European integration. This was also the case for their activities concerning electricity. The ERP not only aimed to reconstruct electricity systems and expand electricity production. It also stimulated cooperation in the electricity sector. European engineers were also willing to work together more closely, inspired by more ideological reasons.

Chapter 5 covers the 1950s until approximately 2001. Its main narrative is the contested nature of interconnections across the Iron Curtain. The chapter focuses on another part of the ERP; the strengthening of Western Europe for a possible new war. At the same time, I show how the NATO alliance actively tried to prevent East-West cooperation, which was mainly propagated by UNECE. East-West co-operation did come about, especially after the process of détente set in. Finally at the very end of the twentieth century the EU begins to play a role in the process of European system-building and thus also enters my narrative.

Chapter 2
"Opening the doors to a revolution"

A dry winter following a hot summer in 1921-'22 led to a lack of water, which seriously decreased hydroelectricity production in Italy.[1] In the Po Valley, in the northern part of the country, this forced local governments to take action. The provinces of Piedmont, Lombardy, and Venice – Italy's industrial heartland – appointed special commissioners to ration the available electricity to industry. Besides this rationing, Switzerland supplied extra electricity. Technically this was possible, as transmission lines crossed the Italian-Swiss border and Italy already imported electricity from Switzerland. Electricity suppliers in France took part as well. French coal-fired plants in Nancy and Vincey supplied electricity to Zurich, Switzerland. The latter town normally received electricity from the Swiss plants in Brusio and Thusis. Northern Italy now consumed that electricity. According to the commissioner for Lombardy, Milanese engineer Angelo Omedeo, these electricity transmissions avoided "consequent shutting down of factories owing to lack of motive power".[2]

At this point in time an international solution – electricity exchanges between countries – seemed obvious to a solve a local problem – electricity shortage in northern Italy. Why this was possible, and how this situation was still rather unique needs historical explanation. By 1921 transmission lines traversed national boundaries for over two decades. The earliest cross-border interconnections, mostly 60-70 kV lines, could not play an important role beyond the local level, however.[3] Often these connections transmitted electricity produced by power plants situated on border rivers.[4]

---

1 Gaetano Salvemini, "Economic Conditions in Italy, 1919-1922," *Journal of Modern History* 23, no. 1 (1951): 32.
2 League of Nations, *Advisory and Technical Committee for Communications and Transit, Procès-Verbal of the Second Session, Held at Geneva, March 29th- 31st, 1922*, LoN document series, C.212.M.116.1922. VIII (Geneva: LoN, 1922), Annex 7, "Report to the President of the Advisory and Technical Committee on Communications and Transit on the Requested Action by the League of Nations for Facilitating the Cession by One Country to Another of Electric Power for Operation of Railways of International Concern," 33.
3 Christophe Bouneau, "La genèse de l'interconnexion électrique internationale de la France du début du siècle à 1946," in *Les réseaux Europééns transnationaux XIXe - XXe siècles: quels enjeux?*, ed. Michèle Merger, Albert Carreras, and Andrea Giuntini (Nantes: Ouest Éditons, 1994), 78-79.
4 Varaschin, "Etats," 136, table 8.

Table 2.1 – Transmission distances and losses per voltage

AC current in kV	Capacity in kW		Transmission distance in km	Cross-section of copper wiring in mm2	Loss of charge in %
	Single line	Double line			
60	19,000	38,000	100	3 x 95	10
110	40,500	891,000	200	3 x 120	10.15
220	110,000	220,000	400	3 x 160	10.2
380	550,000	1100,000	600	3 x 400	10.5
380	500,000	1000,000	1,000	3 x 400	15.7

Source: Legge, *Grundsätzliches*, 8.

But after the Great War, two major developments took place. A first major change was the use of higher voltages for transmission lines. This enabled the transfer of electricity over longer distances, without uneconomical losses in charge (see Table 2.1). Since then, higher voltage transmission lines interconnected the border regions between Germany, Switzerland, France, and to a lesser extent Italy.[5] According to Lundgreen, the use of "high-voltage electrical technology opened the doors to a revolution in machine building, [...] lighting and transportation, [...] to the production, storage and distribution of current via central power stations".[6] Second and related, the average power plant capacity increased with the construction of so-called *supercentrales* or *Überlandwerke*. At the time the rapid increase in capacity resonated in consecutive claims of several new plants to be the largest in Europe.[7] As the name *Überlandwerk* already implies, these plants served consumers far beyond the local.

Networks and plants were not the only aspects of electricity production that operated internationally. The financing – "the nervous system of all construction enterprises for the great technological networks"[8] – and construction of electricity networks were also international in character. Holding companies called *Unternehmergeschäfte* played a dominant role in setting up local and regional electricity systems all over Europe and beyond. These were powerful alliances between manufacturers of electrical equipment on the one hand and banks on the other.

One such company helped engineering the complex electricity transmissions between the three countries in the 1921-22 events described above, namely the

---

5 Bouneau, "La genèse," 78-79.
6 Peter Lundgreen, "Engineering Education in Europe and the USA, 1750-1930: The Rise to Dominance of School Culture and the Engineering Professions," *Annals of Science* 47, no. 1 (1990): 58.
7 Millward, *Private*, 114.
8 Armand Mattelart, *The Invention of Communication* (Minneapolis: University of Minnesota Press, 1996), 99.

Swiss *Unternehmersgeschäft Motor AG*, which had interests in several plants involved in the transmission including *Kraftwerke Brusio AG*.[9] Agostino Nizzola was the technical director of Motor.[10] The company also erected the 50 kV interconnection between Beznau and Löntsch in 1908, and built a plant in Gösgen which connected to the network of the *Compagnie Lorraine d'Electricité* (see Figure 2.1).[11]

According to Nizzola, the electricity transmission involving France, Switzerland and Italy seemed "a first step towards the solution of wider and more interesting problems".[12] He referred in particular to the possibilities of interconnecting different power systems, even across national boundaries. It would allow for a better balancing between thermal and hydroelectricity, and offer avenues for mutual help.

But despite the international character of the industry, Milanese engineer Omedeo stressed that these emergency supplies to Italy only came about due to "the international agreements and goodwill".[13] The obstacles to cross-border transmissions were no longer technical, but political and legislative.[14] Of the three countries involved, Italy had the least restrictive policy. State intervention strengthened in 1919, but mainly to promote further electrification. The 1919 Bill issued uniform measures for public participation in firms, and tariffs and subsidies for building dams.[15] Legislation in France was more restrictive. There, a law issued in October 1919 forbade the export of hydroelectric power without permission from the *Conseil d'Etat*.[16] Since 1912 electricity imports had needed consent of the Minister of Public Works.[17] Switzerland tried to bring unutilized water-power under state ownership in 1891. The construction of export-oriented power plants in the first two decades of the 20th century, among them the two plants in Brusio, led

---

9 Brusio AG was established in 1904, and generated electricity in Switzerland. The main beneficiary of the imported power was the Italian *Società Lombarda per la distribuzione di energia elettricà* (Lombarda).
10 Agostino Nizzola (1869-1961) was born in Lugano, Switzerland. He was trained as an electrical engineer at the EPF in Zurich. Between 1891 and 1913 he worked as an engineer for BBC, before becoming director of Motor, the financial society of BBC. He was a board member on various financial and electricity bodies, under which the Kraftwerke Brusio.
11 H. Niesz, "L'Échange d'énergie électrique entre pays, au point de vue économique et technique," in *Transactions of the World Power Conference, Basle, Sectional meeting*, vol. 1 (Basel: Birkhäuser & Cie, 1926), 1028.
12 LoN doc, ser., C.212.M.116.1922.VIII, Annex 7, "Report to the President," 33-34.
13 Ibid.
14 Varaschin, "Etats," 138-139.
15 Renato Giannetti, "Resources, Firms and Public Policy in the Growth of Italian Electrical Industry from Beginnings to the 30's," in *1880-1980*, ed. Cardot, 44 & 47.
16 Varaschin, "Etats," 139. The Conseil d'Etat is the foremost legal advisor of the French national government.
17 Bouneau, "La genèse," 77.

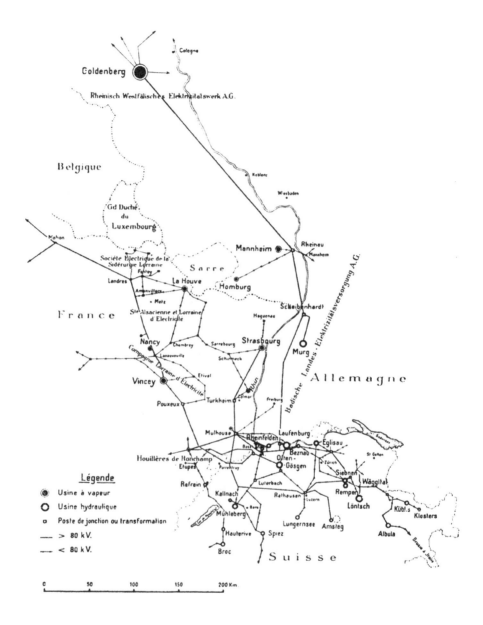

Figure 2.1 – Swiss, French, and German interconnections around in 1926
Source: H. Niesz, 'L'Échange, 1026. Used by permission of the World Energy Council, London,
www.worldenergycouncil.org.

to controversy and fierce debate in Swiss popular press.[18] A 1916 ordinance placed electricity sales to other countries under the control of the Federal government.[19] Thus despite the existence of international connections, national legislation increasingly restricted their use.

Although cross-border electricity transmission was still in its infancy, the use of higher voltage technology in the period between the wars made interconnections beyond national border a serious option.[20] The Franco-Swiss-Italian cooperation answered to this potential. Still, as historian Christophe Bouneau has argued, one could see a paradoxical development in the interwar electricity sector: while the sector was highly international, it became increasingly subjected to national regulations.[21] Next to international transmission lines, a growing international human network had also emerged. A community of electrical engineers, dominant in research and development, and pioneering in entrepreneurship, came to form a transnational class of people. The activities of the *Unternehmergeschäfte* since the 1890s further promoted an engineering and industrial network with international ramifications.[22] This class was developing constantly by holding congresses, conferences, and forming international associations.

But at the same electricity production and transmission became increasingly framed within national boundaries – a process described as *domestication* by Hausmann et al.[23] In part, this was because of government efforts to bring about a more rational organization of electricity generation and supply, inspired by engineering philosophy and wartime experiences with central planning. But it was also to counter the "additional costs" of foreign finance and control of electric power facilities; not only to reduce the major role of foreign finance and manufacturers, but to decrease external dependence in general.[24] This development, which took place during and after WWI, was mainly of a legislative nature. In many European countries, authorities assumed some form of oversight over in- and outbound flows of electricity, and began to develop transmission networks and production capacity, in particular of hydroelectricity. This not only involved import and ex-

---

18 David Gugerli, *Redeströme: Zur Elektrifizierung der Schweiz, 1880-1914* (Zurich: Chronos Verlag, 1996), 287-288.
19 Varaschin, "Etats," 138.
20 Pierre Lanthier, "Logique électrique et logique électrotechnique: la cohabitation des électriciens et des électrotechniciens dans la direction des constructions électriques français: une comparaison internationale," in *Stratégies, gestion, management: les compagnies électriques et leurs patrons, 1895-1945: Actes du 12e colloque de l'Association pour l'histoire de l'électricité en France les 3, 4 et 5 février 1999*, ed. Dominique Barjot et al. (Paris: Fondation Electricité de France, 2001), 35. Also see Kaijser, "Controlling," 32.
21 Bouneau, "Les réseaux," 25, 31-32.
22 Barjot and Kurgan, "Les réseaux," 70.
23 Hausman, Wilkins, and Neufeld, "Multinational," 177.
24 Ibid.

port regulations and concession systems, but also included laws making watercourses "national", and restricting their accessibility to foreign investors.

This development was not without opposition. Fostering the international character of the electricity industry was a concern for most international and professional organizations related to electricity. Electricity producers and *Unternehmergeschäfte* alike wanted to keep the industry as international as possible, and keep borders open. In the eyes of many engineers, the geographical spread of networks and interconnection of power plants led to a more rational organization of electricity production. They often argued that transmission lines should not halt at national borders. The League of Nations took a similar stance. That organization tried to install international conventions that, while respecting the national legislations, sought to simplify the expansion and use of international connections.

The aim of this chapter is to sketch the main national and international context in which electricity networks were developed. It provides a survey of international network-building activities, and the birth of international organizations related to electricity. It will also show the national framing of electricity production and network-development, which displayed itself in this period in restrictive legislation on cross-border developments and in plans for national networks. A transnational class of people – engineers – did not reject this increasing national organization entirely. Rather, engineers mediated to extend electricity networks across borders, while respecting national sovereignty. International interconnections and electricity exchange were legitimated by business interests, but were also seen as more rational. The chapter also shows that debates on system-building did not yet include ideas of specifically European cooperation. Hope was placed on international conventions – and not European ones – as a way of keeping borders open.

An industry expands

Electricity generation and distribution was initially geographically limited to local consumers. Often local governments took part in exploiting gasworks, and were thus not eager to bear risks to support electricity – a potential competitor. Local authorities often granted private initiative with a concession to exploit small-scale electricity plants. Typically, the first application of electricity in the late 19th century

Table 2.2 – Electricity imports and exports from and to Germany, Switzerland, and Sweden, 1925-1930, in kWh

	1925		1926		1927		1928		1929		1930	
Germany	Import	Export	Import	Export	Import	Export	Import	Export	Import	Export	Import	Export
Denmark	–	–	–	–	–	–	–	–	–	–	2.1	320.0
Netherlands	0.0	1.4	0.0	1.3	0.0	3.3	0.0	1.8	0.0	2.0	0.0	2.2
France	37.6	46.0	15.1	59.0	37.7	59.4	46.0	61.5	50.1	60.3	45.0*	46.0*
Lithuania	–	–	–	0.0	–	0.0	–	0.0	–	0.0	–	0.0
Luxemburg	–	0.1	–	0.1	–	0.1	–	0.1	–	0.1	–	0.1
Austria	20.7	0.6	24.3	0.3	47.0	0.4	99.7	0.9	133.9	3.2	218.6	6.7
Poland	11.5	1.4	0.8	10.8	11.1	63.2	3.4	53.4	2.7	51.8	17.6*	52.0*
Sarre	27.8	0.0	17.2	5.0	14.9	7.4	33.4	9.0	50.7	0.6	55.4	0.3
Switzerland	209.4	22.0	148.1	30.1	156.8	27.7	110.5	38.2	166.0	42.7	280.0	68.0
Czechoslovakia	0.0	18.3	0.0	17.0	0.6	17.5	0.0	18.1	0.0	18.8	0.2	20.0
Total	307.0	89.8	205.6	123.5	268.2	178.9	293.1	182.9	403.4	179.5	619.0	515.3
Switzerland	Import	Export	Import	Export	Import	Export	Import	Export	Import	Export	Import	Export
France	40	307	56	395	61	467	70	510	91	565	105	590
Germany	22	210	30	148	28	157	38	111	43	167	68	170
Italy	170	–	225	–	210	–	242	–	150	260	250	175
Total	232	517	311	543	299	624	350	621	284	992	423	935
Sweden	Import	Export	Import	Export	Import	Export	Import	Export	Import	Export	Import	Export
Norway	–	10	–	11.5	–	12	–	13.2	–	17	–	15.8
Denmark	–	16	–	17	–	58	–	43	–	28	–	86
Finland	–	0.02	–	0.02	–	0.025	–	0.04	–	0.1	–	0.12
Total	–	26.02	–	28.52	–	70.03	–	56.24	–	45.1	–	101.9

* Estimates.
Calculated on basis of Kittler, *Der internationale*.

was lighting but other early uses included tramways.[25] In many cases, local governments became involved as network service grew.[26] These first small-scale systems regularly had foreign influences, mainly from the United States and Germany. Diligent patent politics enabled first movers like American firms Westinghouse and General Electric, and the German counterparts *Allgemeine Elektrizitäts-Gesellschaft* (AEG) and Siemens, to expand their empires.[27] Alfred Chandler labeled these the "Big Four". They dominated the industry from the 1880s until the 1940s.[28] They had an interest not only in supplying equipment to produce and distribute electricity, but also in providing consumers with traction systems, electromotors, and other appliances.[29]

Most general histories of electrification regard the 1891 international electrical exhibition in Frankfurt as the emblem of electricity transmission over longer distances. There electricity was transported over 175 kilometers to Frankfurt from its origin, the river Neckar in Lauffen. Only a decade and a half later, the first transmission lines traversed national boundaries.[30] River-run hydroelectric plants on the Rhine fed into Germany, France, and Switzerland. Starting in 1906, a 40 kV line to Guebwiller in France transmitted electricity generated at the hydroelectric plant in Rheinfelden, Germany.[31] Another 40 kV crossed the Rhine and French-German border between Ile Napoléon (near Mulhouse) and Fribourg from 1910. International connections also appeared beyond the Rhine. The first large-scale export-oriented plant was erected in Brusio in 1906. Both 23 kV and 55 kV lines exported hydroelectricity from the Swiss Ticino region to northern provinces in Italy.[32] Scandinavian countries built cross-border linkages as well. During WWI, a submarine cable between Helsingör in Denmark and Helsingborg in Sweden came into operation.[33] Good statistics of international electricity exchanges are available since approximately 1925. By then, countries like Germany. Switzerland and

---

25 See for example Wolfgang Schivelbusch, *Disenchanted Night: The Industrialization of Light in the Nineteenth Century* (Berkeley: University of California Press, 1995). Ginette Kurgan rightly argues that this pattern is varied per country, and was dependent on many factors, like economic and social structure, access to primary energy sources, and the relation between civil society and the State. See Alain Beltran, Ginette Kurgan, and Henri Morsel, "Présentation," *Bulletin d'histoire de l'électricité* 22 (1993): 12.

26 Millward, *Private*, 77.

27 Henri Morsel, "Panorama de l'histoire de l'électricité en France dans la première moitié du XXe siècle," in *1880-1980*, ed. Cardot, 88-89. On AEG and Siemens see Alfred D. Chandler, *The Visible Hand: The Managerial Revolution in American Business* (Cambridge: Belknap Press, 1977), 463-473 and 538-549.

28 Ibid., 464.

29 Hausman, Wilkins, and Neufeld, "Multinational," 180.

30 Persoz, "Les grands," 783.

31 Vivian Saminaden, *Histoire du développement des réseaux interconnectés d'Europe* (Paris: Electricité de France, 1994), 3.

32 Ibid

33 Kaijser, "Trans-Border," 6; and Van der Vleuten, "Electrifying," 120.

Sweden had multiple interconnections with their neighbors, and made increasingly use of these (see Table 2.2; for totals of electricity generation, see Table 2.3).

The use of high voltage transmission lines meant electricity production was no longer restricted to be near consumers. This opened perspectives for harnessing water-power in more distant and isolated mountain areas. Interconnections between thermal and hydroelectric power plants – also over borders – were often built to get a better economic mix.[34] This was the rationale behind the interconnection between Gösgen in Switzerland and Nancy in France. In general, it was more economical to use hydroelectricity rather than burn expensive coal. Switzerland transmitted hydroelectric power to Lorraine in times of plentiful water, often during night-time, and during peak demands in France. The flow reversed in times of low water, during the end of winter or frost.[35] Low hydraulicity impelled Swiss electricity producers to connect not only to French mine-head thermal power units, but also to German ones: Gösgen was connected to Laufenburg as well.[36]

Such projects were the outcome of an emerging field of study in engineering. Since the end of the 19th century, engineers studied the technical-economic planning and operation of electricity systems, to guarantee a maximum productivity and profitability.[37] The emphasis on economic mix and interconnection were two results of this new focus. Another was load management, which aimed at "regularity of load and maximum practical utilization of generating capacity".[38] In other words, it tried to avoid periods of very low and high demand, and ensure a load curve that was as "flat" as possible – resulting in lower prices per kWh. This was done by interconnecting areas with different peak loads, and by distributing to industries with large continuous electricity needs.[39] The introduction of the steam turbine in thermal plants, which was much more efficient than reciprocating steam engines, propelled a search for demand to fulfill the potential of an economy of scale.[40] Another advantage of interconnecting systems or plants was that it allowed mutual assistance in case of incidental shortages.

Working along these engineering principles brought unprecedented challenges in organization and finance, in the form of large plants and vast transmission networks.[41]

---

34 Hughes, *Networks*, 346ff. At p.367 Hughes gives the following definition: "An economic mix is an interconnection of power plants whose energy sources are complementary."
35 Niesz, "L'Échange," 1028.
36 Ibid., 1029-1030.
37 Stier, *Staat und Strom: Die politische Steuerung des Elektrizitätssystems in Deutschland 1890-1950* (Mannheim: Verlag Regionalkultur, 1999), 51. Also see Hughes, *Networks*, 363.
38 Hughes, *Networks*, 219.
39 Kaijser, "Controlling," 32-33.
40 Hughes, *Networks*, 363-364.
41 Segreto, "Financing," 163.

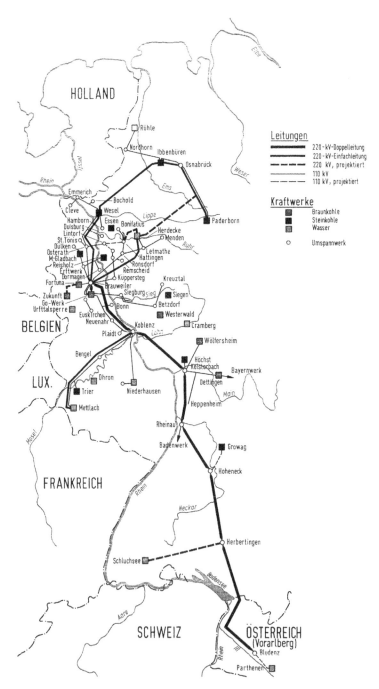

Figure 2.2 – *The RWE system in 1928*
Source: Boll, Entstehung. 45, image 14. Used with kind permission of BDEW Bundesverband der Energie- und Wasserwirtschaft e.V.

The *Unternehmergeschäfte* met these challenges.[42] Shortly after the Frankfurt exhibition, German manufacturers of electrical equipment formed several electrical enterprises, in which Swiss – and to a lesser extent German and Belgian – banks played an important role as financiers.[43] Normally several years passed before electricity plants were in operation, and shares or obligations could not be issued immediately. These holding companies solved the problem this time-lag created by separating the issuing of shares from the long-term finance of new undertaking. This was one reason to incorporate the enterprises in Switzerland, as Swiss legal provisions for issuing bonds were looser than German ones.[44] Switzerland's favorable financial institutional setting helped in generating long-term capital.[45] In 1895 AEG incorporated the *Bank für elektrische Unternehmungen* (Elektrobank), with Swiss and German banks *Crédit Suisse* and Berliner *Handels-Gesellschaft*.[46] In the same year Swiss manufacturers of electrical equipment Brown Boveri & Cie (BBC) founded a financial trust named *Motor für angewandte Elektrizität*, better known as simply *Motor* – the company Nizzola worked for. German financial institutions provided two-thirds of its capital, and BBC itself most of the remaining third.[47] A year later, Siemens created the *Schweizerische Gesellschaft für elektrische Industrie*, better known as *Indelec*.[48] During their first years of existence, the activities of these holding companies were mainly concerned with financial operations, and were aided by a small staff. This changed around 1904-05 when, generally speaking, more managers and technical sections were added to plan and supervise projects.[49]

A good example of the new engineering philosophy combined with financing through *Unternehmergeschäfte* was the system of the *Rheinisch-Westfälischen Elektrizitätswerks Aktiengesellschaft* (RWE, 1898). In the 1910s and 1920s, RWE

---

42 Hertner, "Les sociétés," 342-343. This kind of entrepreneurship was not limited to electricity. Hertner also gives examples of railway undertakings.

43 For Belgium see Ginette Kurgan van Hentenryk, "La patronat de l'électricité en Belgique, 1895-1945," in *Stratégies,gestion*, ed. Barjot et al., 55-69.

44 Albert Broder, "L'Expansion internationale de l'industrie allemande dans le dernier tiers du XIXe siècle: Le cas de l'industrie électrique, 1880-1913," *Relations internationales* 29 (1982): 78.

45 Hertner, "Les sociétés," 342-343, and Barbara Bonhage, "Unternehmerische Entscheidungen im Spannungsfeld gesamtwirtschaftlicher Veränderungen: Eine Fallstudie zum organisatorischen Wandel der Bank für elektrische Unternehmungen in der Zwischenkriegszeit und im Zweiten Weltkrieg" (Lizentiatsarbeit, Philosophischen Fakultät I der Universität Zürich, 1998), 49.

46 It was also known under its French name *Banque pour entreprises électrique*.

47 Patrick Kupper and Tobias Wildi, *Motor-Columbus: From 1895 to 2006. 111 Years of Motor-Columbus* (Baden: Motor-Columbus, 2006), 3. Also see Luciano Segreto, "Stratégie et structure des sociétés financières suisses pour l'industrie électrique (1895-1945)," in *Allmächtige Zauberin unserer Zeit. Zur Geschichte der elektrischen Energie in der Schweiz*, ed. Gugerli (Zurich: Chronos Verlag, 1994), 57-72.

48 Hughes, *Networks*, 164.

49 Ibid., 164-165.

built relative large plants of different generation types, like the 50 MW brown coal-fired Goldenbergwerke (1914) in the Ruhr area. Later it built the hydroelectric plant of Vermuntwerk (1930) in Austria.[50] At the same time, a network of initially 110 kV, and in the 1920s 220 kV, was erected to interconnect them (see Figure 2.2).[51] Elektrobank played a fundamental role in connecting the RWE grid to the south to tap into Rhine, Neckar and Alpine regions in Germany and Austria.[52] Power plant Goldenberg also connected to Gösgen in Switzerland.[53] RWE's system became a *Verbundbetrieb*, a united operation through cooperation between interconnected power plants, which resulted in a well-balanced *economic mix*. The cheapest suppliers of electricity, the brown coal plants at the mine heads, made for the year-round base load. River-run hydroelectric plants performed a similar function. Hydroelectric plants with water storage capacities, like the Vermuntenwerk, covered seasonal shortages.[54] RWE diversified its load in addition to its energy supply. It supplied electricity to municipalities, but its main clientele was industrial. Chemical works in the Ruhr were persuaded to connect to RWE. Their loads were ideal because they took electricity day and night. In addition, RWE had large steady consumers in iron and steelworks. Hugo Stinnes, the chairman of RWE between 1903 and 1924, saw the policy of mass production and large area supply as rational.[55] RWE engineer Arthur Koepchen defined rationalization as "using technology to obtain the economic optimum with a minimum of resources".[56] To facilitate such an optimal system, a main switching station became operational in Brauweiler in October 1929, where interconnected plans and load were centrally controlled and monitored.[57] RWE's *Verbundbetrieb* thus was an example of a rational system that crossed national frontiers.

50 On Goldenbergwerke, in 1914 the largest plant in Europe, see Boll, *Enstehung*, 42-44. For Vermunt-werk, in 1930 by far the largest unit in Austria, see Clemens M. Hutter, "Kriege, Krisen und kein Groschen Startkapital," in *Energie für unser Leben, 1947 bis 1997. 50 Jahre Verbund* (Vienna: Österreichische Elektrizitätswirtschafts-Aktiengesellschaft, 1997), 61.
51 The first 110 kV was built between Lauchammer and Riesa in 1911. Saminaden, *Histoire*, 3.
52 Hughes, *Networks*, 424; and Boll, *Enstehung*, 44.
53 Niesz, "L'Échange," 1030.
54 Ibid., 418.
55 Hughes, *Networks*, 415. For Hugo Stinnes and his policy of integrating firms backward and forward, see Charles S. Maier, *Recasting Bourgeois Europe: Stabilization in France, Germany, and Italy in the Decade After World War I* (Princeton: Princeton University Press, 1988), 209-212.
56 Ibid., 418.
57 Ibid., 423.

Postwar rationalization and regulation

The philosophy followed by RWE (minus its international component) was increasingly put into practice within national territories. The experience of wartime economy strengthened notions of optimized organization and rationalization, in a time when the role of the state in most national economies expanded. This included an increasing state influence on the electricity sector. The war and subsequent reconstruction marked a vital turning point in use of electric power. It also saw electrical engineers making a name in wartime organization and postwar recovery.[58] As the war and postwar period saw an increase of the importance of electricity, an expansion of regulatory measures affected the production and transmission of electric power. Meanwhile, the role of *Unternehmergeschäfte* dwindled, leaving states the most powerful actors in the electricity sector.

In general, the sheer length of warfare during WWI led to a total war economy – an unprecedented feat in modern history. Unaccountable government agencies took care of war mobilization, and led to a corporatist managed society which emerged around the collaboration between state, industry and labor. This went with increased state intervention in production, distribution, and allocating economic resources.[59] Engineers played a profound role in those war agencies and administrations. Their emphasis on rationality, efficiency, and scientific methods thus carved a secure place in administrative thinking. These wartime experiences were at least partially carried over into peacetime. As Thomas Hughes writes "[w]artime government had introduced industrial, technological, and scientific planning and control on an unprecedented scale".[60]

Electricity, which had been introduced in factories to speed up wartime assembly lines, became increasingly associated with rational organization.[61] Governments sometimes took over the role of financier of power plants, and stimulated interconnection to make more electricity available without expanding generation capacity.[62] Wartime administrators themselves were sometimes directly involved in the electricity industry. This was the case in two belligerent countries, France and Germany. German engineer Walther Rathenau (1867-1922), son of AEG-founder Emil Rathenau, was involved in founding Elektrobank. He is regarded

---

58 Barjot and Kurgan, "Les réseaux," 72.

59 Philip Morgan, "The First World War and the Challenge to Democracy in Europe," in *Ideas of Europe*, ed. Spiering and Wintle 69-70.

60 Hughes, "Visions of Electrification and Social Change," in *1880-1980*, ed. Cardot, 327-328.

61 Christophe Bouneau, "L'Économie électrique sous l'Occupation: Des contraintes de la production aux enjeux de l'interconnexion," in *Les entreprises*, ed. Varaschin, 120.

62 Hughes, *Networks*, 288-289.

Figure 2.3 – Louis Loucheur, 1872-1931
Source: League of Nations Photo Archive. Used by
courtesy of United Nations Office, United Nations
Library, Geneva.

one of the vital promoters of the principles of rationalization and (state) planning in Germany.[63] In the service of the Kaiser, Rathenau led the *Kriegsrohstoffabteilung* of the Prussian War Ministry. Already at that time (1915-6), Rathenau proposed to increase state influence in the electricity sector.[64] After the war he became Minister of Reconstruction in the new Weimar Republic, until his murder in 1922.

His French counterpart Louis Loucheur (1872-1931, see Figure 2.3) was an engineer-entrepreneur and co-founder of *Société Giros et Loucheur*, an engineering firm specialized in constructing electricity and electric rail networks.[65] During the war, he served as under-secretary of state for munitions, and later Minister of Armaments. After the war Loucheur became Minister of Reconstruction. In that role, Loucheur aimed to lay the foundations for a strong, efficient and modern France. He encouraged mass production, and stressed the importance of raw materials and energy, in particular coal and hydroelectric power.[66]

Most European countries were in the grip of volatile financial climate and high inflation rates in the first years after the war. This also affected the electro-technical industry. The *Unternehmergeschäfte* were able to continue to play a role, but the character of the industry changed considerably. This was because of a wave of

---

63 W.O. Henderson, "Walther Rathenau: A Pioneer of the Planned Economy," *Economic History Review* 4, no. 1 (1951): 98-108.
64 Stier, *Staat*, 367.
65 Stephen D. Carls, *Louis Loucheur and the Shaping of Modern France, 1916-1931* (Baton Rouge: Louisiana State University Press, 1993), 3-4.
66 Ibid., 129 & 172ff.

mergers and cartels, following the process of horizontal concentration (production, transport, distribution, and finance), and territorial concentration and expansion.[67] After the war Elektrobank, Indelec and Motor underwent complete reorganizations. Motor merged with *Columbus AG für Elektrische Unternehmungen* to *Motor-Columbus* in 1923.[68] These reorganizations were led by the Swiss banks. German firms now only played a minor role in the holding companies. Before WWI the German electro-industry accounted for some 46% of world exports in the sector, this swung between 25 and 28% in the 1920s.[69] The Belgian *Société Financière de Transports et d'Entreprises Industrielles* (SOFINA) saw its large share of German capital shrink in favor of Belgian, American, French, and British capital.[70] Many German stockholders left Elektrobank. Only one-third of the *Aktienkapital* remained German; Swiss banks covered the rest.[71] For a part this change was because of the new Swiss legislation regarding hydropower, the *Wasserrechtgesetz*, which stipulated that at least two-thirds of the stock of the concession-taking companies should be Swiss.[72]

The diminishing role of foreign suppliers of capital and equipment coincided with another development: the encroaching influence of governments on electricity production and transmission. Legislation reinforced the influence of the government on the process. Generally speaking, electricity regulation served a variety of purposes: adjusting prices, replacing coal with hydraulic energy, prioritizing national needs, and making electricity a national public service. The latter involved rationalizing national electricity production by prioritizing interconnections, but also by stimulating electrification, especially of the countryside. In what follows I will discuss these four types of legislation aimed at achieving these four different goals. Although this is not a definitive overview for all European countries, it nevertheless suggests a clear image of the main tendencies in national electricity policy.

The first laws concerned electricity prices. The war seriously disrupted international trade flows, and led to different priorities to employ labor and resources.

---

67 Varaschin, "Etats," 144.

68 Kupper and Wildi, *Motor-Columbus*, 13. These two companies already were a sort of private union, as Walter Boveri was the initial chairman for both.

69 Peter Hertner, "Financial Strategies and Adaptation to Foreign Markets: The German Electro-Technical Industry and its Multinational Activities: 1890s to 1939," in *Multinational Enterprise in Historical Perspective*, ed. Alice Teichova, Maurice Lévy-Leboyer, and Helga Nussbaum (Cambridge: Cambridge University Press, 1986), 153-155. In 1931, at the height of the Depression, it would temporarily regain 32.7%.

70 René Brion and Jean-Louis Moreau, *Inventaire des archives du groupe SOFINA (Société Financière de Transports et d'Entreprises Industrielles) 1881-1988* (Brussels: Archives Générales du Royaume, 2001), XIX.

71 Barjot and Kurgan, "Les réseaux," 75.

72 Bonhage, "Unternehmerische," 50-51.

This led to inflation.[73] Coal was scarce immediately after the war, resulting in higher prices. For many former belligerents this created a situation of *Kohlenhunger*.[74] An employee of the new Austrian republic wrote in 1919 that

> The expansion of water-power is required. The provinces need light and power, the State needs electricity for the railways. The miserable coal situation is widely known.[75]

This led many governments to interfere with electricity prices. Laws on prices of electricity were for example issued in Belgium (1919), Italy (1919), Spain (1920), Germany (1922), and Poland (1920).[76]

A second and related form of legislation stimulated the development of hydroelectricity, also as an alternative for thermal power. For Western Europe, Denis Varaschin concludes that between the wars hydroelectricity became seen as the most important form of national energy to develop.[77] In countries like Switzerland (1916), France (1919), Portugal (1919), and pre-Mussolini Italy (1919) laws on the exploitation of hydraulic power were issued. Usually, such regulations assigned which level of government within the national frame was responsible for granting concessions for exploitation. Austria set up the *Wasserkraft- und Elektrizitätswirtschafts Amtes* (WEWA), in 1918 to study rail electrification and to mobilize capital to expand hydroelectric production.[78] Further laws in 1921 and 1922 gave tax exemptions on all interest payment for loans raised for new power plants, and on running expenses for a maximum of 20 years.[79]

A third form of legislation restricted the export of domestically generated electricity, and against foreign (majority) ownership of plants and installations. In 1916 Swiss Cantons got the right to exploit hydroelectric power, or grant concessions

---

73 Barry Eichengreen, *Golden Fetters: The Golden Standard and the Great Depression, 1919-1939* (London: Oxford University Press, 1992), 71.
74 Varaschin, "Etats," 100.
75 "The expansion of water-power is required. The provinces need light and power, the State needs electricity for the railways. The miserable coal situation is widely known." Staatssekretär Dr. Ellenbogen, "Verhandlungen über die Wasserkraft und Elektrizitätswirtschaft mit den Landesvertretungen Salzburg," 1919, file Z.26064 III, box 2184H, folder 425-1, Österreichische Staatsarchiv, Vienna (hereafter: OS).
76 This often concerned price increases or maximum prices. G. Siegel, *Die Elektrizitätsgesetzgebung der Kulturländer der Erde*, vol. 2, *Westeuropa* (VDI - Verlag, 1930), 21ff, 566ff & 1015ff. For Germany see his *Die Elektrizitätsgesetzgebung der Kulturländer de Erde*, vol. 1, *Deutschland* (VDI - Verlag, 1930), 101ff. For Poland, see Polish National Committee, "Polish Power Resources and their Development," in *The Transactions of the First World Power Conference*, vol. 1, *Power Resources of the World Available and Utilised* (London: Percy Lund Humphries & Co. Ltd., 1924), 1129.
77 Varaschin, "Etats," 100-101.
78 Memorandum on the installation of WEWA, December 18, 1918, file Z.674 III, box 2184H, OS.
79 Bundesministerium für Handel und Verkehr, "The Development of and Utilisation of Water Power in Austria," in *The Transactions of the First World Power Conference*, vol. 1, 698-699.

Table 2.3 – Electricity generation (incl, autoproducers) in Europe in GWh, 1932-37

	1925	1932	1933	1937
Austria	2,300	2,826	2,969	3,082
Belgium	2,274		4,028	5,672
Bulgaria			132	196.5
Czechoslovakia	1,954.5	2,653	3,016	
Denmark	372	657	751	1,104
Estonia		78	89	
Finland		1,479	1,692	2,786.2
France	10,222	15,408	17,156	20,218
Germany	20,328	22,129	13,590	
Hungary			816	
Italy		10,013	11,063	
Latvia		115	133	
Luxembourg		482	461	662.3
Netherlands	945	2,526	2,614	3,318
Spain		2,795	3,066	
Sweden	406 (1926)	4,897	5,334	8,105
Switzerland	2,734	4,867	4,877	6,878
United Kingdom			12,513†	21,888†

† From April 1st of the year considered until March 31st of the following.
Based on: UNIPEDE, *Production et de la Distribution d'Énergie Électrique*, various years; and Kittler, *Der internationale*.

to do so. At the same time, hydroelectricity transmitted across borders needed permission from the Bundesrat.[80] The French regulations of October 1919 had a similar tenor. Without a state authorization or concession, no one was allowed to exploit water-power. Export of electricity generated by French water-power concessionaires required state approval, or an international treaty.[81] In Italy, a separate law of October 1926 subjected both export and import of electricity to approval by the Minister of Public Works. Authorized electricity imports were subjected to a tariff of 0.025 Lire per KWh.[82] Other European countries, too, installed laws governing electricity exports: Czechoslovakia (1919), Finland (1919), Luxemburg (1924), Norway (1917), and Poland (1922).[83] Belgium, Denmark, and Sweden were

---

80 Siegel, *Westeuropa*, 950-951, in particular articles 1 & 8.
81 Ibid., 165-181, and in particular articles 1 & 27.
82 Ibid., 564-565. In 1928 a two-tier tariff for electricity imports was issued; from November 16 until April 15 the levy remained 0,025 Lire per KWh, but between April 16 and November 15 it was lowered to 0,0015 Lire per KWh.
83 Based on the overview in ECE, *Transfers of Electric Power Across European frontiers: Study by the Electric Power Section*, UN doc, ser., E/ECE/151 (Geneva: United Nations, 1952), 62-67.

among the few countries without export restrictions.[84] A nationalistic element was sometimes present in these decisions too. The French government wanted to make French industry superior to German industry. Concession-takers were therefore obliged to use equipment from domestic producers and suppliers since 1928.[85] If this was impossible or impracticable, the Ministry of Public Works granted special permission for foreign purchases.[86]

A fourth type concerned the development of electricity as a national public service.[87] Such national electricity laws aimed to expand production capacity, to interconnect regional electricity systems, and to encourage a wider distribution of electricity. Germany (1919), Portugal (1926), Luxemburg (1921), France (1928), and Belgium (1922) all adopted such laws.[88] Areas still without electricity service often saw the State or subsidiary bodies taking action. Concession-holders were obliged, under certain conditions, to provide electricity to anyone potential customer within their scope, and expand networks of distribution to that. Especially rural areas were electrified in the name of social and economic progress, and sometimes for electoral purposes.[89] This electricity-for-all policy eventually led to discussions about creating national networks. In several countries this led to plans for linking regional networks into national interconnections. This was the case in Switzerland, where toward the end of WWI regional producers agreed to build interconnections between their systems.[90] In Germany, a 1930 plan by engineer Oskar von Miller aimed to provide a general scheme of a national network, which was to serve as a guideline for further "organic" expansion through interconnection.[91] Austrian Staatssekretär Ellenbogen argued in 1918 that in planning large hydroelectricity plants one should think of a transmission network that would integrate newly built power stations with existing ones.[92] Portugal issued a law on a national network in December 1927 with a similar aim.[93] In Italy a north-south transmission line was seen in the early 1920s as the first step toward a national

---

84 This point is also made by Barrère, "La genèse," 45.
85 Harm Schröter, "A Typical Factor of German International Market Strategy: Agreements Between the U.S. and German Electrotechnical Industries up to 1939," in *Multinational Enterprise*, ed. Teichova, Lévy-Leboyer, and Nussbaum, 160.
86 Siegel, *Westeuropa*, 139.
87 Christophe Bouneau, Michel Derdevet, and Jacques Percebois, *Les réseaux électriques au coeur de la civilisation industrielle* (Boulogne: Timée-Editions, 2007), 35.
88 For Germany see Stier, *Staat*, 379-412; Siegel, *Westeuropa*, 802-803 (Portugal), 652-653 (Luxemburg), 138-148 (France), and 23-24 (Belgium).
89 Varaschin, "Etats," 90.
90 Ibid., 104-105.
91 Boll, *Enstehung*, 58-59.
92 "eines Hauptverteilungsnetzes." Memorandum on the installation of WEWA, December 18, 1918, OS.
93 Siegel, *Westeuropa*, 810-815. Also see Matos et al., *A Electricidade*, 323.

Figure 2.4 – Group portrait of CIGRE's first conference in 1921
Source: CIGRE photos d'archive 1921-1982, collection Fondation Electricité de France, 7 Rue de Percier, Paris.

network, which in reality took much longer to realize.[94] Planning such networks and interconnections required a standardization of frequency and tension. Over the 1920s, 50 Hz triple phase alternating current became the standard in most of Europe.[95] The French Ministry of Public Works recommended the use of 50 Hz as early as April 1918. This was adopted soon after in Portugal, Luxemburg, Belgium, but also in Hungary and Czechoslovakia.[96]

International organization in the field of electricity

While governments took on the issue of electricity supply, electrical engineers were organizing themselves in new international professional societies. In the 1920s, most of these societies discussed national legislation, and how international collaboration could be continued. Generally speaking, membership of these organizations was often arranged through national committees and national professional organizations. Though they were open to all nationalities, the organizations were

94 Giannetti, "Resources," 48-49.
95 Varaschin, "Etats," 142. Varaschin can not pinpoint the exact development that made 50 Hz the standard.
96 Siegel, *Westeuropa*, 806 (Portugal), 672 (Luxemburg), and 40 (Belgium) L, de Verebélÿ, "General Survey of Hungary's Power Resources and Their Future Development, with Special Reference to Electrification," in *Transactions of the World Power Conference*, vol. 1, 924; and Masarykova Akademie Práce, "Review of the Natural Sources of Energy and Their Use in Czechoslovakia," in *Transactions of the World Power Conference*, vol. 1, 760.

in effect dominated by countries with an advanced electricity industry. The earliest organization, the *International Electrotechnical Commission* (IEC), was founded in 1906 in London. It essentially made the *International Electrotechnical Congress,* held since 1881, into a permanent organization. The first discussions in London were between representatives of national (electrical) engineering organizations.[97] The aim of the IEC was "to consider the question of standardization of the nomenclature and ratings of electrical apparatus and machinery".[98]

The 1920s saw the foundation of three more international organizations. One them was the *Conférence Internationale des Grands Réseaux de Transport d'Énergie Électriques à Très Haute Tension* (CIGRE), which gathered for the first time in Paris in 1921. CIGRE brought together engineers interested in electricity-transmission from related national professional organizations. Conferees were not present as national representatives, but as private people, however. Overall, CIGRE's objective was to study technical issues related to the construction and exploitation of large electrical networks at high voltage. But the 1921 conference participants also looked beyond technical subjects. They also devoted their attention to legislation on distribution, and imports and exports of electricity.[99] Thus, the first part of the conference was devoted to papers describing national legislation about high voltage transmission lines.[100]

Four years later another organization was founded. In 1925 the electro-technical industries of Italy, France and Belgium set up the *Union Internationale des Producteurs et Distributeurs d'Énergie Électrique* (UNIPEDE).[101] In the following years more members joined, including Poland, Switzerland, and the Netherlands.[102] In the first years, UNIPEDE was made up of national professional groups related to electricity generation, transmission, and distribution. The first congress held in Rome in 1926 – with a keynote address by Benito Mussolini – had 220 delegates from 13 countries.[103] Within UNIPEDE, too, national regulations were a

---

97 L. Ruppert, *History of the International Electrotechnical Commission - L'histoire de la Commission Electrotechnique Internationale* (Geneva: Bureau Central de la Commission Electrotechnique Internationale, 1956), 1. Austria, Belgium, Canada, France, Germany, Great Britain, the Netherlands, Hungary, Italy, Switzerland, Spain, Japan, the United States of America were represented. Norway, Sweden, and Denmark were not present but had expressed their interest in joining. Spain and Hungary were represented by their respective ministries of commerce. Canada sent a delegate from the Standardisation Commission.
98 Ibid.
99 Jean Tribot Laspière, ed., *Construction et exploitation des Grands réseaux de transport d'énergie électrique à très haute tension. Compte-rendu des travaux de la Conférence Internationale tenue à Paris du 21 au 26 novembre 1921* (Paris: l'Union des Syndicats de l'Électricité, 1922), 5. "[...] les participants indiquaient qu'ils entendaient écarter de leur examen et de leurs discussions tous autres sujets, notamment ceux qui concernent la législation des distributions et l'importation ou l'exportation du courant".
100 Ibid., pp.63-360.
101 UNIPEDE did not see a lot of historical attention. In 2000, the remnant of the organisation commissioned a historical study, providing an overview of its activities. See Lyons, *75 Years*.
102 For UNIPEDE, see Henri Persoz, "40 ans d'interconnexion internationale en Europe: Le rôle de l'UNIPEDE," in *Electricité et électrification*, ed. Trede, 293-303; and Lyons, *75 Years*, 12-13.
103 Ibid.

widely discussed topic. At the UNIPEDE's first meeting in Rome. Italian engineer Domenico Civita presented a report on existing legislation in a wide number of countries.[104]

Finally, the *World Power Conference* (WPC) was formed in 1924 to serve as a forum to discuss the world's emergent energy questions.[105] The institutional roots of this organization lay within the British electro-technical industry, while its inspiration lay in the atrocities of 1914-1918. The war, wrote WPC's first chairman Daniel N. Dunlop, "revealed the need for a conference of practical men, scientist, engineers, manufacturers, financiers and politicians, to consider the utilization of the forces of nature, in the light of new internationalism [...]".[106] The WPC took their internationalist attitude seriously, and invited Germany to join in order to, in Dunlop's words, "seal the spirit of complete goodwill in which the Conference assembled".[107]

The organization consisted of an International Executive Committee of 23 members, each representing their respective national electricity industries. Geographically, the Committee consisted mainly of European countries, and their (former) colonies.[108] In addition, a structure of National Committees existed, populated by leading figures from electricity companies, equipment producers, technical universities, and related state bodies. This was complimented by a permanent secretariat based in London. The first conference saw an attendance of 2,000 delegates from over forty countries.[109] Although electricity (mainly hydroelectricity) was only one of many energy-related issues the Conference dealt with, national electricity regulation was widely discussed there.

Within these international circles of electrical engineers, producers and entrepreneurs, a consensus emerged: national embedding of electricity regulation was seen as unavoidable, but should it not harm cross-border cooperation and flows of electricity. As an example, I will review a special session at the 1926 World Power Conference in Basel, Switzerland devoted to international exchange of elec-

---

104 D. Civita, "Sur la situation électrique dans les différents pays. Législation et statistique," in *Comptre rendu des travaux du premier congrès international tenu à Rome en septembre 1926*, ed. UNIPEDE (Rome: L'Universale Tipografia Poliglotta, 1926), 489-600.

105 Scarce histories of this organisation are Hans-Joachim Braun, "Die Weltenergiekonferenzen als Beispiel internationaler Kooperation," in *Energie in der Geschichte: Zur Aktualität der Technikgeschichte. 11th symposium of ICOHTEC*, ed. Braun (Düsseldorf: Verein Deutscher Ingenieure), 10-16; and Fells, *World Energy*.

106 Cited from Dunlop's foreword in *The Transactions of the First WPC*, vol. I, VII. This idealistic motivation of Dunlop is also acknowledged in Fells, *World Energy*, 42.

107 Ibid., IX. Germany did form a National Committee, presided by Klingenberg and Von Miller as member.

108 In 1924 countries represented on the Committee were the Australian Commonwealth, Austria, Belgium, the Dominion of Canada, Czechoslovakia, Denmark, the Dutch East Indies, France, Germany, Great Britain, the Netherlands, the Indian Empire, Italy, Japan, Dominion of New Zealand, Norway, Russia, Spain, Sweden, Switzerland, Union of South Africa, United States of America, and Yugoslavia.

109 *The Transactions of the First WPC*, vol. 1, IX.

tricity. Etienne Génissieu, prominent French engineer and supporter of interconnecting electricity systems, gave an outline of existing interconnections between Switzerland and France.[110] To him there was no general solution for the exchange of electricity between nations. Such a solution was not dependent on technical factors, but on sheer diplomacy.[111] For one, Génissieu thought that electricity should be free from regular custom and fiscal duties. He argued that it was far more difficult to fix the value of the "cargo" on transmission lines than it was on regular goods. What is the value of a delivery that is variable, mobile, changeable, and that should be immediately be consumed after production?, asked Génissieu.[112] Prices were not uniform, but dependent on a multitude of factors; time, place, quantity, use, season etc. He was supported by German engineer Robert Haas, characterized as a supporter of U.S. style *laissez-faire* in the electricity industry.[113] He gave examples of electricity flows between Germany and Switzerland. To Haas it was remarkable that energy-rich countries fenced off their potential with laws and controls. To him, "the European countries today are mentally and economically not yet completely ripe for the alternately exchange of the electricity".[114]

Both Haas and Génissieu underlined the fact that international exchange was already taking place. But without legislation, larger exchanges would be able to take place resulting in a more rational use of resources.[115] Without exception, all papers in the session argued for a laissez-faire regime for international electricity transmission. Swiss Professor Landry underlined this in his General Report on the session. "In spite of all advantages which national interconnection brings with it", he wrote, "there will be in certain countries either a periodical or permanent surplus or shortage of energy".[116] Based on the examples named by Haas and Génissieu. Landry valued that international connections "can never have any but a useful and beneficial effect from all points of view".[117] Landry added that

---

110 On Génissieu see Bouneau, Derdevet, and Percebois, *Les réseaux*, 41-43.

111 E. Génissieu, "Échanges d'énergie entre pays," in *Transactions of the World Power Conference*, vol. 1 , 1001 and 1015.

112 Ibid., 1014-1015.

113 The characterisation is made in Stier, *Staat*, 433. Haas was the director of the *Rheinischen Kraftwerke* at Rheinfelden. He should not be confused with the French Robert Haas (1891-1935), who was a pivotal figure in the *Organisation on Communications and Transit* of the League of Nations.

114 "die europäischen Länder sind heute geistig und wirtschaftig noch nicht ganz reif für den wechselweisen Austausch der elektrischen Energie." Robert Haas, "Austausch Elektrischer Energie zwischen verschiedenen Ländern," in *Transactions of the World Power Conference*, vol. 1, 987.

115 A point also made by Niesz, 'L'Échange', 1049.

116 Professor Landry, "Exchange of Electrical Energy Between Countries: General Report on Section B," in *Transactions of the World Power Conference*, vol. 1, 1116

117 Ibid., 1117.

From an economic and technical point of view [...] everything speaks in favor of the exchange of energy between countries. Everything possible must be done therefore, to develop this exchange.[118]

The League of Nations and electricity transmission

Efforts were in fact made to regulate international electricity exchange. In their report to the WPC session, both Haas and Génissieu mentioned the work of the League of Nations (LoN) on international electricity transmission. This might seem surprising, as the League is far better known for its – allegedly ailing – political work.[119] In general, the three mains tasks for the newly found League were to enforcing the Paris Peace Treaties, promote international security, and to develop international collaboration.[120] The League's main bodies were the Assembly, where every country was represented, and the Council, which was the exclusive domain of the "Great Powers".[121] The Secretariat, a permanent international administrative service, took care of the overall coordination (see Figure 2.5).[122]

The LoN engaged in a wide range of so-called "technical activities", in particular through its *Health Organization, Economic and Financial Organization*, and *Organization for Communications and Transit*.[123] These organizations worked in relative autonomy because both Council and Assembly, staffed with ministers and diplomats, were "ill-suited" to oversee work for which they had "limited knowledge,

---

118 Ibid., 1124.
119 For histories of the League, see F.P. Walters, *A History of the League of Nations* (London: Oxford University Press, 1952); and the more recent Pierre Gerbet, Marie-Renée Mouton, and Victor-Yves Ghébali, *Le rêve d'un ordre mondiale de la SDN à l'ONU* (Paris: Imprimerie Nationale, 1986). Also the thematic edited volume UN Library Geneva, *The League of Nations in Retrospect: Proceedings of the Symposium* (Berlin: Walter de Gruyter, 1983).
120 Gerbet, Mouton, and Ghébali, *Le rêve*, 42.
121 The Assembly met every September. Each country had one vote. Through history, the Council consisted of three to six permanent members, and between four to eleven elected member states, usually represented by foreign ministers. The original Council members were Great Britain, France, Italy, and Japan. Germany and the Soviet Union later became permanent members, too.
122 Ibid., 36.
123 For an early overview of the League's technical work see H.R.G. Greaves, *The League Committees and World Order: A Study of the Permanent Expert Committees of the League of Nations as an Instrument of International Government* (London: Oxford University Press, 1931). Recently, an excellent study of the work of the Economic and Financial Section has appeared: Patricia Clavin and Jens-Wilhelm Wessels, "Transnationalism and the League of Nations: Understanding the Work of its Economic and Financial Organisation," *Contemporary European History* 14, no. 4 (2005): 465-492.

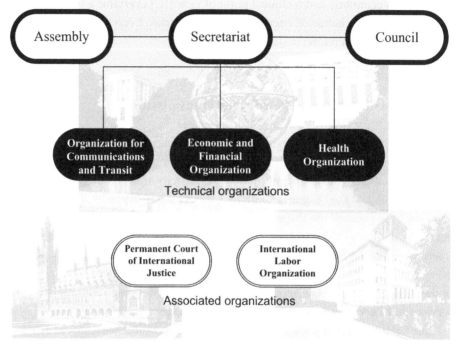

Figure 2.5 – The basic structure of the League of Nations
Adapted from The League of Nations: A Pictorial Survey (1929). *The pictures in the background represent (clockwise) the Palais des Nations (used by the LoN between 1936 and 1946, currently the United Nations Office at Geneva), the William Rappard Centre (International Labor Organization 1925-1975, currently World Trade Organization) and the Peace Palace in The Hague (Permanent Court of International Justice, still in use).*

interest, and time".[124] These organizations thus had very little political account-ability, and worked mainly with experts. Contemporaries therefore often equated "technical" with "non-political".[125] According to one observer, the difference be-tween political and technical was "the distinction between the volitional and the scientific attitude and action upon any given matter".[126]

---

124 Martin David Dubin, "Transgovernmental Process in the League of Nations," *International Organization* 37, no. 3 (1983): 490. A similar point is made in Gerbet, Mouton, and Ghébali, *Le rêve*, 108. According to Pierre Le Marec, the Assembly was "incompetent" for such "technical" work, and needed permanent commissions within the League's structure. See his "L'Organisation des Communications et du Transit" (PhD diss., Université de Rennes, 1938), 28.
125 Schot and Lagendijk, "Technocratic Internationalism," 198ff.
126 Pitman B. Potter, "Note on the Distinction Between Political and Technical Questions," *Political Science Quarterly* 50, no. 2 (June 1935): 268. A precise definition of the *technical* approach is hard to establish, as it is not completely limited to the work of engineers. According to Potter "'political' refers to policy or general principle or theory of action, 'technical' to application in detail of previously adopted policy or law".

The organization that dealt with electricity was the Organization for Communications and Transit (OCT). A body like the OCT was foreseen during the Paris Peace conference.[127] This sentiment was further reinforced by contemporaries' conception that the progress of transport technologies made borders seem obsolete. To South African minister of foreign affairs Jan Smuts, British representative at the Peace Conference in Paris, transport and communications were "bursting through the national bounds and (…) clamoring for international solution".[128]

At the same time, the League's built on the fruitful inter-Allied cooperation during WWI. During the war, so-called *Inter-Allied Councils*, in which Italy. Great Britain and France joined forces, had controlled and rationed food, shipping, coal, and munitions. The good experiences with these Inter-Allied Councils inspired the idea to use the LoN for common economic needs.[129] In practice the OCT dealt with transport issues (road, rail, maritime, inland waterways, air), aiming to standardize and create international regulatory regimes for them.[130] In 1920, the Council agreed to host a conference dealing with such issues. The resulting *General Conference on Freedom of Communications and Transit* met in Barcelona in 1921 and laid the basis for the OCT. The agenda included ways to restore pre-war free trade and unhindered travel, in the form of a *General Convention on the Freedom of Communications and Transit*.

Electricity issues were discussed for the first time as part of talks on an international regime of railways. Most members of the Barcelona Conference were in favor of electrifying international lines. But as these international routes crossed borders, the overhead power lines would, too. Who would be responsible for the necessary electricity became a point of discussion, however. The Italian delegation proposed that countries with large hydroelectricity resources should be responsible for the traction. The suggestion was rejected by 16 votes to 6. But delegates

---

127 By Covenant article XXIII (e) the League bore responsibility 'to secure and maintain freedom of communications and of transit and equitable treatment for the commerce of all Members of the League'. "Subject to and in accordance with the provisions of international conventions existing or hereafter to be agreed upon, the Members of the League will make provisions. In this connection, the special necessities of the regions devastated during the war of 1914-1918 shall be borne in mind."
128 J.C. Smuts, *The League of Nations: A Practical Suggestion* (London: Hodder and Stoughton, 1918), 43.
129 J.A. Salter, *Allied Shipping Control: An Experiment in International Administration* (London: Clarendon Press, 1921).
130 See Frank Schipper, Vincent Lagendijk, and Irene Anastasiadou, "New Connections for an Old Continent: Rail, Road and Electricity in the League of Nations' Organisation for Communications and Transit," in *Europe Materializing?*, ed. Badenoch and Fickers. Communications at that time was not equated to telecommunications, but to means of transport. Telecommunications was a minor part of League activities, but mostly reserved for other international organisations. For the League's activities concerning radio, see Antoine Fleury, "La Suisse et Radio Nations," in *The League of Nations in Retrospect*, 196-220.

nevertheless thought the issue interesting enough for further study.[131] This provided the first impetus to study the issue of international cession of electricity, for which Paolo Bignami was assigned as expert.[132] His primary tasks were to decide whether the issue fell within OCT's competences, and whether it was desirable to devise detailed regulations.[133]

Judging from Bignami's report, the matter did fall within the mandate of the OCT, as electric traction did make for a great improvement in the means of transport.[134] Based on his report, the OCT decided to leave further study of electrifying international railway lines to its Rail Committee. At the same time, however. Bignami saw the need to take up international electricity transmission as a topic of study. According to him, his study only concerned one aspect "of the much wider, and consequently much more complicated, question of the value of international agreements in assisting to bring about a rational exploitation of power [...]".[135] He used the 1921-2 electricity transmission from France, via Switzerland, to Italy as an example. International agreements enabled a better regularization of international electricity exchanges. Bignami thought. As state control increased, these agreements should not hamper the principle of sovereignty.[136]

The OCT approved his suggestion, and therefore appointed a temporary Subcommittee for Hydro-Electric Questions. It presented its first findings in 1923. Whereas rail and waterway transport knew earlier international conventions, the Subcommittee found itself working on a novel issue.[137] The Subcommittee therefore refrained from stipulating detailed codes of law, and drew up two Conventions in "very general and elastic terms".[138] These Conventions only gave general governing principles. It expected that, in practice, special agreements between states were

---

131 "Report to the President of the Advisory and Technical Committee on Communications and Transit on the Requested Action by the League of Nations for Facilitating the Cession by One Country to Another of Electric Power for the Operation of Railways of International Concern," 1922, registry file 14, box R-1120, League of Nations Archive, Geneva (hereafter: LoN).

132 Bignami, an engineer, was present at the 1921 Barcelona conference, member of the Italian Chamber of Deputies, and former Under-Secretary of State.

133 "Report to the President of the Advisory and Technical Committee on Communications and Transit," 1922, LoN

134 LoN doc, ser. C.212.M.116.1922.VIII, Annex 7, "Report to the President", 31.

135 Ibid., 33. Bignami actually used the French-Italian-Swiss collaboration in 1921-'22, which also opened this Prelude.

136 Ibid., 34.

137 LoN, *Second General Conference on Communications and Transit*, vol. 3, *Electric Questions: Report Concerning the Draft Conventions and Statutes Relating to the Transmission in Transit of Electric Power and the Development of Hydraulic Power on Watercourses Forming Part of a Basin Situated in the Territory of Several States*, LoN doc, ser. C.378.M.171.1923.VIII (Geneva: LoN, 1923), 3-4

138 LoN, *Advisory and Technical Committee for Communications and Transit: Minutes of the 4th Session: Report of the Sub-Committee for Hydro-Electric Questions*, LoN doc, ser., C.486.M.202.1923.VIII (Geneva: LoN, 1923), 9.

needed.[139] The first Convention, the *Convention on the transmission in transit of electric power*, was an attempt to settle matters of international transmission and transit of electricity. In general, all measures and solutions should fit within the "limits of national laws".[140] This includes the construction of new lines and installations, either directly by states or concessionary companies. The choices made for new transmission lines should be technical considerations, and not political ones or national frontiers. Transit of electricity should be free of special dues, besides charges for expenses made and services delivered.

The second Convention concerned the *Convention relating to the development of hydraulic power on watercourses forming part of a basin situated in the territory of several states*.[141] It aimed to arrange the construction of power plants in rivers or lakes with two or more riparian states. Such plants were already in existence on the Rhine, for example. Here, too, the method of building hydroelectric plants and installations should be a technical consideration, without looking at political borders. Navigable waterways remained subject to the General Convention of the Regime of Navigable Waterways of International Concern. Generally speaking, both Conventions were highly theorectical, and lacked examples from practise.

Although fourteen countries initially signed the transit Convention, and thirteen the Convention on hydraulic power, the ratification turnout was low.[142] Only a handful of states ratified the Conventions; four for the one on transmission in transit, and five for the one on development of hydraulic power on international watercourses.[143] As the group of ratifying countries did not include neighboring states, the Conventions had little practical value. Although the attempt was made to codify the possibilities of continuing and expanding of international electricity flows, it hardly materialized in the form of an international agreement.

---

139 LoN, doc, ser. C.378.M.171.1923.VIII, 4.
140 Ibid., 5,
141 Ibid.
142 "Conventions adoptées par la Deuxième Conférence générale des Communications et du Transit, Genève, novembre-décembre 1923. Transmit aux Gouvernements les instruments officiels approuvés par la Conférence", 1923, registry file 14, box R-1144, LoN
143 By 1938 this number had increased to respectively eleven (Czechoslovakia, Danzig, Denmark, Egypt, Great Britain, Iraq, Greece, New Zealand, Panama, Spain, and Western Samoa) and ten (Danzig, Denmark, Great Britain, Iraq, Greece, Hungary, New Zealand, Panama, Siam and Western Samoa). See Sir Osborne Mance, *International Road Transport, Postal, Electricity and Miscellaneous Questions* (London: Oxford University Press, 1946), 148-150.

Conclusions

To contemporaries, the emergency electricity delivery to Italy showed the potential of international interconnection of electricity systems. The introduction of larger power plants and especially higher transmission voltages opened new opportunities for collaboration between regional systems. But the first decades of the 20th century saw a double development. On the one hand, the international character of the electricity industry strengthened. The number of transmission lines crossing borders grew. *Unternehmergeschäfte* financed and built of plants and networks all over Europe and beyond. In addition, a transnational community of electrical engineers emerged through several non-governmental organizations.

Yet on the other hand, the Franco-Swiss-Italian collaboration was a rare event. Technically, transmitting electricity between interconnected electricity producers and distributors across borders was possible with relative ease. But politically, international electricity flows became increasingly subjected to the consent of national authorities. Since the end of WWI, most European governments had installed an array of legislation to regulate electricity. On a whole, authorities took an active hand in electrification and provided a framework of rationalization with national borders. One outcome of this development was that in many countries the in- and outflow of electricity needed a form of state approval. Concession systems and other restrictive measures limited the possibilities of international holding companies and previously unchecked international electricity flows.

In their first years of existence, international conferences devoted significant attention to such national legislation. To electrical engineers, the national framing became a reality in the first decade after WWI. Their international organizations –CIGRE, UNIPEDE, and WPC – all had national committees or national professional unions as the branches of their organizational tree. But legislation restricting the free flow of electricity across borders was a contested issue, and many pleaded for a more open system. Not only entrepreneurs argued for a laissez-faire regime for international electricity flows. Many engineers thought that international interconnections enabled a better economic mix, improved load factors, and opened perspectives for mutual help. In sum, international cooperation was seen as more rational.

International arrangements for easing cross-border electricity flows were tried by LoN. The LoN took up the study of international electricity transmission – and generation – in 1922. It fitted well within the overall work of its OCT, which promoted the freedom of communications and transit. The two Conventions tried to respect national legislation – and sovereignty – as far as possible. They were hardly a success, however, because only a few states ratified them. Because the first efforts of the LoN had little impact, a different course was taken towards the end of the 1920s, as the subsequent chapter will show. In response to the League's failing global attempt, possible solutions became framed within an emerging push for European unity. This was done both in terms of a liberal European exchange regime, but also in the form of a European electrical network.

Chapter 3
Planning a European network, 1927-34

In 1932 the journal *L'Européen* featured a front-page article by Marcel Ulrich.[1] Ulrich was laureate of the French *Ecole de Polytechnique* and *Ecole des Mines de Paris*.[2] At the time he also was president of UNIPEDE.[3] He earlier served as president with CIGRE. Ulrich thus was distinguished French engineer but also a well-known figure within the international electro-technical community. His article certainly appealed to the latter community, as Ulrich described on-going discussions about a European electricity network. Engineers proposed such schemes starting in 1929, which received supported from the electro-technical community. About at the same time, the International Labor Organization and LoN took similar plans into consideration. Between 1930 and 1937, these Geneva organizations studied its feasibility. To engineers, a European interconnected network enabled a better economic mix by linking thermal and hydroelectric power plants.

As the idea of a European network was essentially a technological project, Ulrich's article seemed out of place in *L'Européen*. This journal provided a forum for different visions on European values and the future of Europe.[4] With other journals like *L'Europe, L'Europe nouvelle, Paneuropa, l'Européen* was an outgrowth of the idea of European unity, which gained significant momentum and became a movement in the 1920s. To Europeanists – a loosely grouped elitist alliance of people promoting and believing in European unification – "Europe" seemed a way to overcome economic nationalism and political disagreement, and to restore Europe's pre-war global prestige. Ideas for unifying Europe often included technological projects as a unifying force. The European movement showed fascination with electricity, as well as with rational organization and technological solutions. It

---

1 Marcel Ulrich, "Un projet de réseau européen. Le transport de l'énergie electrique," *L'Européen* 25 (1932). I thank Waqar Zaidi of Imperial College for point my attention to this article.
2 *Annales des Mines : Biographies relatives à des ingénieurs des mines décédés*, s.v. "Jacques Marie Marcel Ulrich", http://www.annales.org/archives/x/ulrich.html (accessed July 11, 2007).
3 Ulrich ((1880-1933) was UNIPEDE president from September 1930 until July 1932. See Lyons, *75 years*, 110.
4 Etienne Deschamps, "L'Européen (1929-1940): A Cultural Review at the Heart of the Debate on European Identity," *European Review of History - Revue européenne d'histoire* 9, no. 1 (2002): 85-95.

is therefore not surprising that Europeanists saw a European electricity network as a tool for forging European unity. Many Europeanists believed that such a network could increase material and social progress in Europe. Some even went further: they believed that interconnecting Europe's countries also encompassed a dimension that I would label an *ideological mix*. In their eyes, the *immediate* construction of a European high-voltage network could relieve unemployment, spark economic growth, modernize Central and Eastern European economies, and at the same time create a spiritual and unifying European bond. In other words, they regarded the rationalization of Europe's energy economy as a panacea for a multifariousness of interwar issues. Many engineers, however, including Ulrich, did not see immediate prospects for such a network. Rather, they saw it as a long-term and gradual process whereby Europe's electricity structure was rationalized and expanded.

This chapter discloses the particular history of the idea of a European electricity network in the 1930s, and traces its origins. This idea originated in the electro-technical community, with support from industry, but it gradually became a regular topic on the international political agenda. A network of engineers, entrepreneurs, and politicians was responsible for spreading this idea. All were infused with European ideas, and convinced that European unification could not only be a political and economic project. "Europe" needed a technological dimension as well. Generally speaking, these actors motivated their ideas by pointing at the economic crisis and deteriorating international relations, but also demonstrated a strong belief in planning, coordination, and rationalization.

But the ideal of a European electricity network was not uncontested. A proposal made by Belgium met substantial opposition from national economic interests groups. Many questioned the technological and economic feasibility of such an undertaking. Still, although (national) authorities checked those exchanges of energy flows across borders, in practice electricity exchanges between countries *were* taking place. Political turmoil eventually brought studies of a possible European network to a halt.

European unification and electricity

Ideas of European unification gained significant strength after WWI. Such ideas often had roots in much older notions of shared European values, as Europe was seen as a centuries old geographical and cultural concept.[5] After WWI, ideas on European unification were more connected to precarious circumstances of the time

---

5 See for example den Boer, "Europe."

and on the options for shaping a better future. During interwar years, "Europe" was envisaged as a possible solution to several lingering political, cultural, and economic issues. WWI itself was interpreted as a low point for Europe's civilization. According to historian Michael Adas "it was clear to virtually all Western thinkers that European civilization had entered a period of profound crisis".[6] Historian Jo-Anne Pemberton writes that "visions of despair and warnings that the social and intellectual foundations of Western civilization were disintegrating featured prominently in philosophical and social commentary".[7]

Politically, the 1919 Paris Peace Treaties restored a balance among European powers. This was however a brittle and precarious one. The dissolution of the Austrian-Hungarian Empire and the re-creation of Poland led to border changes in Central and Eastern Europe. This, in turn, caused problems with minority groups and displaced persons. In Western Europe, fierce hostility still existed between France and Germany, especially over the system of reparations established by the Peace Conference. Economically, these reparations contributed to an unstable conjuncture. Most European countries experienced high inflation during and immediately after the war.[8] Fear of inflation and attempts to regain pre-war markets led to inward-looking national economic policies, resulting in a spree of tariff walls and volatile exchange rates. The years after 1929 saw an even further slide into the economic abyss.[9] Meanwhile, the United States closed domestic markets to European products, restricted immigration and abdicated from international politics by not joining the League of Nations. The new communist regime in the Soviet Union also turned its back to the international political arena, only to join the League in September 1934.

The wish for unifying Europe was a response to these issues.[10] Unification – either economically, politically, or both – was a way to restore pre-war European power and prestige.[11] A well-defined way towards European unity did not exist.

---

6 Adas, *Machines as the Measure of Men: Science, Technology, and Ideologies of Western Dominance* (Ithaca: Cornell University Press, 1989), 381.

7 Pemberton, "Towards a New World Order: A Twentieth Century Story," *Review of International Studies* 27 (2001): 312.

8 Eichengreen identified a postwar boom to 1919-1921. See Eichengreen, *Golden*, 107ff.

9 An excellent introduction into the European economic situation after WWI and the Great Depression is Clavin, *The Great Depression in Europe, 1929-1939* (Basingstoke: Macmillan, 2000).

10 For an overview of all sorts of European-inspired manifestations during the Interwar, see Pegg, *Evolution*; and Michel Dumoulin and Yves Stelandre, *L'Idée européenne dans l'entre-deux-guerres* (Louvain-la-Neuve: Academia Bruylant, 1992).

11 Analytically speaking, historians often a make distinctions between a political, economical, and cultural path and unity is often made. In practice, these different paths are obviously intertwined. See Sylvian Schirmann, "Introduction," in *Organisations internationales et architectures européennes 1929-1939. Actes du colloque de Metz 31 mai - 1er juin 2001. En hommage à Raymond Poidevin*, ed. Sylvian Schirmann (Metz: Centre de Recherche Histoire et Civilisation de l'Université de Metz , 2003), 11.

On the whole, economic unification was seen more viable than, and a precondition for, political unification.[12] Without economic cooperation, competition was likely to plunge Europe into another major conflict. Economic unification would not only end "beggar-thy-neighbor" policies, but would result in a large market as well. The United States with its large domestic market, was observed with a mix of envy and admiration, and often compared to Europe.[13] In the 1920s, entrepreneurs and politicians looked across the Atlantic for ideas on how to improve efficiency and rationalization, promoted by the technocracy movement and proponents of scientific management. By applying these ideas, not only in factories and electricity systems but on Europe's economy as a whole, they tried to mimic the economic success of the United States.[14]

Many argued that to arrive at similar levels of economic prosperity and technical progress, and to be able to resist American economic supremacy, a United States of Europe had to be created as a counterweight. Count Richard Coudenhove-Kalergi was one of them. Coudenhove was the founder of the Pan-European movement in 1922 and an important Europeanist thinker in the Interwar period. He thought that only an economic and political organized Europe could compete on an equal footing with the United States, the Soviet Union, and the British Empire (see Figure 3.1).[15] Europe should become the fourth world power. The notion of Pan-America, the association of sovereign states in North and South America, inspired Coudenhove to come up with the term "Pan-Europe".[16]

Next to Coudenhove, another important ideologue of the European movement was Francis Delaisi (1873-1947). This French left-wing journalist started to publish on international economy and politics after WWI.[17] Delaisi identified two contradictions in postwar Europe. Firstly, he condemned the subjection of economic policy to narrow national political interests. To Delaisi, this ran counter

---

12 Michel Dumoulin, "La reflexion sur les espaces regionaux en Europe à la aube des annees trente," in *Organisations internationales*, ed. Schirmann, 24.

13 Contemporary Dannie Heineman explicitly drew potential lessons from the American experience for Europe. See Heineman, *Outline of a New Europe* (Brussels: Vromant, 1930), 16ff. More recently historian Victoria de Grazia has also written about comparisons being made between the two. See her *Irresistible Empire: America's Advance Through 20th-Century Europe* (Cambridge: Belknap Harvard, 2005), 78-95.

14 Charles S. Maier, *In Search of Stability: Explorations in Historical Political Economy* (Cambridge: Cambridge University Press, 1987), 22ff. Also see Pemberton, "New Worlds for Old: the League of Nations in the Age of Electricity," *Review of International Studies* 28 (2002): 320.

15 R.N. Coudenhove-Kalergi, *Paneuropa* (Vienna: Editions Paneuropéennes, 1928), 4. A recent biography on Coudenhove is Vanessa Conze, *Richard Coudenhove-Kalergi. Umstrittener Visionär Europas* (Zurich: Muster-Schmidt, 2004).

16 Richard Coudenhove-Kalergi, *Paneuropa ABC* (Vienna: Paneuropa-Verlag, 1931), 3.

17 Michèle Pasture, "Francis Delaisi et l'Europe, 1925-1929-1931 (extraits)," in *L'Idée européenne*, ed. Dumoulin and Stelandre, 43.

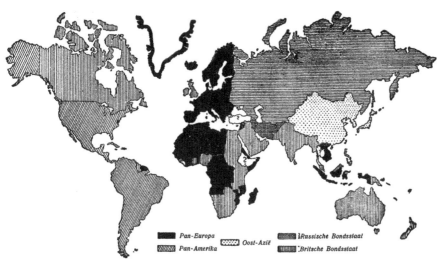

Figure 3.1 – Coudenhove-Kalergi's Paneuropa (in black) in the world
Source: Coudenhove-Kalergi, Paneuropa ABC, *32.*

to existing economic interdependencies between European countries.[18] Secondly, Delaisi identified a paradox between what he regarded the "two Europes"; a horse-power-Europe (Europe A) and horse-drawn-Europe (Europe B).[19] In "Europe A", Delaisi argued, a mechanized industry came about with the steam engine as key technology. This also led to a new entrepreneurial bourgeoisie that broke the political power of old aristocratic elites. Besides increasing production, these changes triggered democratisation.[20] To Delaisi "[h]orse-power [was] the natural supporter of democracy".[21] "Europe B", on the other, relied on animal power rather than on steam engines, and knew a *latifundia* subsistence. A seeming lack of democracy followed the lack of development.[22]

State intervention could not solve these contradictions, Delaisi argued. Rather, it needed liberal economic principles. For Delaisi, abolishing protectionist policy was the first step towards a peaceful and united Europe. In addition, rationalizing production methods would further strengthen interdependent economic re-

---

18 This is the main thesis of his *Les contradictions du monde moderne* (Paris: Payot, 1925). I used the English translation: *Political Myths and Economic Realities* (London: N. Douglas, 1927).
19 This was the theme of Delaisi's influential *Les deux Europes* (Paris: Payot, 1929). The dividing line ran across Danzig, Cracow, Budapest, Florence, Barcelona, and Bilbao.
20 Ibid., 47ff.
21 "[l]e cheval-vapeur est le support naturel de la démocratie". Ibid, .50.
22 Ibid., 49.

lations.[23] He favored international institutions to guide this process, stressing the triangle of LoN, ILO, and the International Chamber of Commerce (ICC, 1920).[24] Although his ideas were sometimes seen as simple, if not simplistic, they became popular within the international trade union circles and the European movement.[25] Delaisi's emphasis on planning and rationalization was equally en vogue. This was a notion that would come to infuse European ideas, especially after 1927.

While Delaisi saw an important role for technology, the supposed relation between European unification and technology went much further, in particular for network technologies. Many contemporaries regarded these as a unifying force, and fundamental precondition for cultural, economic, and political unity. Starting with railways, argues sociologist Armand Mattelart,

> the image of the network served as a guide for the first formulation of a redemptive ideology of communication. Networks of communication were envisaged as created of a new universal bond.[26]

Electricity transmission systems enable certain forms of transport and communication networks.[27] While these latter two physically circulate messages and ideas, and potentially bring people together, electricity is not able to do this directly.

But figuratively electricity was nonetheless seen as a means of connecting people and carrying ideas. Some saw electrification as an incentive to collaboration. For example American engineer Charles P. Steinmetz claimed that "to get the economy of the electric power, co-ordination of all the industries is necessary, and the electric power is probably today the most powerful force tending towards co-ordinations, that is cooperation".[28] In addition, electricity network also served as a powerful symbol. For example, the French internationalist magazine *Notre Temps* introduced a weekly column in 1929 named *La Jeune Europe*, which reported on the progress on European unification.[29] The headers used in this of *Notre Temps*

---

23 Franck Théry, *Construire L'Europe dans les années vingt: L'action de l'Union paneuropéenne sur la scène franco-allemande, 1924-1932* (Geneva: Institut européen de l'Université de Genève, 1998), 53; and Delaisi, *Les deux*, 193.

24 Théry, *Construire*, 56.

25 Dumoulin, "La reflexion," 25; and Patrick Pasture, "The Interwar Origins of International Labour's European Commitment (1919-1934)," *Contemporary European History* 10, no. 2 (2001): 226-227.

26 Mattelart, *The Invention*, 85.

27 This is stressed in Nye, *Electrifying*, 26.

28 Steinmetz is cited in Ibid., 167.

29 The column was written by Pierre Brossolette, who was a well-established French journalist and member of the *Section Française de l'Internationale Ouvrière* (SFIO), a socialist party. He also wrote for *L'Europe nouvelle*. During the German occupation he was active in the Resistence movement. On the role of *Notre Temps* within the Interwar Europeanist circle, see Klaus-Peter Sick, "A Europe of Pluralist Internationalism: The Development of the French Theory of Interdependence from Emile Durkheim to the Circle Around Notre Temps (1890-1930)," *Journal of European Integration History* 8, no. 2 (2002): 45-68.

Figure 3.2 – Headers in Notre Temps
Headers from La Jeune Europe, a column printed in the journal Notre Temps, from different years. I am indebted to Waqar Zaidi for providing me with these images.

confirm electricity's prominent role in Europe's (see Figure 3.2).[30] The first image shows two male figures reaching out to each other, while standing in from of electricity poles. The second shows a birds' view of Europe, with electricity lines in the fore cover the continent. The asymmetric crescendo directions of the power lines also suggest progress. While the first images hints at a European electricity network, the second invokes a form of European cooperation and progress through electricity.[31] In particular, electricity networks were regarded bearers and indicators of progress. Rural electrification was often associated with a modernization mission. It brought an "urban" technology into the hinterland, and made its inhabitants equally "modern".[32] The halo of progress and cooperation surrounding electricity functioned like a magnet.[33] Thus, "Europe" and electricity had symbolic overlap in this period.

An explicit combination of such ideas is the foreword to Delaisi's *Les deux Europes*, written by Dannie Heineman.[34] Heineman, a German-trained electrical engineer of American origin, was administrator of SOFINA. This was one of the largest *Unternehmergeschäfte* in the 1920s and 1930s. In the foreword, Heineman argued that the war had deprived Europe of its former grandeur and markets.[35] European countries responded by protecting domestic markets, while subsidising export industries. Heineman saw two main problems. First, a market crisis

---

30 The first image of the two men seems to anticipate the journal's later cooperative stance towards the national-socialistic ideology, especially when paying attention the right arm of the person on the right.
31 I thank Dr. Alexander Badenoch for helping me in analyzing this imagery.
32 Coutard, "Imaginaire".
33 Schivelbusch, *Disenchanted*, 75. Nye makes a similar point in *Electrifying*, 168.
34 Heineman, "Préface," in Delaisi, *Les deux Europe* (Paris: Payot, 1929), 7-20.
35 Ibid., 8.

in "Europe A" leading to unemployment, and second, an agricultural crisis in "Europe B".[36] Heineman envisaged electricity to restore the "broken economic harmony" between "Europe A" and "B", and to help mend both crises.[37] Electrification would help lowering costs of manufactured products in Europe A, thus making its products more competitive on world markets. At the same time, production and purchasing power of agricultural communities in Europe B would be raised. According to Heineman it was electricity that enabled every European region to industrialise.[38] "The imbalance caused by horse-power", wrote Heineman, "is abolished by kilowatt".[39] An International Clearing House should help finance large works of public interest, like railways but in particular power plants and networks.[40] In addition, Europe should rationalise its economy; not only its production, but also its sales and the transport of products.

The European project taking shape

Despite this wide range of ideas about European unification, no central rallying point existed for the European movement. This changed in 1929. On September 5 of that year, Aristide Briand addressed the Assembly of the LoN, and proposed to seek a way to forge a United States of Europe. The initiative of the French Minister of Foreign Affairs in retrospect seems a supreme attempt to forge European security and stability, both politically and economically. His appeal to the Assembly underlined the need for "some sort of federal bond" between the people of Europe to tackle the political and economic issues. Briand aimed to provide a political dimension to on-going "technical and economic initiatives".[41] It helped to carve a niche for a regional and European policy in the LoN. That niche would be the *Commission for Enquiry on European Union* (CEEU).[42] Set up by the Assembly in September 1930, this commission was the main vehicle within the League on European collaboration. It worked closely with other League organizations and commissions. But it also radiated outside the League's sphere.

---

36 Ibid., 11-12.

37 Ibid,, p.17. The disturbance between Europe A and B was, according to Heineman, primarily caused by the introduction of steam power.

38 Ibid.

39 "Le déséquilibre que le cheval-vapeur a provoqué c'est le kilowatt qui le supprime". Ibid., 17.

40 Ibid., 11-12.

41 LoN, *Verbatim Record of the 10th Ordinary Session of the Assembly of the League of Nations, 6th Plenary Meeting*, LoN doc, ser., A.10.1929 (Geneva: LoN, 1929), 5.

42 One of few studies on the CEEU is Antoine Fleury, "Une évaluation des travaux de la Commission d'Étude pour l'Union Européenne 1930-1937," in *Organisations internationales*, ed. Schirmann, 35-53.

While Briand's proposal placed European unification firmly on the international political agenda, it was preceded by several initiatives in the economic sphere. For one, within the international labor movement "Europe" functioned as "a unifying concept" since the early 1920s.[43] For another, support for European economic co-operation gained a foothold, especially in the financial and corporate world.[44] The first initiatives came from politician-industrialists, and were inspired by continuing Franco-German antagonisms. In 1921 the French Minister of Liberated Areas, Louis Loucheur, and the German Minister of Reconstruction, Walther Rathenau, struck an agreement in Wiesbaden, on paying German reparations in kind.[45] The Wiesbaden agreements were however revoked because of domestic opposition.[46]

Further rapprochement between France and Germany was reached, however. Many considered 1924-1925 a turning point.[47] The 1924 Dawes Plan restructured German reparations payments and led to an influx of capital which ended high inflation in German.[48] The next year the Pact of Locarno fixed the Franco-German border, politically rehabilitated Germany's position in Europe, thus solving another major issue haunting the European scene. Germany's reentry in international politics sparked a wave of commercial agreements and 14 international cartels were formed between 1924 and 1926.[49] In particular the *Entente Internationale de l'Acier* was regarded as an economic counterpart to Locarno.[50] Comprising an iron and steel production cartel of Belgian, French, German, and Luxembourg companies, this entente was signed in 1926 after eight months of negotiation.[51] According to one historian, before 1925 the debate on schemes for European unification was disparate, but "[w]hat followed after 1925 was characterized by the fact that the discussion became more concentrated, more purposeful".[52]

---

43 Pasture, "The Interwar," 222ff.

44 Éric Bussière, *La France, la Belgique et l'organisation économique de L'Europe, 1918-1935* (Paris: Comité pour l'histoire économique et financière de la France, 1992), 315. Also see Théry, *Construire* 63ff.

45 See Ibid., 64-65; Bussière, *La France,* 131-135; and Louis Loucheur and Jacques de Launay, *Carnets secrets, 1908-1932* (Brussels: Éditions Brepols, 1962), 84-95.

46 This opposition was not just domestic. In particular Great Britain was, within the International Reparations Commission, against such a scheme. See Carls, *Louis Loucheur,* 228-234.

47 For positive changes between Germany and France see Théry, *Construire,* 9-13. He points to three developments in particular. First, the accession of Gustav Stresemann as Chancellor, who was willing to fulfill Germany's obligations as laid down in the Versailles Treaty. Second, the adoption of the Dawes Plan in August 1924. The third event was Germany's recognition of its western border vis-à-vis Belgium and France.

48 Patrick O. Cohrs, "The First 'Real' Peace Settlements after the First World War: Britain, the United States and the Accords of London and Locarno, 1923-1925," *Contemporary European History* 12, no. 1 (2003): 1-31.

49 Théry, *Construire,* 57-58.

50 Maier, *Recasting,* 542.

51 Czechoslovakia, Poland, Austria and Hungary later joined. Théry, *Construire,* 60.

52 Peter Krüger, "European Ideology and European Reality: European Unity and German Foreign Policy in the 1920s," in *European Unity in Context: The Interwar Period,* ed. Peter M.R. Stirk (London: Pinter, 1989), 86.

One such purposeful development was set in motion by Louis Loucheur in that year. Loucheur proposed to host an international economic conference, under the auspices of the LoN.[53] The European economy in particular was to be a central topic. Loucheur, active in both politics and industry, envisaged an economically unified Europe, based on industrial cooperation.[54] Historian Stephen Carls stressed how Loucheur realized during the Paris Peace negotiations that "the Germans would eventually outstrip the French economically, regardless of the measures taken at the conference".[55] From that moment he was a proponent of a European economic system with Germany as a cornerstone. Loucheur envisaged such a European economy existing of private ententes in the industrial sector – like coal, steel, iron, chemicals, and electricity –, and in particular along a German-Franco axis. Such a "Europe des producteurs" had two main advantages, according to Loucheur. First, it enabled processes of rationalization beyond the scope of a single country, encompassing the whole of Europe. Second, international agreements could help transform the existing climate of custom barriers, and restore pre-war purchasing power.[56] The International Economic Conference eventually took place in Geneva, in May 1927. During the previous eighteen months, the League's Economic Organization and the appointed Preparatory Committee worked to achieve a consensus. They decided that the Conference participants should be experts in economics, trade, industry, and scientific management.[57] The subsequent Conference succeeded in passing resolutions on lower trade tariffs. Negotiations on tariff truces were one topic, and another was economic rationalization within a European framework – along the lines of Loucheur.

According to a report by ILO on the conference, "[t]he whole work of the Conference was dominated by the idea of rationalization".[58] In particular, the Conference discussed the ideal of a rational distribution of work between nations, including relations between agricultural and industrial countries. International industrial agreements were equally seen as a measure of rationalization.[59] The closing resolution of the Conference stressed that these measures were of a European nature:

---

53 The whole international and French context surrounding this proposal is best explored in Chapter II of Bussière, *La France*, 257ff.
54 Veronique Pradier, "L'Europe de Louis Loucheur: Le projet d'un homme d'affaires en politique," *Études et documents* V (1993): 295. Also see Bussière, "L'Organisation économique de la SDN et la naissance du régionalisme économique," *Relations internationales* 75 (1993): 304.
55 Carls, *Louis Loucheur*, 171.
56 Pradier, "L'Europe", 295; and Théry, *Construire*, 65-66.
57 Pemberton, "New Worlds", 319.
58 International Labour Office, *The Social Aspects of Rationalisation: Introductory Studies* (Geneva: P.S. King, 1931), 5.
59 Ibid.

> [T]he Conference has fully carried out its task of setting forth the prin-
> ciples and recommendations best fitted to contribute to an improvement
> of the economic situation of the world and in particular to that of Europe,
> thus contributing at the same time to the strengthening of peaceful rela-
> tions among nations.[60]

From Loucheur's suggestion for an economic conference, inspired by his quest for economic unification, to Briand's politically oriented proposal seemed a logi-cal next step. In September 1930 a Japanese delegate to the LoN noted that "the European federation, that is Briand and Loucheur".[61] Adding a technological part to these economic and political initiatives for uniting Europe seemed almost equally logical.

This technological part also included electricity networks. At the International Economic Conference, electricity was one topic on the table. Among many other cartels under discussion Loucheur himself pleaded for forming an electricity car-tel, based on Franco-German cooperation.[62] At the same time, the Conference rec-ognised the electricity industry as one where international rationalisation made sense, which should lead to lower prices and increased production. Direct refer-ence was made to the potential role of international connections between various hydroelectric and thermal power plants:

> From year to year co-operation between hydroelectricity power stations
> and coal-fired power stations improves as a result of the increasingly high
> voltages used for transmission. […] Thus the idea of an international
> linking-up of water- and steam-produced electrical energy is advanc-
> ing towards realization, and wholly new vistas are opening for interna-
> tional co-operation in power generation. (…) By this system the question
> of world power supply might perhaps be more economically solved than
> ever before.[63]

Although electricity was part of discussions on international rationalization, it was not directly linked to European cooperation. It was about to happen, however, as within the international electro-technical community ideas of Europe and ideas of rationalization were invoked simultaneously in the form of a common electricity system.

---

60 LoN, *World Economic Conference: Discussion and Declarations on the Report of the Conference at the Council of the League of Nations on June 16th,1927* (Geneva: LoN, 1927), 14.

61 "la Fédération européenne, c'est Briand-Loucheur." Cited in: Pradier, "L'Europe", note 39.

62 René Brion, "Le rôle de la Sofina," in *Le financement de l'industrie électrique, 1880-1980*, ed. Monique Trédé-Boulmer (Paris: Association pour l'histoire de l'électricité en France, 1994), 226.

63 LoN, *International Economic Conference, Geneva, May 1927*, vol. 16, *Documentation: Electrical Industry* (Geneva: LoN, 1927), 17.

Imagining Europe electrically

The first idea for a European-wide electricity network was put forward in May 1929.[64] This was two years after the International Economic Conference, and several months before Briand's speech. French engineer George Viel presented a paper on the potential of 400 kV technology and its application in France, at a conference hosted by *Groupe du Sud-Est de la Société Française des Electriciens*. He argued that exploiting distant hydroelectric resources was difficult without transmission voltages higher than 220 kV, regardless of the precise location.[65] At 400 kV electricity could be transmitted over 1,000 km without substantial losses. This would enable France to construct connections with neighboring countries like Spain and Italy, but also with the Ruhr and Sarre regions.[66] Seasonal exchange with these countries thus resulted in saving large amounts of precious coal. Viel argued that a 400 kV grid could connect centers of hydroelectricity production, and therefore enabled the exchange of seasonal surpluses.[67]

In the last part of his paper, Viel pondered on the possibilities of 400 kV on the European mainland.[68] Here similar results could be achieved: a better economic mix, better connections between generation and consumption, resulting in lower electricity prices. The main difference, however, was the increase of scale of rationalization. This in addition enabled peak load savings because of the longitudinal time differences. He added a map of a possible scheme for such a European network (see Figure 3.3).[69]

Viel's interest in long-distance transmission predated his 1929 plan. As director of the *Compagnie électrique de la Loire et du Centre*, he pioneered in erecting interconnections at 52 and 120 kV. He also planned an interconnection between the Massif Centrale and the Alpine regions by higher voltages, which was gradually brought into service under Viel's guidance between 1925 and 1940.[70] His ponderings on an electricity network beyond French borders were therefore not startling.

---

64 Several of these plans have been mentioned elsewhere, but mostly to illustrate Interwar thinking or as examples of technocratic utopias. Never before have its impact been properly assessed. See for example Fridlund and Maier, "The Second."; Maier, "Systems Connected: IG Auschwitz, Kaprun, and the Building of European Power Grids up to 1945," in *Networking Europe*, ed. Van der Vleuten and Kaijser, 129-158. The earlier mentioned Atlantropa project by Hermann Sörgel will not be dealt with here. This plan never saw serious consideration on the international level.
65 Georges Viel, "Etude d'un reseau 400.000 volts," *Revue generale de l'électricité*, no. 28 (1930): 729.
66 Ibid., 740.
67 Ibid.
68 Ibid., 741-744.
69 Ibid., 742-743.
70 Claire Seyeux, "Gestion du personnel: La réponse de Loire et Centre 1912-1932," in *Stratégies, gestion*, ed. Barjot et al., 382.

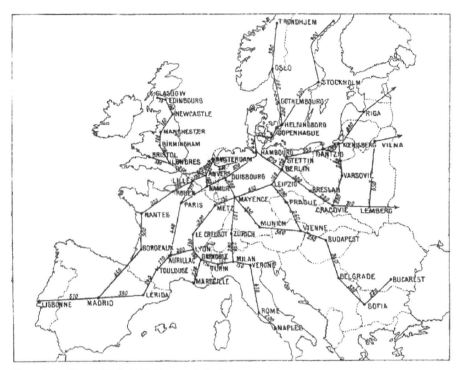

Figure 3.3 – George Viel's 400 kV network for Europe
Source: Viel, *"Étude,"* 743, figure 14.

Why Viel thought in terms of a *European* 400 kV network is more difficult to explain. Viel was the first to think in terms of a European system, but his paper does not explain what inspired him to think in European terms. Still, in retrospect, there appears to be a possible source of inspiration. The *Compagnie électrique*, Viel's employer, belonged to the *Société Giros et Loucheur*, partly owned by Louis Loucheur.[71] Taking his ideas on Europe and rationalization into consideration, and his activities in the electricity sector, it seems fair to assume that Louis Loucheur's ideas were of influence on Viel.

Viel clearly set a trend. Only one year later, in June 1930, Ernst Schönholzer championed an electricity plan for Europe.[72] The scheme of this engineer from Zurich resembled Viel's. Schönholzer agitated against the "waste" of coal, and argued for a better utilization of hydropower in Europe. He envisaged a grid interconnecting major consumption areas, in particular the cities of London, Berlin,

71 Ibid., 378-381.
72 Ernst Schönholzer, "Ein elektrowirtschaftliches Programm für Europa," *Schweizerische Technische Zeitschrift* 23 (1930): 385-397.

Table 3.1 – European network proposals in size and costs (including plants)

Architect	Size	Costs (in 1930 Swiss Fr)*	Load	Saving per year
Georges Viel	3,000 km[†]	10.4 billion Fr.	79.5 million kW[†]	7 million kW
Ernst Schönholzer	3,800 km	25 billion Fr.	6.4 million kW	24 mil, tons of coal
Oskar Oliven	9,750 km	240 billion Fr.	20 million kW	-

* Converted on basis of League of Nations Statistical Yearbook of 1930.
[†] New network necessary in France for national grid and high-capacity transmission lines into neighboring countries. Load represents the hydro-electric potential in Europe as a whole. Viel did not indulge in extensive calculations for his European scheme.

Paris, and Vienna.[73] While Viel assumed the use of 400 kV, Schönholzer calculated his plan based on a transmission voltage of 660 kV. The Channel would be traversed by use of an overhead transmission line between Calais and Dover.

A main difference concerned Schönholzer's invocations of Europeanist ideas. Although Schönholzer cannot be linked to any prominent Europeanist, he listed both the initiatives of Briand and Coudenhove-Kalergi as inspiration. He argued that Briand's plan for a United States of Europe needed "an electrical-economic program striving for a uniform and rational use of *white and black coal*".[74] According to Schönholzer, if Europeans could curb their internal political tensions, international HV transmission lines could serve as a symbol of a yet existing European "Kulturgemeinschaft".[75] Schönholzer remained a rather anonymous figure and he did not make a lasting impact on the electro-technical community.

But a German colleague of him did. In the same month, German engineer Oskar Oliven gave a General Address at the second World Power Conference in Berlin, in which he pleaded for a European electricity system.[76] Oliven, the Director-General of the *Gesellschaft für Elektrische Unternehmungen* (GESFÜREL) in Berlin, was the first to introduce this idea at an international event, which explains why his Address arguably had the biggest impact within the international electro-technical

---

73 Ibid.
74 "ein elektrowirtschaftliches Programm zum Zwecke der einheitlichen, rationellen Ausnützung der weissen und der schwarzen Kohle". Ibid., 385. "White coal" was an oft-used expression for hydro-electricity.
75 Ibid.
76 Oskar Oliven, "Europas Großkraftlinien. Vorschlag eines europäischen Höchstspannungsnetzes," *Zeitschrift des Vereines Deutscher Ingenieure* 74, no. 25 (June 21, 1930): 875-879. Oliven's contribution can also be found in the proceedings of the 1930 Berlin WPC. It was also published as a separate booklet, in French, German, and English, being "European Super Power Lines: Proposal for a European Super Power System" (General Address presented at the World Power Conference, Berlin, 1930).

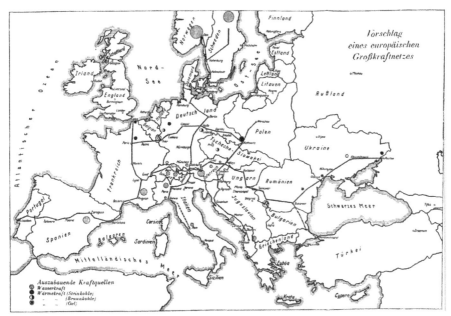

Figure 3.4 – Oskar Oliven's scheme for a European super power system
Source: Oliven, "Europas,". Used by permission of the World Energy Council, London, www.
worldenergycouncil.org.

community.[77] In later years, any notion of a European network was often referred
to as "the Oliven-plan".

In his Address, Oliven reminded his fellow engineers how electricity supply
grew from a local to regional service. Like Viel and Schönholzer, he too looked at
a further scale increase, arguing that it was time to look ahead:

> [T]o-day we are facing the fact that exchange of energy and compensation
> of load are taking no heed of political frontiers. Now is the time for us to
> realize that we have not yet considered that this exchange and compensa-
> tion is a question of the greatest importance for the whole of Europe and
> we have not yet done anything in this matter to ensure and organized co-
> operation of the political and economic factors of our Continent.[78]

He envisaged a network of approximately 9,750 km, consisting of five main lines
(see Figure 3.4). Three lines ran from north to south: from Norway to Rome, from

---

77 Viel would present his paper only one year later at a CIGRE conference. See Georges Viel, 'Etude d'un
réseau à 400.000 volts', in *Compte rendu des travaux de la sixième session de la C.I.G.R.E.* (Paris: Union des
Syndicats de l'Électricité, 1931).
78 Oliven, *European*, 1.

Calais to Lisbon, and from Warsaw into Yugoslavia. These were complemented by two east-west lines: from Paris to Katowice, and from Rostov to Lyon. Together they combined a tight coupling between areas with hydro and coal-fired power stations on the one hand, and large centers of consumption on the other. Like the two other proposals, this European system would exploit existing energy sources to a better extent, and help to shave peak loads. It also allowed exploitation of hydropower all over Europe, whereby Oliven targeted the Danube and the Dalmatian coast as well.[79] Oliven hoped that his "super power lines" would open up these regions economically.

Technologically, Oliven did not see insurmountable problems. He pointed out that new 200 kV lines were built to eventually operate at 400 kV.[80] In his eyes, 400 kV thus was possible, or at least would soon be possible. Outside technological issues, Oliven expected that in particular "personal and political motives" were potential barriers.[81] Such motives earlier had prevented otherwise sound interconnections of plants and systems on smaller scales, and prevailed over economic-technical logic. Oliven, unlike Schönholzer, did not directly legitimate his idea by referring to plans for European unification, but by pointing to the economic advantages and efficiency of such a network. Still, Oliven recognized that the existing old European culture provided the most suitable grounds for an "Elektro-Verbund-Wirtschaft".[82]

To Oliven, the effectuation of a general electricity plan for all of Europe was 'a self-evident fact for the coming generations'.[83] This did however not imply that Oliven expected his "europäischen Großkraftliniennetzes" to be realized in the short term. Crucially, Oliven did not see his grand vision to be completed before the coming generations.[84] He recognized a growing number of interconnections between emerging national systems. Oliven regarded these "a very good interim solution for the period until the time when the difficulties standing in the way of a common European high voltage system are removed by international agreements".[85] The first practical step towards a rational electricity supply in Europe was to create a European electricity network. Such an undertaking should be studied within the scope "of a very large organization", argued Oliven.[86] Although not specifying

79 Ibid., 3-4.
80 Ibid., p.2. From 1929 on, RWE in Germany constructed 220 kV, which were also equipped to carry a voltage of 380 kV. See Boll, *Entstehung*, 46.
81 Oliven, *European*, 1-2.
82 Oliven, "Europas," 879.
83 Oliven, *European*, 1.
84 Ibid.
85 Ibid., 6.
86 Ibid., 10.

particular organizations, he urged scientists, politicians and engineers at the conference to use their influence with their respective governments.

This appeal by Oliven resonated with ideas articulated by Dannie Heineman. In his foreword to *Les deux Europes* in 1929, he too proposed to take up the concept of an electrified Europe as object of a general study.[87] During UNIPEDE's third congress in September 1930, he made another point similar to Oliven. There, Heineman proclaimed that "the great revolution of tomorrow" was an international entente or cartel between electricity producers and distributors that could establish a comprehensive economic plan for the electrification of Europe.[88] However, Heineman added that such collaboration had to be preceded by national cooperation between electricity companies.

Heineman did not only have a message similar to that of Oliven, there was also a personal link. The two studied together and since 1922 Heineman's SOFINA owned a quarter of the shares of Oliven's enterprise GESFÜREL.[89] Thus, the two men most certainly knew of each other's lecture. Like Viel, Heineman also knew Loucheur. Together they set up a consortium for a traction system in Constantinople in 1911.[90] In 1927 Heineman, like Loucheur, had argued for an international cartel of electricity producers and distributors. According to him, only international collaboration enabled a technical and economic rational exploitation of natural resources.[91] Taken together, their visions about Europe and electricity combined encompassed both an economic mix as well as an ideological mix. While Oliven stressed the rationalizing effects of connecting consumption and production centers, Heineman hoped to raise Europe out its industrial and agricultural depressions.

The idea of a European network became known outside engineering circles. By 1929, Heineman was well-entrenched within the European movement, and was a crucial promoter. He was a member of Count Coudenhove-Kalergi's Paneuropa Union, which included also Briand and Loucheur, and involved in setting up its Economic Office.[92] Towards the end of 1930, Heineman gave several lectures in

87 Heineman, "Préface," 18-19.
88 "la grande révolution de demain". "Discours de D. Heineman," in *Congrés international de l'UNIPEDE à Bruxelles, 1930, Compte rendu*. Cited in Brion, "Le rôle," note 31. This event is also mentioned in Liane Ranieri, *Dannie Heineman, patron de la SOFINA: Un destin singulier, 1872-1962* (Brussels: Éditions Racine, 2005), 181-182.
89 GESFÜREL, "Contrat de collaboration," 1922, file 5663, box 26, collection SOFINA, Belgium State Archives, Brussels (hereafter BSA). Oliven was already involved with SOFINA as representative on the management board since at least 1912.
90 Ranieri, *Dannie Heineman*, 68-73.
91 Heineman, "Internationale Elektrizitätswirtschaft," *Wirtschaftshefte der Frankfurter Zeitung*, 1927, 26.
92 The Economic Office would be housed in SOFINA's office in Brussels. Ranieri, *Dannie Heineman*, 327.

German and French entitled "Sketches of a new Europe", in which he conveyed ideas from *Les deux Europes*.[93] This lecture, eventually published in three languages and two Europeanist journals, made both Heineman and his ideas more widely known – including his emphasis on the potential role of electricity.[94] Paul Hymans (1865-1941), Belgian minister of foreign affairs, was clearly inspired by Heineman's lecture.[95] In early 1931, Hymans sent the text around the Belgian diplomatic service in Europe.[96] Likely, Hymans also knew about Heineman's suggestion to start a study into the electrification of Europe, made in the foreword of Delaisi's book. Already in January 1930, Belgian embassies and consulates in Europe started to send information about electricity laws of their respective host countries to Hymans' Brussels ministry.[97] Soon, the Belgian foreign ministry took up Oliven's suggestion to bring such a study within the scope of a large organization; the League of Nations.

The League and a European electricity network

The League's OCT studied electricity in an international context starting in 1921. The two 1923 Conventions were however hardly successful. A change of course took place after that. Since 1924 the Subcommittee dealing with electricity became a permanent one, renamed as the *Committee on Electric Questions* (CEQ). In ad-

---

93 Heineman, *Outline*. His lecture shows all elements of the typical European project of the Interbellum. Heineman hoped to tackle the economic and financial troubles of his time– heavily inspired by the America experience –, and give "the vision of an engineer", with technological integration reinforces the political authority. According to Heineman three crucial elements were needed for forging a "United States of Europe". Firstly, a financial organism comparable to the U.S. Federal System of Banks. Heineman thought that the Bank for International Settlements (BIS, 1930) would be a good starting point. Second, an administrative organism was needed, similar to the Interstate Commerce Commission. Thirdly, means of transport and communications had to expand between the European states, enabling a more optimal mode of trade.

94 It was issued in an English, German and French version. In 1930 it was published as "Esquisse d'une nouvelle Europe," *L'Européen* 7 (1931): 1-7. One year later it was again printed as "Das Wirtschaftliche Gleichgewicht Europas," *Paneuropa* 6, no. 2 (1930): 48-56

95 Paul Hymans (1865-1941) studied law in Brussels, and acted as minister of foreign affairs in four Interwar cabinets (1918-1920, 1924-1925, 1927- 1934, and 1935-1935). He was minister of economic affairs during the last two years of WWI, and represented Belgium at the Paris Peace Conference. He was the first chairman of the General Assembly of the League of Nations in 1920.

96 Letter by Hymans to diplomatic service, 19 January 1931, file 11440: Commission consultative des Communication et transit, Diplomatic Archive of Belgium, Brussels (Diplobel). Hymans introduced Heineman as "a friend from business".

97 Dossier "Documentation sur de la législation et la réglementation concernant l'importation et l'exportation et le transit d'energie électrique dans divers pays," 1929-1933, file 4643: Pan-Europa, Diplobel. The dossier includes letters from ambassadors from Sweden, Greece, France, Latvia, Yugoslavia, Hungary, and Luxembourg.

dition, its competence increased as electrical engineers and other specialists now staffed the Committee.[98] The CEQ got in touch with the IEC, WPC and CIGRE, and offered them representation on the Committee.[99] Still, it did not have the expected result as the Committee was rather inactive. The CEQ gathered in 1927 and 1928, but without taking new issues into consideration. This was about to change in 1930 as ideals of a European electricity network were to gain momentum within the League of Nations.

In the slipstream of Briand's proposal and setting up the CEEU, the CEQ was about to rejuvenate its work. The Belgian government triggered this by making several proposals to the CEEU in December 1930. One of these related to international electricity exchanges.[100] In recent years, according to the Belgian proposal, the main industrial countries in Europe with common frontiers built cross-border electricity lines, and electricity exchange gained importance. Belgium thought that these exchanges were increasingly important, but at the same time ever more controlled – sometimes restricted – by national laws. The Belgian government stressed that "national legislations should not stand in the way of such a program and that a definite statute should be established to enable it to be carried into effect".[101] So far, the proposal stayed close to the earlier international Convention on electricity transmission and transit, whose disappointing results were regretted by the Belgian government.

But an important deviation from the previous ideas was that Belgium considered the issue – under present technical conditions – essentially a "continental one". Belgium opted for a European solution, which it expected to have immediate effects. The CEEU was therefore requested to study electricity transmission in a European framework. This was to be able to "already look forward to the time when these exchanges can no longer be limited to two neighboring countries, but when they will have to extend the whole continent, which will have to be covered

---

98 New members were the director of the Elektrobank, J. Chuard, the Swede and Director-General of Hydraulic Power and Canals F.W. Hansen, and the Frenchman G. Arbelot who held the position of Director of Hydraulic Power and Electricity Distribution in the Ministry of Public Works. LoN, *Advisory and Technical Committee for Communications and Transit: Minutes of the 6th session Held at Geneva, March 12th – 14th, 1924*, LoN doc, ser., C.196.M.61.1924.VIII (Geneva: LoN, 1924), 4 and 6.

99 "Permanent Committee on Electric Questions: Report on the Work of the First Session," 23 November 1926, registry file 14, box R-1144, LoN I could however not find any interferences or interruptions of IEC, WPC, and CIGRE in minutes of the Committee. In other words, although there was a live correspondence between those organisations and Geneva, physical representation cannot be confirmed.

100 LoN, *Proposals put Forward by the Belgian Government for the Agenda of the Commission of Enquiry for European Union, on December 11th, 1930*, LoN doc, ser., C.706.M.298.1930.VII / C.E.U.E.3 (Geneva: LoN, 1930), 1.

101 Ibid.

by an immense network of power distribution".[102] Belgium entrusted this task to the CEEU as it saw electricity networks as a part of European unification. The latter process was described in the proposal as "to lay the foundations is to establish a system of constant co-operation among the peoples of Europe", and "to strengthen the links uniting these peoples".[103] This thus included physical links as well.

The LoN Council and the CEEU accepted the Belgian proposal in May 1931.[104] Because of its technical nature, the matter was left to the CEQ, which was not without doubt when discussing the issue in June. In particular, OCT Secretary-General Robert Haas pointed out that not only technical aspects were of importance, but that "economic and legal aspects were far from negligible".[105] Chairman Silvain Dreyfus mentioned the two previous Conventions, which had been ratified by only a few members. He asked why a strictly European approach would receive a warmer welcome. The OCT nevertheless accepted to study the question, and proposed two things. First, as the Belgian request was concise and did not contain a plan for action, the OCT asked the Belgian government for more information. Only after receiving Belgium's additional information, a competent committee would be set up to study this question. This decision postponed concrete steps by several months.[106] Second, the OCT invited the League's Secretariat to prepare documentation on national legislation and international agreements in force in various European countries.

The Belgian government sent a note with additional information to the League's Secretariat on November 4, 1931.[107] In the note, the Belgian government clearly expressed which steps should be taken to arrive at an ambitious goal: the creation of a European electricity network. According to the Belgian government argued that there were two main advantages to such a project. First, a European electricity network created a "communauté d'intérêts" between countries, helping to consolidate peace. Second, such a network was the only possible way to an intensive and rational exploitation of Europe's energy resources. According to the note, proper coordination between the electricity policies of the various countries was lacking in the current situation.[108]

---

102 Ibid.
103 Ibid.
104 LoN, *Resolution Adopted by the Commission of Enquiry for European Union Relating to Transport and Transit of Electric Power*, LoN doc, ser., C.417.M.173.1931.VIII (Geneva: LoN, 1931), 79-80.
105 Ibid., 44.
106 Ibid.
107 "Note. Divers aspects de la question du transport et du transit de l'énergie électrique et notamment du problème de la création d'un réseau européen," 4 November 1931, registry file 9E, box R-2572, LoN The accompanying letter was address to Sir Eric Drummond, the League's Secretary-General at the time.
108 Ibid, The French text read: "L'un des results de la création d'un réseau électrique européen serait d'établir entre les differents pays une communauté d'intérêts bien propres à consolider la paix. La création d'un réseau électrique européen peut seule rendre possible l'exploitation rationnelle et intensive, de toutes les sources d'energie de l'Europe, exploitation qui, à l'heure actuelle, este entravée par le manque de coordination des politiques électriques des différents pays."

The new note identified three distinct elements for study. The first concerned national legislations on production, transport, distribution, and exchange of electricity. The second element was of a technical nature, and entailed technical parameters and security regulations in network and power stations currently in force. This could help to determine standards for operating electricity networks in Europe. A last object of investigation was of an economic nature. The Belgian government wanted an inquiry into possibilities to mobilize international credit for certain countries, as well as a study of possible rates of return on capital investments.[109]

The OCT Secretariat responded cautious to this additional note. Secretariat members regarded the plan as complicated, and therefore proposed careful incremental steps. Given the technical, political and juridical complexity concerning a European electricity network, work should start by examining issues that could be solved with relative ease.[110] The intent to set up a committee of experts that should have representatives from both various governments as well as electricity producers was discussed again.[111]

The international electro-technical community was quick to express its interest. In February 1932, UNIPEDE president Marcel Ulrich wrote the League Secretariat about the pending study into a European electricity network. In his letter he explained that industrialists within his Union were very interested in creating a European electricity transmission network, since they expected eventually be called upon to realize and operate it.[112] In December 1932, then UNIPEDE-president Robert A. Schmidt enquired whether the special committee "for studying the Oliven project" had already been formed, and if so, who its members were.[113] The response from Geneva was negative. In addition, the OCT stressed that they planned to study a broader issue than Oliven's proposal.[114] The OCT meanwhile had become familiar with that latter scheme. While asking the texts of the Belgian proposal made to the CEEU, WPC Chairman Daniel Dunlop sent along a copy of paper by Oskar Oliven. He also offered his services for documenting electricity legislation in Europe.[115]

---

109 Ibid., 2-4.
110 The response stated that work should commence with "questions qui pourraient être résolues plus vite et plus facilement". Emil Hauswirth to Pietro Stoppani, 25 February 1932, registry file 9E, box R-2572, LoN
111 Ibid.
112 Marcel Ulrich to Pietro Stoppani, 16 February 1932, registry file 9E, box R-2572, LoN Ulrich wrote that "[l]es industriels groupés au sein de notre Union sont, en effet, des plus directement intéressés au projet de création de réseaux européens de transport d'énergie électrique, puisque ce sont eux qui seront éventuellement appelés à les réaliser et à s'en servir".
113 "pour l'étude du projet Oliven." R.A. Schmidt to Robert Haas, 7 December 1932, registry file 9E, box R-2572, LoN Schmidt had succeeded Ulrich in July 1932. See Lyons, 75 Years, 110.
114 Robert Haas to president of UNIPEDE, 1 December 1932, registry file 9E, box R-2572, LoN
115 Daniel Dunlop to Robert Haas, 16 July 1931, registry file 9E, box R-2572, LoN

The Belgian government announced in June 1932 that "its study of the questions not being at an end".[116] In other words, it anticipated to supply more information on the issue. This once more postponed appointing the special committee. Meanwhile the Secretariat found the WPC willing to help collecting information on European electricity statistics and legislation.[117] The chairman send Siegel's *Die Elektrizitätsgesetzgebung der Kulturländer de Erde*, and additions to that book from national committees of the WPC.[118] But in a return letter Gijsbert van Dissel, the secretary of the CEQ, hinted at the unfavorable perspectives of the project. Van Dissel wrote that the original plan was to send out a questionnaire to acquire statistics, plans, and legislation of concerning countries. This was cancelled because of "the general economic crisis and the fact that most countries are at the present moment suffering from an over-production of energy and a decrease in consumption".[119]

Albert Thomas' European public works

The economic crisis did not go unnoticed in Geneva. Many contemporaries interpreted the October 1929 Wall Street crash as a turning point in Europe's economic fortunes, not in the least because it coincided with a renewed effort to settle reparation issues.[120] Although many European countries faced similar and interrelated problems, they nevertheless chose to tackle them nationally.[121] 1929 witnessed a growth of protectionist measures. Resolutions on relaxing commercial and tariff policy as agreed on at the International Economic Conference of 1927 did not stand.[122] The overall tense economic situation led to a drastic increase of unemployment in European countries.

The depression inspired Albert Thomas, the director of the International Labour Organization (ILO), to design a comprehensive plan for the construction

---

116 LoN, *Various Communications by the Secretariat: 3. Transmission in Transit of Electric Power*, LoN doc, ser., C.531.M.265.1932.VIII (Geneva: LoN, 1932), 27.
117 Ibid.
118 C.H. Gray to G, van Dissel, 21 March 1932, registry file 9E, box-R-2572, LoN The concerned book is Siegel, *Die Elektrizitätsgesetzgebung*.
119 G, van Dissel to C.H. Gray, March 1932, registry file 9E, box-R-2572, LoN
120 Clavin, *The Great*, 88-89, & 99.
121 Ibid., 5.
122 LoN, *Work of the Second Conference with a View to Concerted Economic Action: Statement by M. Colijn*, LoN doc, ser., C.144.M.45.1931.VII (Geneva: LoN, 1931), 13.

Table 3.2 – Unemployment in European countries, 1928-34 (in thousands of men)

Country	Austria	Belgium	Czecho-slovakia	France	Germany	Poland	Italy	Sweden
1928	182	5,300	39	16	...	126	324	10.6
1929	192	5,600	42	10	1,899	129	301	11.2
1930	243	16,500	105	13	3,076	227	425	12.2
1931	300	41,100	291	64	4,520	300	734	17.2
1932	378	71,800	554	301	5,575	256	1,006	22.8
1933	406	62,400	738	305	4,804	250	1,019	23.7
1934	370	72,300	677	368	342	2,718	964	18.9

Source: B. R. Mitchell, *European historical statistics, 1750-1920* (New York: Columbia University Press, 1975), 166-172.

of a wide range of European public works.[123] His public works included a system of railways and highways, as well as an electricity transmission network. For several reasons, Thomas saw these public works as an apt solution to the problems Europe was facing. First, the construction of public works provided much needed jobs in a time of high unemployment. Second, it offered Central and Eastern European countries a prospect for further industrialization. This line of thinking was strongly influenced by Delaisi's *Les deux Europes*.[124] Third, the increase and improvements of infrastructures led to more mobility and market formation in that part of Europe. Thomas also hoped to "induce investors to put out money which at present time they are keeping hidden in their stockings".[125] A final reason for Thomas was to create "the elements to construct a New Europe".[126] At the same time, the plan fitted well with ILO's – and Thomas' – interest in rational organization and planning.

This intended creation of a New Europe resembled an earlier ideal of Thomas, but only on a larger scale. During the early phase of mobilization during WWI, Thomas was entrusted with organizing a productive war economy, working to-

---

123 Albert Thomas (1878-1932) was born in Champigny-sur-Marne, as son of a baker. An excellent pupil, he went to study history and literature at the *École normale supérieure* in Paris. When Thomas moved into municipal politics in 1904, he already was on his way to become a spokesman for French Socialism and the leading reformist of the socialist party. Several biographical publications on Thomas and his ideas have appeared. Presumably the earliest to appear is B.W. Schaper, "Albert Thomas: Dertig jaar Sociaal Reformisme" (PhD diss., Leiden University, 1953). A French edition appeared in 1959. A more recent biography is Denis Guérin, *Albert Thomas au BIT, 1920-1932: De l'internationalisme à L'Europe* (Geneva: Institut européen de l'Université de Genève, 1996).
124 Schaper, *Albert Thomas*, 307-308.
125 Albert Thomas to Hon. R.H. Brand, Messrs. Lazard Bros, & Co Ltd, 30 May 1931, fonds Cabinet Albert Thomas (hereafter: CAT), file 6B.7.3, Archives of the International Labour Office, Geneva (hereafter: ILO).
126 "l'un des élements de construction d'une Europe nouvelle." Note by Banque générale pour l'industrie électrique, "Reseaux internationaux," 14 December 1931, CAT file 11A.2.3, ILO.

gether with Louis Loucheur. When he became minister of armaments, Thomas closely collaborated with industrialists and directed the French war economy to significant increased production. He wondered how the "spirit of war", which caused a new sense of national belonging, could be transferred into peacetime. Thomas proposed creating "a new France", whereby the close cooperation between state, industry, and labor was continued.[127] According to historian Martin Fine, Thomas used the war as vast testing laboratory where he applied new methods on various areas of economic and social activity.[128] Albert Thomas brought these experiences to Geneva in 1919 as the first director of the ILO. Thomas made sure that its Secretariat had a relative autonomous position within the Organization.[129]

His ideas further were shaped by his growing interest for optimization and scientific management. He already had observed the introduction of Taylorist practices in France.[130] During a trip to the United States, Thomas came in touch with progressive businessmen Henry Ford and Edward A. Filene. Both exposed the ILO-director to American ideas on scientific management and rationalization.[131] With Filene's financial support, he set up the International Management Institute (IMI) in 1926. This organization, headed by Thomas' ILO colleague Paul Devinat, collected and spread knowledge about scientific management.[132] Thomas linked rationalization with the economic future of Europe, too. In an introduction to a handbook on scientific management, he wrote that this novel approach was a revelation for many Europeans, who saw the economic progress of the United States as a threat to Europe.[133] Thomas, with Devinat, applauded the 1927 resolution of the International Economic Conference that stressed the need of rationalization in Europe.

Two years later, Albert Thomas also welcomed Briand's initiative, albeit critically. Thomas appreciated the momentum created by his former prime minister.

---

127 Martin Fine, "Albert Thomas: A Reformer's Vision of Modernization, 1914-'32," *Journal of Contemporary History* 12, no. 3 (1977): 551.
128 Ibid., 549.
129 Schaper, *Albert Thomas*, 206ff. The ILB was divided into three parts; a diplomatic division preparing general conferences, a political division communicating with organisations of employers and workers, and a research division taking care of inquiries. Thomas' heart in particular laid with the latter. Emil Walter-Busch, "Albert Thomas and Scientific Management in War and Peace, 1914-1932," *Journal of Management History* 12, no. 2 (2006): 219.
130 Ibid., 214.
131 Fine, "Albert Thomas," 554. For Filene and his European activities see de Grazia, *Irresistible*, 130ff.
132 This history is best described in Walter-Busch, "Albert Thomas," 219-222.
133 Scientific management "a été la révélation pour un grand nombre d'Européens que ces progrès économiques de l'Amérique menaçaient la situation du vieux continent et qu'il n'y avait de salut pour lui, à son tour, que dans une rationalisation de la production". Paul Devinat, *L'Organisation scientifique du travail en Europe* (Geneva: Bureau International du Travail, 1927), VII. The introduction to this book was written by Thomas.

Figure 3.5 – Albert Thomas, 1878-1932
Source: League of Nations Photo Archive. Used
by courtesy of United Nations Office, United
Nations Library, Geneva.

He applauded that European unification gained a political dimension, but he dis-
approved the adopted method of the LoN. He in particular felt that other Geneva
institutions – like ILO – where passed over in the process that led to the establishment of the CEEU.[134] He blamed Aristide Briand for not inviting the most prominent international officials to the first discussions in 1929 – probably including
him.[135] In addition, he was skeptical about concrete results, as Briand's proposal
seemed ill-prepared.[136] The Briand initiative and the resulting Commission of
Enquiry nevertheless became the focal point of Thomas' European efforts, as he
tried to provide a more concrete and technical focus to its work.

In April 1931 Thomas presented a memorandum about unemployment in
Europe to the ILO Secretariat, which he wished to send to the CEEU. He wanted
to install two sub commissions; one studying the possibility of creating a European
Labor Exchange, and another one to launch a vast program of European public

---

134 Guérin, *Albert Thomas*, 65.
135 Schaper, "Albert Thomas," 304.
136 That was characteristic for Briand according to Thomas. He once said of Briand that he did not prepare his speeches by searching in books and notes , but by dreamingly staring at the smoke of his cigarette
("Lui, il prépare ses discours non pas en cherchant dans les livres, non pas en cherchant dans des notes. Il
regarde la fumée de sa cigarette qui s'envole, et il rêve à l'idée nouvelle à laquelle il peut s'attacher"). Cited
in Guérin, *Albert Thomas*, note 31.

works.[137] At that time many national governments issued public works projects to relieve unemployment. These programs not only provided jobs. The newly built railways, roads, drainages and other works should benefit the whole society. Thomas's ambition was to coordinate these national projects into large-scale European schemes. When geared to one another, public works not only benefited the country of construction, but also neighboring countries, Thomas argued. He also hoped that countries would order equipment and material from each other.[138] At the same time, wrote Thomas, it "would thus develop that spirit of collaboration, that European spirit which is the object of the Commission of Enquiry for European Union to foster".[139] His three prime projects were an extensive international road system[140], a system of navigable waterways, and finally an international electricity transmission system. Thomas, like others before him, envisaged this network to work at 400 kV. He also recognized the current work of the OCT and stressed the importance of the Belgian memorandum.

But the responses from the ILO Secretariat were rather skeptical.[141] Thomas' co-workers challenged the economic viability of his program, and preferred a national framing over his European approach.[142] Thomas decided to include these comments in the memorandum which he submitted to the CEEU. It was discussed by the CEEU Unemployment Committee in early July 1931. This Committee was created two months before, in close collaboration with ILO.[143] Generally speaking, it endorsed the intended positive effects of the proposed scheme of European public works by Thomas. It invited countries to propose plans within this program. In addition, the Committee stressed the need of international collaboration, and the requirement of capital and credits.[144]

Thomas' vision of European public networks met considerable opposition from Pietro Stoppani, LoN Secretariat member and head of the Economic section. Stoppani told Thomas that his plan encompassed "projets de luxe", and that only

---

137 LoN, *Memorandum from the Director of the International Labour Office on Certain Questions Dealt with by that Office, of Special Interest to European States*, LoN doc, ser., C.39.M.19.1931.VII (Geneva: LoN, 1931).
138 LoN, *Unemployment: Proposals of the International Labour Organisation*, LoN doc, ser., C.275.M.127.1931.VII, Annex 14 (Geneva: LoN, 1931) It is explicitly mentioned that the proposals to combat unemployment were "made on the Director's responsibility", being Thomas.
139 Ibid.
140 The history of Thomas' efforts for the road network has been disclosed in Frank Schipper, *Driving Europe: Building Europe on Roads in the Twentieth Century* (Amsterdam: Aksant, 2008).
141 Thomas wrote about the response to Raoul Richard. Thomas to Richard, 8 May 1931, CAT file 6B-7-3, ILO.
142 Guérin, *Albert Thomas*, 71.
143 LoN, *Mémoire du Bureau International du Travail. Genève, le 29 juin 1931*, LoN doc, ser., C.E.U.E./C/1 (Geneva: LoN, 1931), 1 .
144 LoN, *'II. Public works*, LoN doc, ser., C.395.M.158.1931.VII (Geneva: LoN), 56-57

public work programs in backward countries should be considered. In addition, Stoppani regarded improving roads a better stimulus for local economies than electricity networks.[145] Stoppani left Thomas under the impression that the LoN would thwart his activities. To the ILO director, the LoN was unwilling to take the initiative. It let him to assume the LoN was not the proper route to his European networks. He decided to rely on engineers instead.[146]

Therefore Thomas assembled a group of experts around him from engineering and finance. He contacted Marcel Ulrich, and other prominent French engineers Ernest Mercier, and Henri Cahen, and also Dannie Heineman. In December 1931 he met Georges Lemaître, delegated administrator of the *Banque Générale pour l'Industrie Électrique*, who offered his services The *Banque Génerale* collaborated with *Elektrobank* and *Motor-Columbus*, and was active in Germany, Argentina, France, Italy, Poland, and Yugoslavia.[147] Besides being a financial institute the *Banque Générale* had an engineering department, which frequently conducted technical studies.[148]

Lemaître was however convinced that a "super network" at 400 kV was not an "immediate technical and economic necessity".[149] According to Lemaître, the advantages of 400 kV were only useful for transmitting electricity over very long distances of around 1,000 km.[150] He argued that a dense patchwork of networks was developing, but mainly within national boundaries. What was necessary according to Lemaître was to "weld" together these national networks.[151] This was not far from what Oliven had proposed. Although connecting centres of production and consumption made sense from an economic point of view, Lemaître also saw a political obstacle to Thomas' network. Lemaître argued that it was politically unacceptable to any state to be dependent on another country for meeting one's energy needs. What he therefore proposed was a reduced programme, limited to bilateral projects between "horse-powered" countries. Such an undertaking could be carried out rapidly and still create employment.[152] The French electrical engineers, with whom Thomas was in touch, backed Lemaître's opinion on 400 kV. Marcel

---

145 Thomas wrote Richard about his episode. Thomas to Ricard, 18 July 1931, CAT file 6B-7-3, ILO.
146 Ibid. English translation reads: "We will not be able to succeed if it were not on behalf of the technicians and the great groupings of interests of the coherent and effective initiatives".
147 "Electrification de l'Europe. Note sur une conversation avec M. Lemaître, administrateur-délégue de la Banque Générale pour l'Industrie Électrique," 10 December 1931, CAT file 11A.2.3.1, ILO.
148 Georges Rabinovitch, "Electrification de l'Europe. Note sur une conversation avec M. Lemaître, administrateur-délégue de la Banque Générale pour l'Industrie Électrique," 10 December 1931, CAT file 11A.2.3.1, ILO.
149 Ibid., 2-3.
150 Ibid., .3.
151 "Ce qu'il faut, par conséquent, c'est provoquer la soudure des réseaux nationaux.". Ibid.
152 Ibid., 4.

Ulrich was one of them.[153] At a small conference on December 12, Thomas again discussed options with Lemaître. Thomas underlined what he regarded the two prime aims of his plan: to reduce unemployment, and to create a "New Europe". Lemaître, on the other hand, reiterated his thoughts on using 400 kV.[154] Thomas was clearly disappointed seeing his original 400 kV plan amended. Describing this episode to Henri Cahen, Albert Thomas wrote that "our electrician friends have thrown me a small disillusionment".[155]

Responses to the plan

Until now, I have only highlighted those directly involved in plans for a European electricity system. But how did engineers, industrialists and politicians not directly involved in these initiatives look at the notion of a European electricity network? Although it is hard to provide a definitive overview of opinions, this section reviews two rather insightful sources. The first is a report by the LoN on the WPC in 1933. A LoN official attended this meeting and actively documented the response by engineers to the plan. Second, the Diplomatic Archive of Belgium harbors a collection of responses from domestic actors. Together, they provide more insight in arguments used by both proponents and opponents, both internationally and domestically.

Domestically, the Belgian proposal to CEEU met significant opposition.[156] Politically, the Minister of Public Works reprimanded Hymans for launching such an initiative without consulting the Minister of Defense, and industrial circles. Especially that latter group made its grievances heard. In general, industry protested against possible dependency on foreign-generated electricity and the potential harm to Belgian economic interests. The *Comité Central Industriel*, an employer's association, contended that electricity imports were far from desirable from the viewpoint of both national economy and defense. These arguments were in line with Lemaître's expectations. The *Comité* contended that if the "Oliven project" was

---

153 Thomas to Dannie Heineman, 29 December 1931, CAT file 6B.7.3, ILO.
154 Report of a conference on "Reseaux internationaux, " 12 December 1931, CAT file 11A.2.3, ILO.
155 "nos amis électriciens m'avait jeté une petite douche ."Thomas to Henri Cahen, 29 December 1931, CAT file 6B.7.3, ILO.
156 Besides the groups and associations named in this section, others wrote the Ministry of Foreign Affairs. This included the *Compagnie Générale d'Entreprises Electriques et Industrielles, Union Belge des Producteurs d'Electricité, Union des Villes et Communes Belges.* The same archival material has been used in Ranieri, *Dannie Heineman,* and I kindly thank Miss Ranieri for pointing my attention to these files.

carried out, "Belgian interests" should at least play a role in its building.[157] More straightforward was the opinion of the *Association des Constructeurs de Matériel Electrique de Belgique*. It wrote that the effect of a European electricity network was nothing less than the "the death of our extensive electrical industry".[158]

Arguably the most interesting comments on the proposal came from the *Union des Exploitations Électriques en Belgique*. This Union represented the interests of private concession-holding undertakings that exploited power stations, distribution networks, tramways and electrified railways.[159] It argued that high voltage technology did not allow establishing a European network according to plans put forward by engineers. In other words, the *Union* regarded 400 kV as technologically unfeasible. From a financial point of view, the *Union* regarded the calculated returns on investments as very optimistic, especially considering the general economic situation in 1932. The *Union* thus concluded that creating a European electricity network was not feasible from both a technical and financial point of view, and therefore not interesting for Belgium.[160] The influential engineer colonel Emil Weyl, administrator of Electrobel and board member of SOFINA, also deemed the prevailing economic situation unsuitable to begin such an undertaking. He nevertheless expressed his full support for the LoN study into the political and administrative organization of such a network.[161]

The stress placed on unfavorable economic circumstances can be illustrated by fate of an attempt to float a new company, the *Compagnie Européenne pour Entreprises d'Electricité et d'Utilité Publique* (EUROPEL). This joint venture between SOFINA, *Elektrobank*, and the *Compagnie Italo-Belge pour Entreprises d'Electricité et d'Utilité Publique* (Italo-Belge), three of the large *Unternehmergeschäfte* in Europe, was signed in June 1929.[162] EUROPEL would finance and setup electricity systems in for example Silesia and Hungary.[163] But this never materialized. In 1933 the partners decided to liquidate EUROPEL, as SOFINA was unable to place the

---

157 "Si donc l'on juge opportun de ne pas pousser le projet Oliven, il est non moins essentiel de veiller à ce qu'il ne soit pas réalisé par d'autres en dehors des intérêts belges." Note by the *Comité Central Industriel,* 13 January 1931, File 4643 II, Diplobel.

158 "la mort de notre grosse industrie électrique [...]." Note by the *Association des Constructeurs de Matériel Electrique de Belgique,* 4 March 1932, File 4643 II, Diplobel.

159 Ginette Kurgan van Hentenryk, "Le régime économique de l'industrie électrique belge depuis la fin du XIXe siècle," in *1880-1980,* ed. Cardot, 120.

160 Director-General and President of the *Union des Exploitations Électriques en Belgique* to Mr. Van Caenegem, 24 November 1931, File 4643 II, Diplobel.

161 Weyl to Van Caenegem, 16 March 1932, File 4643 II, Diplobel.

162 Draft statutes of "Cie Européenne pour Entreprises d'Electricité et d'Utilité Publique ~ 'Europel'", 2 June 1929, Box 12, File 5890, collection SOFINA, BSA.

163 Brion, "Le rôle," 231.

company on the Brussels Stock Exchange and raise the necessary capital.[164]

Similar arguments were expressed by engineers at the 1933 sectional meeting of the WPC, held in Stockholm, but they also added new arguments and visions on how to organize electricity supply in Europe.[165] Despite its apparent pessimism, League Secretariat members had taken up the invitation to visit the meeting. The report of the conference provides an interesting insight into the different prevailing visions on how to organize electricity supply in Europe. The best-known proposal was the one presented by Oliven. Generally speaking, engineers agreed that such a network enabled a better economic mix and load factor.[166] But a great divergence between countries with well-developed electricity infrastructure, and those still building one, also had to be taken into account. According to the report, several engineers therefore expressed doubts about the possibility to immediately create a European electricity network. Not only would it need a vast amount of capital, lesser developed countries were not ready for such a "rational development".[167]

But to many engineers Oliven's plan was a theoretical one. Some remarked that transmission lines in Oliven's plans hardly matched with existing ones. Several engineers regarded developing a European system through gradual growth a more practical alternative; from local and provincial networks to national ones, before arriving at a "supranational network".[168] There seemed to have been a consensus on the argument that international connections should be built first between regional and national networks. Cross-border electricity exchange could cover immediate needs before a European system was in place.[169] According to the report this was the most probable development. This was in line with Lemaître's vision, but also corresponded with Oliven's own expectations.

Based on these sources, it seems as if a "super" European network was seen as undesirable by some, and by many others as impossible in the short term. In Belgium, national economic interests clearly were an important issue. But elsewhere the notion of international collaboration was not refused, nor was the planning on a European scale. Rather, it was technological and economic arguments that led many engineers to believe the scheme was not yet do-able. The more grad-

---

164 Newspaper clipping from unknown paper, "Compagnie Européenne pour Entreprises d'Electricité et d'Utilité Publique – EUROPEL. Assemblée extraordinaire du 31 mai 1932," 1 June 1932, Box 12, File 5890, collection SOFINA, BSA.
165 "Session spéciale de la Conférence Mondiale de l'Énergie, Stockholm 1933," n.d., registry file 9E box R-4286, LoN The report is without an author's name, but likely written by Gijsbert van Dissel, then the responsible Secretariat member for the CEQ.
166 Ibid.
167 Ibid.
168 Ibid.
169 Ibid.

Table 3.3 – Electricity exports relative to national production, indexed (base year = 1925)

	1926	1927	1928	1929	1930	1932	1933	1934	1937
Germany	100.3	100.6	100.5	100.3	100.5	104.9	100.7	99.0	
France	99.9	100.2	100.2	100.4	100.3	99.7	99.5	99.6	99.7
Netherlands	100.5	100.1	99.9	99.9	99.8		99.0		
Austria	100.1	101.2	102.9	105.1	104.2	109.0	110.2		112.6
Switzerland	100.1	100.1	100.0	100.0	100.0	99.8	99.8	99.9	99.9
Czechoslovakia			105.0	101.8		99.0	99.0	99.0	

Calculated from: UNIPEDE, *Production et de la Distribution*, various years; and Kittler, *Der internationale*.

Table 3.4 – Electricity imports relative to national consumption, indexed (base year = 1925)

	1926	1927	1928	1929	1930	1932	1933	1934	1937
Denmark	99.9	101.7	101.0	100.2	101.1	102.7	100.4		100.0
Germany	99.6	99.7	99.7	99.8	99.9	99.4	101.6	99.0	
France	100.2	100.3	100.3	100.3	100.3	100.2	100.0	100.0	100.0
Netherlands	100.0	100.0	100.5	104.2	103.6		101.7		
Norway	100.1	109.8	100.1	100.3	99.0				
Austria	99.5	99.7	100.4	104.7	100.6		100.5		155.0
Switzerland	101.2	100.6	101.0	104.0	106.2	99.2	99.1	99.1	99.2
Czechoslovakia	99.9	99.8	99.7	99.7	99.0	99.0	99.6	99.6	

Calculated from: UNIPEDE, *Production et de la Distribution*, various years; and Kittler, *Der internationale*.

ual approach, by building interconnections between regional and national networks was seen as the way forward, towards a European system. These opinions matched those expressed by the engineers consulted by Albert Thomas. They did not see the immediate need and possibility of a 400 kV network, and therefore proposed to use the emerging national networks as a backbone for a future and gradually emerging system.

The available statistics of international electricity flows for this period show that this vision made sense. Stronger even, international exchange expanded alongside national production. Since 1925 electricity exports represented only a few per cent of total national production – except for Switzerland, and gradually Austria. In the period 1925-1937, the relative amount of electricity flowing either in or out European countries hardly altered. Considering the growth of domestic production between 1925 and 1937 (see Table 2.3), electricity production more than doubled in many countries despite a severe economic crisis. But Tables 3.3 and 3.4 show the relative importance of import and export did not change substantially. In other words, whereas production increased, electricity exports rose accordingly – with Austria as the sole exception (see Table 3.5). This seems to suggest a status quo of national versus international developments; both national networks and international exchange grew gradually and hand-in-hand.

Table 3.5 – Electricity exports as percentage of national production

	1926	1927	1928	1929	1930	1932	1933	1934	1937
Belgium	-	-	0.24	0.62	0.64	-	0.37	0.29	-
Germany	0.58	0.71	0.66	0.55	0.66	2.61	0.74	-	-
France	0.75	0.97	1.00	1.15	1.12	0.62	0.41	0.48	0.62
Netherlands	0.00	0.00	0.00	0.00	0.00	-	-	0.00	-
Austria	1.00	1.98	3.57	5.58	4.74	9.09	10.17	-	12.33
Switzerland	27.16	25.15	25.05	23.86	23.33	19.03	20.03	21.54	22.62

Calculated from: UNIPEDE, *Production et de la Distribution*, various years; and Kittler, *Der internationale.*

The demise of the projects

In August 1932 the Belgium government sent a third and complementary note to Geneva.[170] The contrast with its previous memorandum was remarkable. Gone were projections of a European network and invocations of its potential contributions to stability in Europe. The aspect of system-building seemed to be replaced by a more regulatory approach. Now, the main focus was on the study of two issues; one, problems relative to the political and administrative regime of electricity, and second, issues related to technologies of production and transmission, and economic aspects of their exploitation.[171] The Belgian government nevertheless suspected that these issues could be addressed best in the European framework of the CEEU.[172] The primary object was to draw up European conventions. Studying both issues should lead to a road map which allowed for a gradual development of an international electricity system.[173] In that light, the CEEU sent a letter to all participating European governments in May 1933, asking to supply the Secretariat with information on existing power stations, existing systems, and planned expan-

---

170 "Suggestions préliminaires et informations complémentaires relatives à la question du transport et du transit de l'énergie électrique," 13 August 1932, registry file 9E, box R-2572, LoN
171 Ibid.
172 Ibid.
173 Ibid.

sion.[174] The original Belgian proposal and the two additional notes were included with the letter. With the emphasis on a European network downplayed, the final aim of the study became how to establish a European liberal exchange regime for electricity.

At the 1933 OCT meeting it became clear that the present circumstances were unfavorable. This was directly related to the economic depression, which according to the CEQ caused an overproduction of electricity.[175] The CEQ therefore decided that "the present situation [does] not render it possible to anticipate in the near future either the institution of a more liberal regime for the exchange of electric power or the constitution of a European electric system".[176] But political tensions in Europe were also rising. This was underlined by resignation of all German OCT members in 1933. However, the CEQ decided that the documentation should be updated until a more favorable moment presented itself.

The Secretariat reported in 1935 that a detailed study was being prepared, despite the unfavorable conditions.[177] The study reviewed the structure of each country's electricity sector. In addition, it included an abstract of existing laws on the import and export of electricity. In 1937 the Secretariat expressed that despite the deteriorating political situation in Europe the study would be finished and presented to the CEQ in "the near future".[178] This optimism was shattered the year after. Because of political changes in Europe, and in particular in Central and Eastern Europe, peaceful perspectives of international electricity exchanges in Europe had become very uncertain – to say the least.[179] Therefore the study was abandoned. In August 1939, three weeks before Germany's invasion of Poland, it was registered into the LoN's archive and never to be consulted for its intended purpose.[180]

Albert Thomas' idea of a European electricity network had already suffered

---

174 "Transmission and Transit of Electric Energy. Circular letter no.81," 4 March 1933, registry file 9E, box R-4286, LoN Responses were received from Austria, Belgium, Denmark, Estonia, Finland, France, Germany, Hungary, Latvia, Lithuania, Luxembourg, the Netherlands, Norway, Poland, Portugal, Switzerland, Turkey, Romania, the United Kingdom, and Yugoslavia. For an overview see LoN, *Transport and Transit of Electric Power and Regime of the International Exchange of Electric Power in Europe*, LoN doc, ser., C.98.M.33.1934.VIII (Geneva: LoN), 97ff.

175 LoN, *Memorandum of the Secretary-General of the Committee on Transport and Transit of Electric Power and the Regime of International Exchange of Electric Power in Europe*, LoN doc, ser., C.C.T.566 (Geneva: LoN), 97.

176 LoN doc, ser., C.98.M.33.1934.VIII, 22.

177 Ibid. 38.

178 LoN, *Transport and Transit of Electric Power, and Regime of the International Exchange of Electric Power in Europe*, LoN doc, ser., C.380.M.256.1937.VIII (Geneva: LoN), Annex 23.

179 LoN, *Transport and Transit of Electric Power, and Regime of the International Exchange of Electric Power in Europe*, LoN doc, ser., C.266.M.159.1938.VIII (Geneva: LoN, 1938), 13.

180 v.B. (unknown initials) to Mr. Lukac, 8 August 1939, registry file 9E, box R-4286, LoN

a major setback in December 1931, after his expert-advisors denounced the use of 400 kV. Thomas wrote Heineman that he had not given up on his "European electricity union". He asked Heineman's advice on whether to follow Lemaître's suggestion to forge collaboration between Western European electricity producers and interconnect national systems.[181] But Thomas also moved on to a new venture. Since early 1932, he took significant interest in Francis Delaisi's *Plan quinquennal européen*, a European five-year plan. Thomas took part in a meeting on this plan in January 1932, organized by the *Comité Fédérale de Coopération Européenne*.[182] Like before, Delaisi stressed the need to bridge the divide between Europe A and Europe B, but now his main focus was on constructing roads in Eastern Europe.[183] This would help lowering transport costs, which in turn made agricultural products more competitive on the world market.[184] A report on the electrification of Central Europe was written by a French engineer, but it stressed that it was primarily to help developing transport infrastructures, most notably rail.[185]

What was left of ILO's efforts on European public works, including its electricity part, died with its inspirer Albert Thomas on May 8, 1932. In September 1932, the reports of CEEU's Unemployment Committee were handed over to a commission preparing the Monetary and Economic Conference, to be held in London one year later.[186] National governments filed proposals that hardly resembled Thomas' initial schemes. In addition, only Central and Eastern European countries' plans were proposed. They included plans for new roads and railway connections towards adjacent countries, but the overall European character was lost.[187] The International Conference on Monetary and Economic Questions in 1933 eventually rejected the international public works program as a whole. Without ambiguity the United States – the most important creditor at the time – stressed that every

---

181 Thomas to Heineman, 29 December 1931, CAT file 6B.7.3, ILO.

182 "Comité Fédérale de Coopération Européenne, Commission agricole et des travaux publics," 30 January 1932, CAT file 11C.7.3, ILO. The Comité Fédérale was created in 1928 by French mathematician Émile Borel. See Jean-Michel Guieu, "Le Comité fédérale de Coopération européenne: L'action méconnue d'une organisation internationale privée en faveur de l'union de l'Europe dans les années trente (1928-1940)," in *Organisations internationales*, ed. Schirmann, 73-91.

183 Delaisi, "Un plan quinquennal européen," in *Bulletin du Groupement français pour la paix par la SDN*, 4, (May 1931), 6. Found in CAT file 11C.7.3, ILO.

184 "Comité Fédérale de Coopération Européenne, Commission agricole et des travaux publics," 30 January 1932, CAT file 11C.7.3, ILO.

185 No mention was made to previous ideas for a European network. A. Guiselin, "Rapport pour 'Union Douanière Européenne. Complémentaire au Plan Quinquennal de Francis Delaisi. Electrification de l'Europe Centrale," 8 January 1932, CAT file 11.C.7.5, ILO.

186 LoN, *Monetary and Economic Conference: International Questions Relating to Public Works*, LoN doc, ser., C.377.M.186.1933.VIII (Geneva: LoN, 1931), 1.

187 The list of proposals presented to the London Conference can be found in LoN, *Report on the Fourth Session of the Committee*, LoN doc, ser., C.379.M.188.1933.VIII (Geneva: LoN, 1933); and LoN, doc, ser., C.377.M.186.1933.VIII.

country should raise its own funds. U.S. representative Paul Warberg stated that the United States opposed any idea of financing "somebody else's program".[188]

The CEEU, once the focal point of the European movement, was barely in existence in 1932. The main items on the 1932 agenda were electing a new chairman, as the CEEU lost its chair and spiritual father Aristide Briand.[189] Five years passed before the CEEU met again. At the final meeting in 1937, only a handful of persistent believers were left, who thought the CEEU "ought to meet even if it had nothing on its agenda".[190] This was literally the case at the meeting. The only resolution adopted was one that asked the Secretariat to draw up an agenda for the CEEU's next meeting, one that was never scheduled. The CEEU never really lived up to its expectations. According to historian Antoine Fleury, this was primarily due to the failure of the political activities of the League, aggravated by the political and economic crisis, and not so much to the underlying idea of European union as such.[191]

The European movement lost much of its momentum due to the death of two prominent proponents of European unity. Loucheur had already died in 1931. Added to that was the rise of Hitler Germany after 1933. Following Austria's *Anschluss* to the Third Reich, Coudenhove-Kalergi traded Vienna for Bern, and later New York.[192] This also had consequences for the promoters of a European system. Nation states turned to strategic network-building, anticipating a possible new war. Two important proponents of a European system left the scene. Oskar Oliven, of Jewish descent, fled from Germany to Zürich following the aryanisation of GESFÜREL in 1934.[193] He died in 1937. Dannie Heineman, also of Jewish origins, equally left Europe and eventually settled in New York. The start of WWII in 1939 sealed the fate of the Interwar projects. But as we shall see, the idea of a European electricity system had taken root.

---

188 Charles P. Kindleberger, *The World in Depression, 1929-1939* (London: Allen Lane, 1973), 210.
189 LoN, *Commission of Enquiry for European Union*, LoN doc, ser., C.724.M.324.1932.VII (Geneva: LoN, 1932).
190 The quote is from Mr. Paul-Boncour, representing France. LoN, *Minutes of the Seventh Session of the Commission*, LoN doc, ser., C.532.M370.1937.VII (Geneva: LoN, 1937).
191 Fleury, "Avant-propos," in *Le Plan Briand d'Union fédérale européenne: Perspectives nationales et trans-nationales, avec documents*, ed. Antoine Fleury and Lubor Jílek (Bern: Peter Lang, 1998), XV.
192 Conze, *Richard Coudenhove*, 51-53.
193 Joseph Walk, *Kurzbiographien zur Geschichte der Juden, 1918-1945* (Munich: Saur, 1988), 286.

Conclusions

Around 1927-1930 an intriguing convergence took place between engineers aiming to keep the electricity sector international, and ideas on the economic and political unification of Europe. Intellectually underpinned by men like Coudenhove and Delaisi, "Europe" became part of the policy of both the LoN and ILO. In the slipstream of these initiatives, a number of plans for a European electricity network were presented. While previously cross-border electricity transmissions were discussed as "international" and "bilateral", engineers now increasingly spoke of a European network. "Europe" represented a unit of optimization, where energy resources and electricity demand could be rationalized to a maximum extent. In addition, the network maps of engineer like Oliven and Viel not only represent a future electricity system. They also are a vision of what Europe should be, showing which countries are "European", and which are not.

Initially these schemes circulated only within engineering circles. However, through the close relations between the worlds of engineering, industry, and politics – exemplified by men like Heineman, Loucheur, Thomas –, these plans for a European network gained wider knowledge. It was carried by a network of people who sympathized with Delaisi and Coudenhove, and believed in both rationalization and European unification. In particular the role of the Belgium government – in the person of Paul Hymans – was instrumental. Hymans was connected both to the European movement and Heineman. Eventually the idea of a European network transformed into an agenda item of the CEEU. In parallel, Albert Thomas and the ILO took up a similar study, related to both battling economic depression and securing a European peace.

The notion of a European network found an easy entrance into ongoing processes aiming at unification, for two reasons. First, it fitted well with ideas of international rationalization and cartelization, resonating since the International Economic Conference of 1927. Such notions were equally popular within engineering circles. Second, it served what I call an ideological mix of expectations. Electrifying Europe would create employment, and increase the productivity of Eastern European ("Europe B") agriculture and Western European industry ("Europe A"). To some, a European electricity network would symbolize European unity, and provide a foundation for a New Europe.

Although they both wished a European system, there were important differences between engineers and Europeanists.[194] Several Europeanists, in particular Thomas, hoped to construct a European grid in the short term. They saw the con-

---

194 The distinction between the two is analytical. In practice, one could be an engineer and Europeanist at the same time.

struction of such a vast grid contributing to unemployment relief and improving the economic structure all over Europe. Electrical engineers, however, stressed that European interconnected system was a project for the coming generations. An immediate construction of such a network was in their eyes unattainable. It needed to use a transmission voltage of 400 kV or higher, which was neither technically feasible nor economically justified. In addition, the international financial climate was hardly favorable.

In looking at available responses to the plans, I found many critical remarks by engineers on the economic, financial, political, and technical feasibility of building a European network. But this opposition was primarily directed at a particular reading of Viel's and Oliven's proposals: the need to build a "super" network, in the form of new-to-built European arteries. These plans seemed to suggest a *planned* system. For many engineers, this planned European network did not sufficiently take into account the ongoing processes of network planning and building on the *national* level. Thomas' adviser Lemaître saw a political obstacle as well. Recognizing the protective legislation of national governments, he argued that no country would be willing to accept to be dependent on a third country for covering energy needs.

Most commentators therefore proposed to interconnect national networks. This would also improve economic mix, and open possibilities for mutual assistance. Oliven himself already mentioned that constructing interconnections between emerging national systems was a good "interim solution for the period until the time when the difficulties standing in the way of a common European high voltage system are removed by international agreements".[195] By this approach a European system would *gradually* grow. This approach also was close to ongoing processes. Statistical evidence shows how national production and consumption, as well as import and export of electric power *together* grew. Although cross-border electricity transmission remained rather modest, national and international electricity flows experienced a balanced growth. As an alternative to European network plans, this process was to be continued, alongside the possible removal of restrictive policies.

This new consensus did however have some consequences. Interconnecting national systems at that point was possible in only the most industrialized part of Europe. This can perhaps be best explained by looking at the presupposed dichotomy between Europe A and B. Men like Thomas and Delaisi wanted to develop economies in the eastern and southern part of Europe with electrification. But with national systems forming the backbone of an organically growing European

---

195 Oliven, *European,* 6.

system, "Europe B" fell out of scope as it was hardly as electrically advanced as Western European countries. This dichotomy would be strengthened in following decades, because of economic and political causes.

This chapter showed how and when the movement to keep the electro-technical industry "international" transformed into a movement in favor of organizing electricity supply on a *European* level. Although plans for a European electricity network were subjected to criticism, crucially, their *European* dimension was never really in doubt. At the same time, the development of national systems was not questioned either. Engineers did not plead for building a planned European network in the short term. Rather, they foresaw a future European system as the outcome of gradual growth. "The European electricity economies together, not as a single unit", argued one German engineer, "constitutes the European electricity economy".[196]

---

196 "Die europäischen Elektrizitätswirtschaften in ihrer Gesamtheit, nicht als Einheit, sind die Europäische Elektrizitätswirtschaft." Joseph Legge, *Grundsätzliches und Tatsächliches zu den Elektrizitätswirtschaften in Europa* (Dortmund: Gebrüder Lensing, 1931), 4.

Chapter 4
(Re)Constructing regions, 1934-51

In April, 1949, a group of European engineers was welcomed by their American hosts, and presented to the press at a location not far from the White House in Washington D.C. The conference they attended there kicked off a five-week tour of power plants and control centers around the United States. The visitors from Europe, most of them system operators in their respective countries, flew across the Atlantic to see firsthand the American state-of-the-art in the electricity industry. This Technical Assistance (TECAID) Mission was an integral element of the electricity programs set up within the framework of the *European Recovery Program* (ERP), also known as the Marshall Plan. The overall intention of the ERP with regard to electricity was to expand generation capacity, by building national and international power plants on the one hand, and making better use of new and existing capacity by creating European power pools on the other. These power pools, should be brought about by building both physical and institutional interconnections between countries.

To Paul G. Hoffman, administrator of the ERP, the mission was about more than increasing the amount of electricity available in Europe. In his address to the European engineers, Hoffman named two other important aspects of the TECAID Mission, which also applied to the ERP general. First, increasing the availability of electricity should help increase productivity in industry. Hoffman linked productivity to welfare, stating that it was "impossible for any people to enjoy a better standard of living unless within the confines of that country the people produce more".[1] At the same time, expanding generation capacity was directly related to economic recovery. The ERP's most prominent advisor on electric power, Walker Cisler, considered electricity to be "one of the greatest resources for the revival of Western Europe".[2]

The adjective "Western" reflected the absence of Central and Eastern European countries in the ERP. What is less obvious in Cisler's mention of "Western Europe"

---

1 "Address of Welcome to European Electric Systems Operators Group and Press Conference," 22 April 1949, Speech and article file 1949, Paul. G. Hoffman Papers, Truman Library, Independence (Missouri), Paul. G. Hoffman papers. I thank Frank Schipper who providing me a copy of the press conference transcript.
2 Ibid.

is that, Scandinavian engineers also did not come to Washington as part of the TECAID mission. In this, the meeting was a harbinger of how Europe would eventually be organized electrically. By 1964, within each of these three "regions", Western Europe, Scandinavia, and Central and Eastern Europe, international electricity flows were institutionalized as a permanent power pools. This division in regions reflected historical continuity, as well as the technical-economic possibilities for network connection. As we saw in the previous chapters, Western Europe had a history of international electricity exchanges before 1940. In Scandinavia initiatives towards regional cooperation were undertaken in that same period. On the other hand, overland connections between Scandinavia and the European mainland were only possible between Finland and Soviet Union, and Denmark and Germany. In all other cases submarine cable technology was necessary, which required new technological solutions and vast investments. Central and Eastern European countries generally had lower levels of electrification than their Western and Nordic counterparts. Linking to Northern or Western Europe was thus hardly possible without substantial technological progress and, again, major investment. Yet technology and geography were far from the only reasons for this division in regions. It also reflected political and socio-economic differences. Within the emerging Cold War world, the division between East and West reflected different ideological points of view. This was to a lesser extent also true for the *status aparte* of Scandinavian countries.[3]

As an outcome of these efforts, organizations representing regional power pools eventually became the face of European cooperation. Inherent in these pools were American ideals of productivity and integration, as well as specific European views on collaboration. Not only the power pools themselves, but also the UN and ERP institutions were guided and steered by a cohort of – mainly Western – European electrical engineers, who had their own beliefs regarding the future shape of a European system and what "Europe' should be about. UNIPEDE's Study Group on International Connections was a crucial forum for these engineers, as many of its members held positions on postwar Committees and Commissions. European engineers clearly had differing opinions from American ERP officials, who argued for international – and even supranational – ownership and operation of power plants and networks. The ideas of Western European engineers showed remnants of interwar plan, in stressing the solidarity effects of a European network. At the

---

3 Spain also – largely involuntarily – held an exceptional position in international relations. Franco's Spain was absent or denied from nearly all postwar international organisations and other forms of collaboration. See for example Edward Johnson, "Early Indications of a Freeze: Greece, Spain and the United Nations, 1946-47," *Cold War History* 6, no. 1 (2006): 43-61.

same time, their proposed way of creating such a network was rather similar to the consensus that emerged in the course of the 1930s that national and international interconnections should develop side-by-side. To them, a European system should consist of nationally operated networks, working in close coordination.

In this chapter, I will review how collaboration *within* regions came about and what the underlying assumptions behind it were. I will start by reviewing ideas of Europe during WWII and immediately afterwards and show how they related to network-building plans and activities shortly before and during WWII. Here I emphasize the increased priority given to network control and national interconnections, not only for reasons of rationalization but for strategic and sometimes military motives as well. After that, I will provide an extensive account of reconstruction efforts with an emphasis on the ERP. I will reconstruct the discussions related to plans for the European electricity sector within the framework of the ERP, and how European ideas fused with American beliefs on interconnected systems. Most attention will be dedicated to cooperation in Western Europe. The chapter shows how U.S. visions for Europe's electricity structure, which entailed international ownership of electric plants and pooling of resources, were neither rejected nor accepted uncritically. Instead, U.S. ideas were adjusted to fit the prevailing notions of European engineers. These engineers shared the idea that European cooperation was useful, but should be of an informal character, and the importance of European electricity exchanges was to meet national electricity needs. The outcome was a lasting form of international collaboration, which was successful in liberalizing regulations for international electricity transfers. At the same time, as interdependencies between countries grew, this was done without giving up national control over the electricity sector.

This chapter touches only briefly upon the question why collaboration *between* regions did not come about in this period. The strategic intentions of American policy are examined more closely in the subsequent chapter on electricity connections between East and West. Because these factors still need to be taken into consideration, this chapter will conclude with a review of the reconstruction period, rather than true conclusions. These will be drawn at the end of chapter 4 for the postwar period as a whole.

Wartime and postwar ideas of Europe

Ideas on Europe unification remained alive, even as economic problems and political tensions between nations persisted in the course of the 1930s. Another ideology presented itself in the form of Hitlerite fascism. The debate whether Hitler's

Nazi ideology contained a specific European element is still open. According to Pierre Gerbet, Hitler sought a grand Germany rather than a grand Europe.[4] Peter Bugge supports this by stating that National Socialism "was a program for Germany and not for Europe".[5] By contrast, John Laughland has attempted to prove that "Europe" was more than propaganda to the Nazis.[6] It is however fair to say that on the surface Nazi ideology had elements in common with ideas of Europe. Hitler's intentions to create a unified and efficient European economy, a *Großraumwirtschaft*, were hardly far from the ideals of interwar Europeanists. Yet the goal of this Nazi New Europe, a "social and racial reconstruction of European society", was different, as was the means to establish it: war.[7]

Another similarity between Europeanists and National Socialists was their intended use of network technologies. To forge the union and create a European space, Nazis envisaged using *Großraumtechnik*. They argued that construction of vast networks of motorways (*Autobahnen*), railways, and airlines would facilitate European economic integration.[8] Still, this integration was not intended to share resources, enable free trade, and create dependencies. Rather it was meant to create a self-sufficient autarkic German (war) economy and improve the means to wage war.[9] Both Hitler and Mussolini appealed to a "technocratic impulse" and drew on people "with economic and technological expertise".[10] Some fervent Europeanists, who shared some of these values, eventually chose to support this German Europe. One of them was Francis Delaisi. In his 1942 *La révolution européenne*, the darling economist of the interwar European movement interpreted German dominance as a means to rationalization, stability, and the creation of a unified European economy.[11]

---

4 Pierre Gerbet, *La construction de L'Europe* (Paris: Imprimerie nationale, 1983), 43.
5 Bugge, "The Nation Supreme: The Idea of Europe 1914-1945," in *The History*, ed. Wilson and Van der Dussen, 107.
6 Laughland's motivation to prove this point seems not to come from historical interest alone, but also serves his skeptical outlook on the current state of European integration. See his *The Tainted Source: The Undemocratic Origins of the European Idea* (London: Little, Brown and Company, 1997). When juxtaposed, Bugge and Laughland have total opposite views. Bugge states that "Hitler rarely used the concept of 'Europe' and the little he said, other than in propagandistic connections, is fully in accordance with his racial philosophy and the 'Drang nach Osten'". Laughland, on the other hand, claims that "Hitler made regular references to Europe throughout his entire time in office, including before the war".
7 Alan S. Milward, *War, Economy and Society: 1939-1945* (Berkeley: University of California Press, 1977), 10-11 and 14.
8 Helmut Maier, "Systems connected: IG Auschwitz, Kaprun, and the building of European power grids up to 1945," in *Networking Europe: Transnational Infrastructures and the Shaping of Europe, 1850-2000* (Sagamore Beach: Science History Publications, 2006), 138-139; and Laughland, *The tainted*, 28 and 31.
9 Charles S. Maier, *In Search of Stability: Explorations in Historical Political Economy* (Cambridge: Cambridge University Press, 1987), 86-87.
10 Ibid., 76-78.
11 Laughland, *The Tainted*, 41. Also see de Grazia, *Irresistible*, 127.

Despite German hegemony, these New Order ideas of Europe were contested. Since 1941, writes historian Walter Lipgens, "leading personalities and elite of the resistance groups in all countries had [...] expressed in almost identical terms their realization that 'from the English Channel to the Aegean Sea' the same battle was being fought against the same enemy, on the basis of the same faith in human dignity and the rule of law, and in the conviction that the resistance was a single unity which would overcome past discords and in due time bring about a federation of Europe".[12] Historian Peter Bugge notes that as an exception Scandinavian resistance movements seemed to favor an Atlantic order.[13] Many Western European governments found themselves in exile in London, offering possibilities to discuss a post-Hitler Europe. Belgium, the Netherlands and Luxembourg agreed in September 1944 to form an economic and customs union, the Benelux. Around the same time, a French official named Jean Monnet proposed to place coal and steel from the Ruhr under the supervision of a European supranational authority, and to create a large common market.[14]

As after WWI, the ending of WWII witnessed a growing number of initiatives in favor of European unity. In general, the initiative for European cooperation moved from private movements to the international governmental stage. During the interwar period the only intergovernmental body aiming to stimulate European collaboration was the CEEU, which had little tangible results. In 1947-1948, European cooperation became a policy objective of many countries, which consequently entered into a patchwork of new organizations.[15] These organizations all generated more results than the CEEU. These new nationally-based organizations did not end private initiatives, however. Richard Coudenhove-Kalergi remained a tireless promoter of European unity, and was, for example, the driving force in setting up the *European Parliamentary Union*.[16]

A notable difference from the interwar period was the role of both the United States and Soviet Union.[17] Both had deliberately played a minor role on the international stage in the 1920s and 1930s. The two emerged out of WWII as superpowers, and to a large extent dominated international politics, but hardly in harmony with each other. At the Yalta Conference in 1944 they claimed separate spheres of

---

12 Walter Lipgens, *Documents in the History of European Integration*, vol. 1, *Continental Plans for European Union, 1939-1945* (Berlin: Walter de Gruyter, 1985), 662.
13 Bugge, "The Nation," 111.
14 Gerbet, *La construction*, 46.
15 Ibid., 59.
16 Elisabeth du Réau, *L'idée d'Europe au XXe siècle: Des mythes aux réalités* (Brussels: Editions Complexe, 1996), 130.
17 Maier, "The Two Postwar Eras and the Conditions for Stability in Twentieth-Century Western Europe," *The American Historical Review* 86, no. 2 (1981): 161.

influence and consequently divided postwar Europe.[18] The United States' vision of European cooperation was "more in accordance with the will of the local populations" than Stalin's conception of the future of Europe.[19] His vision more closely resembled Hitler's imperialistic ambitions, as he tried to remake Central and Eastern Europe in the image of the Soviet Union. The very thought of European cooperation including Western Europe was repressed, leaving "'Europe' [...] mainly a term and idea employed by dissidents signifying western, democratic, humanist or other similar orientations".[20] Between some Eastern European and West German intellectuals, the idea of reviving Central Europe, or *Mitteleuropa,* was very much alive in the early 1980s.[21] The revitalization of the term was, on a whole, to resurrect the "center" of Europe from the destructive effects of Yalta, but also to reassert nationalistic aspirations of the Soviet satellites.[22]

While Central and Eastern Europe were coerced into withholding participation European cooperation, another region chose voluntarily to stay at arms' length. The choice to create a separate Nordic organization reflected the overall Scandinavian attitude towards European cooperation, which embraced postwar European integration with "mixed feelings".[23] During the Cold War, the Nordic international political position was centered on the so-called *Nordic balance*; "a political balance [...] whereby Nordic countries could enjoy a lower level of tension than Central Europe and yet keep both [...] superpowers at a distance".[24] The foundation of the Nordic Balance consisted of the NATO membership of Norway and Denmark, Sweden's policy of non-alignment, and the *Treaty of Friendship, Cooperation and Assistance* between Finland and the Soviet Union (April 1948).[25]

---

18 The role of "Yalta" is particularly stressed in Timothy Garton Ash, *In Europe's Name: Germany and the Divided Continent* (New York: Random House, 1993). Great Britain was also part of the Yalta discussions.
19 Geir Lundestad, "Empire by Invitation? The United States and Western Europe, 1945-1952," *Journal of Peace Research* 23, no. 3 (1986): 263.
20 Ole Wæver, "Europe Since 1945: Crisis to Renewal," in *The History*, ed. Wilson and Van der Dussen, 164 and 161.
21 Thomas Masaryk coined the term as a political concept in the 1920s, believing that there were strong opportunities for a *New Europe* consisting of small nations between Germany and Russia. Josette Baer, "Imagining Membership: The Conception of Europe in the Political Thought of T.G. Masaryk and Václav Havel," *Studies in East European Thought* 52 (2000): 203-226. For the historical and topographical roots of the term see Hans-Dietrich Schultz and Wolfgang Natter, "Imagining Mitteleuropa: Conceptualisations of 'its' Space in and Outside German Geography," *European Review of History - Revue européenne d'histoire* 10, no. 2 (2003): 273-292.
22 Hans-Georg Betz, "Mitteleuropa and Post-Modern European Identity," *New German Critique* 50 (1990): 173.
23 Thorsten B. Olesen, "Choosing or Refuting Europe? The Nordic Countries and European Integration, 1945-2000," *Scandinavian Journal of History* 25 (2000): 147.
24 Wæver, "Nordic Nostalgia: Northern Europe after the Cold War," *International Affairs* 68, no. 1 (1992): 78-79.
25 Mikael af Malmborg, "Swedish Neutrality, the Finland Argument and the Enlargement of "Little Europe'," *Journal of European Integration History* 1 (1997): 65.

Instead of joining the Western European developments, the Scandinavian countries often went ahead with their own integration process. One example was the Nordic Council, set up to promote political integration in Scandinavian countries. Beyond these regional alliances, generally speaking, Scandinavian countries either favored cooperation through an Atlantic alliance, as well as within new global organizations over any sort of pan-European cooperation.

In Western Europe cooperation and integration was not only on the agenda of countries themselves, but was also heavily stimulated by the United States. After WWII, the U.S. officially committed itself to assist Europe by providing substantial aid through the ERP. Recovery and integration were part and parcel of the ERP agenda. According to the first report to the U.S. Congress, the attainment of the ultimate recovery goals depends largely on raising industrial efficiency and output in Europe. It is in planning this part of the program that the participating countries have perhaps the greatest opportunity to make the fundamental adjustments required to redirect the use of European resources along the lines of economic cooperation.[26]

Alan Milward adds that the ERP was placed in the framework of a sort of customs union theory, which posits that if "all restrictions on the movement of factors of productivity were removed from a particular area this would maximize the efficiency with which those factors were used and thus maximize output [...]".[27] The Foreign Aid Act proposed to the U.S. Congress by President Truman spoke of the intention to create a larger common market without internal borders like the U.S. itself, and the Congress insisted on a common reconstruction program and organization.[28] According to diplomatic historian Michael Hogan, the United States envisaged two steps towards an integrated Europe; first, at least some merger of economic sovereignty, and second, the rationalizing power of the market together with a modern belief in economic planning and bureaucratic management.[29]

---

26 ECA, *First Report to Congress of the Economic Cooperation Administration* (Washington, D.C.: U.S. Government Printing Office, 1948), 4.
27 Milward, *The Reconstruction of Western Europe, 1945-'51* (Berkeley: University of California Press, 1984), 56-58. The quote is on page 58. Also see Pascaline Winand, *Eisenhower, Kennedy, and the United States of Europe* (New York: St. Martin's Press, 1993), 5.
28 Gerbet, *La construction*, 69.
29 Michael J. Hogan, *The Marshall Plan: America, Britain, and the Reconstruction of Western Europe, 1947-1952* (Cambridge: Cambridge University Press, 1987), 293.

Preparing for war

In the years before the war, national dispatch stations were installed in several – mostly Western – European countries. This was the case in Belgium, for example, where the foremost private electricity producers founded the *Coordination de la Production et du Transport de l'Énergie électrique* (CPTE) in 1937, headed by Louis de Heem. CPTE's main task was coordinating the various existing systems through interconnected operation.[30] Although the rationalization of existing networks was the main impetus for coordinating networks on a national basis, it was also connected to preparations for an anticipated war. This was the case in several Western European countries.

One of the nations most concerned with potential war preparation was France. In June 1938 the French government announced its national interconnection program.[31] The program included setting up a central dispatching bureau under the direct supervision of the Ministry of Public Works. Its core activities included coordinating information exchange between existing regional dispatch offices and creating an economic mix between thermal and hydroelectric power.[32] Both the French government and a large labor union argued that the new measures could immediately contribute to national defense as well. Several prominent electrical engineers, including Pierre Ailleret,[33] had voiced similar opinions, arguing that it would provide an instrument to allocate electricity to key sectors and areas in case of a war economy.[34] Network-building activities envisaged in the program struck a similar balance between issues of economy and defense. Of a planned network expansion of some 4,85 km costing 1.5 billion French Francs (see Table 4.1), some 541 million of the funds were earmarked for lines in the interest of national defense. This involved strengthening networks in the north-east of France, where power plants were vulnerable in case of a German attack.[35] In this region the state built a 150 kV network, supplying electricity to the Maginot Line to provide elec-

---

30 CAPAS, "Évolution du système électrique européen. Nouveaux défis pour la recherche" (Académie royale des Sciences, 2006), 52.

31 Bouneau, "Transporter," in *Histoire générale*, vol. 2, ed. Lévy-Leboyer and Morsel, 792-793.

32 Ibid., 796.

33 Pierre Ailleret was born on March 10, 1900, graduated from the Ecole des Ponts et Chaussées and the Ecole superieure d'Electricité. Early on in his career, he worked in the French Ministry of Public Works. In 1929 he became professor at the National Institute of Agronomy, and since 1938 he taught at the Ecole de Ponts. He was one of the founders of *Electricité de France* (EDF). During the first postwar years he was the French representative on the Public Utilities Committee of the Allied Kommandatura of Berlin. He was appointed vice-general-director, until 1967. He died in 1996. His son, François Ailleret, also held a high positions within EDF.

34 Ibid., 793.

35 Ibid., 794-795.

Table 4.1 – 1938 French National Interconnection Program (length of lines in km)

	220 kV	150 kV	90 kV	Total
Lines of first urgency	540	376	153	1,069
Urgent lines	592	916	33	1,541
Other lines	733	596	246	1,575
Total	1,865	1,888	432	4,185

Source: Bouneau, "Transporter," 794.

tric traction for provisioning trains, enable ventilation systems, and electrify gun turrets.[36] The French interconnection program long outlasted the Maginot Line, and was aborted by the Vichy government in 1943, mainly because of shortages of equipment. Measures to safeguard existing lines and plants were taken in the same year. The Ministry of Industrial Production even set up a special police force to guard electrical installations. Later in 1943, German troops performed similar tasks, with two regiments assigned to protect the crucial interconnection between Paris and the Massif Centrale.[37]

In Italy strategic and military considerations played a key role in network building and administration as well, both before and during the war. Since 1922 the Mussolini administration increased efforts to prepare for warfare and a war economy. The electricity sector was a key part of these efforts. Especially the north of Italy was crucial, as it harbored 71.8 per cent of all installed capacity, and also was the expected theatre of war.[38] Measures included making hydroelectric dams less sensitive to aerial attacks through camouflage techniques, standardizing frequencies, and increasing the interconnectedness of regional systems.[39] The stress placed upon the latter aspect was not new and already discussed during WWI, and the years immediately after.[40] Now, a T-shaped grid was planned: an east-west line traversing the Po Valley from Turin to Venice, and the north-south line from Verona to Terni (80 km north from Rome).[41] In 1941 the project of the 230 kV North-South line was finally planned, connecting Florence and Verona. Although the line was completed during the war, it was taken out of service in 1944. Contrary to earlier expectations, the North remained relatively free of military action.[42]

---

36 Morsel, "Industrie électrique et défense, en France, lors des deux conflits mondiaux," *Bulletin d'histoire de l'électricité* 23 (1994): 7-18; and Hervé Bongrain, "L'Électricité au service de la Défense nationale," in *Histoire générale*, vol. 3, ed. Morsel, 560.
37 Bouneau, "Transporter," 848-851.
38 Segreto, "Stratégies militaires et intérêts économique dans l'industrie électrique italienne: Protection ou interconnexion des installations électriques, 1915-1945," *Bulletin d'histoire de l'électricité* 23 (1994): 68-71.
39 Ibid. The proposed means of camouflage was artificial fog.
40 Ibid., 65, and Giannetti, "Resources."
41 Segreto, "Stratégies militaires," 73.
42 Ibid., 75-78.

Germany, the other fascist regime, also prepared itself for a new war. The 1936 Four-Year-Plan aimed at economic self-sufficiency and rearmament, whereby electricity was a basic element of the war economy.[43] Due to the Depression, the electricity sector had an overcapacity. But with the armaments productions at full steam and economic recovery on its way, this surplus quickly turned into deficit.[44] In the fall of 1939 reserve capacity in Germany was practically non-existent.[45] Therefore a *Reichslastverteiler* – load dispatcher – was assigned to directly intervene in the operation of power plants and networks in September 1939, shortly following the invasion of Poland. Historian Bernhard Stier argues that an autarkic electricity policy for the Reich was impossible. Not only was Germany a net importer since the 1920s, but the war economy required even more electricity in order to become self-sufficient in other sectors.[46] The production of aluminum, and in particular *Buna*, a type of synthetic substitute for natural rubber, required substantial kWh per ton.[47] It was therefore not surprising that new sources of electricity were sought in recently absorbed and occupied countries.

This was done within the second Four-Year-Plan of November 1940, which aimed to develop Germany into a European *Großwirtschaftsraum*.[48] The Plan identified the expansion of hydroelectric production as well as the full technical interconnection of the German system as its essential elements. In addition, new interconnections to adjacent countries should help to increase reserve capacity. This included the exploitation of resources in countries under German occupation, and countries collaborating with the Nazi regime. Also in Austria, already interconnected to Germany before the *Anschluß* of 1938, many hydroelectric plants were planned. These included hydroelectricity plants on the rivers Inn, Enns, and Danube. Alpine storage plants, like the *Tauern-Großkraftwerk* at Kaprun, were planned in particular to cover peak loads.[49] In 1941 the Nazis discussed building

---

43 "Grundlage der Kriegswirtschaft." Stier, *Staat,* 475.
44 Stier, "Expansion," 271.
45 Stier, *Staat,* 478.
46 Ibid., .479 and 483.
47 Whereas the production of ton of aluminium – a known energy-intensive process – required 20.000 kWh, a ton of Buna required 40.000. See Maier, *Erwin Marx (1893-1980), Ingenieurwissenschaftler in Braunschweig, und die Forschung und Entwicklung auf dem Gebiet der elektrischen Energieübertragung auf weite Entfernungen zwischen 1918 und 1950* (Verlag für Geschichte der Naturwissenschaften und der Technik, 1993), 259-261. Stier calculated a ton of aluminium at 25.000 kWh. See "Expansion," 272.
48 Maier, *Erwin Marx,* 285.
49 Ibid., 270-271. A recent and impressive study of the Nazi electricity programme in Austria is Oliver Rathkolb and Florian Freund, eds., *NS-Zwangsarbeit in der Elektrizitätswirtschaft der 'Ostmark' 1938-1945: Ennskraftwerke - Kaprun - Draukraftwerke - Ybbs-Persenbeug - Ernsthofen* (Vienna: Böhlau Verlag, 2002).

new connections from Austria to Bulgaria, Slovakia, and Croatia.[50] The occupation of Norway in April 1940 revived ideas of importing Norwegian hydroelectricity.[51]

Also in Germany the vulnerability of electrical installations was recognized. Already in 1934 the *Reichsluftfahrtministerium* (Ministry of Aviation) tested the potential damage of air raids by tying explosive charges to transmission lines. Similar analyses were made for possible Belgian and French artillery attacks.[52] Sections of the German *Wehrmacht*, particularly the air force, favored developing underground transmission lines.[53] The current standard of AC was not fit for that, which stimulated research into the feasibility of DC cables. This even resulted in a scheme quite similar to Oliven's interwar plan, but for HVDC.[54] Towards the end of the war, a first part of the HVDC system was completed between the Elbe and Berlin.[55]

In the Netherlands, military considerations were an argument to interconnect local systems within the western and most urbanized part of the country.[56] Shortly after that work had started, however, the German occupation in 1940 changed priorities. Besides interconnecting local and provincial systems within the Netherlands, the Nazis also wanted to construct linkages with Germany.[57] The new German authorities left matters as much as possible to Dutch actors, including G.J.Th. Bakker of the Ministry of Economic Affairs and J.C, van Staveren of the union of Dutch electricity producers (*Vereeniging van Directeuren van Electriciteitsbedrijven in Nederland*). They supervised the building of interconnecting lines which had mostly already been discussed during the 1930s.[58] Representatives of the Dutch provincial electricity company and the German RWE

---

50 "Niederschrift über die Sitzunf des Fachausschusses I (Wasserkraftplannung) am 27, und 28.1.1942 in Berlin, Pariser Platz 5a," Collection Wasserwirtschaftsstelle für das untere Donau-gebiet 1940-1942, Box 134, OS.

51 Such plans were first presented at the 1930 WPC in Berlin. See Maier, *Erwin Marx*, 94-100.

52 Maier, "'Nationalwirtschaftlicher Musterknabe' ohne Fortune. Entwicklungen der Elektrizitätspolitik un des RWE im 'Dritten Reich,'" in *Elektrizitswirtschaft zwischen Umwelt, Technik und Politik. Aspekte aus 100 Jahren RWE-Geschichte, 1898-1998*, ed. Helmut Maier (Freiberg: TUB, 1998), 143-144.

53 Maier, "'Lauchhammer', 'Döbern' und 'Ragow': Imaginäre und reale Verknotungen der Niederlausitzer Landschaft in die Elektrizitätswirtschaft des 20. Jahrhunderts," in *Die Niederlausitz vom 18. Jahrhundert bis heute: Eine gestörte Kulturlandschaft?, Band 19 der Cottbuser studien zur Geschichte von Technik, Arbeit und Umwelt*, ed. Günter Bayerl and Dirk Maier (Münster: Waxmann, 2002), 149-195.

54 Maier, *Erwin Marx*, 286-292.

55 Maier, "Systems Connected," 145.

56 G.P.J. Verbong, L.van Empelen, and A.N. Hesselmans, "De ontwikkeling van het Nederlandse koppelnet tijdens de Tweede Wereldoorlog," *NEHA-Jaarboek* 12 (1998): 277-278.

57 Ibid., 284 & 287.

58 For the continuity between 1930s discussions and wartime building, see G.P.J. Verbong, A.N. Hesselmans, and J.L. Schippers, "Crisis, oorlog en wederopbouw," in *Techniek in Nederland in de twintigste eeuw*, vol. 2, *Delfstoffen, energie, chemie*, ed. J.W. Schot et al. (Zutphen: Stichting Historie der Techniek/Walberg p, 2000), 190-201.

reached an agreement in 1941 on an international connection between Nijmegen and Kleef. Each party would be responsible for building the line on its own side of the border. This line was completed in April 1944 but only taken into service for a short while.[59] Another line, which involved Belgium as well, was projected for the most southern province Limburg. This 220 kV line between Lutterade (Netherlands), Zukunft/Brauweiler (Germany), and Jupille (Belgium) was completed in 1944, but only gained importance after WWII.[60] Transmission lines with France were also planned, but never built.[61]

Worries over the vulnerability of electricity systems and the according precautionary measures were certainly justified. Electricity was no longer merely the object of fascination, but had become essential to modern economies. According to a 1945 U.S. bombing survey, electricity was "an essential of all modern industry". During WWII, this was certainly the case for Germany. The U.S. survey claimed that the German electricity system was in a precarious state. It stated that "any loss of production would have directly affected essential war production, and the destruction of any substantial amount would have had serious results".[62] While recognizing electricity's strategic importance, the Allies never explicitly targeted German electrical installations; the British Royal Airforce only dropped 0.04 per cent of its bombs on electric utilities, and the U.S. Airforce 0.05 per cent.[63] Albert Speer ironically remarked at the Nuremberg Trails that the Allies prolonged the war by not launching a coordinated attack on the German electricity system.[64] The Allied forces had a similar policy for Italy, as they decided not to bomb the industrial North. That, in combination with the unexpected southern front left many electrical installations relatively unharmed. Most damage was inflicted in central Italy, by both Allied actions as well as retreating German troops.[65]

In France, the electricity system was seriously damaged, in particular in the summer of 1943, when an upsurge of Resistance actions targeting electrical installations coincided with massive aerial bombardments by the Allies. The situation worsened with the Allied invasion of Normandy. By August 1944 the French high-voltage network was nearly paralyzed. Shifting priorities in favor of war-related in-

---

59 Verbong, Empelen, and Hesselmans, "De ontwikkeling," 301-302.

60 See Louis De Heem, "Expérience acquise dans le fonctionnement interconnecté du réseau belge avec les réseaux des pays voisins," in *Report to UNIPEDE Congres: Comité d'études des interconnexions internationales*, IV.1 (Rome: UNIPEDE, 1952), 2-3.

61 Stier, "Expansion," 286.

62 United States, *The United States Strategic Bombing Survey: Over-all report (European War)* (Washington, D.C.: Government Printing Office, 1945), 83 and 85.

63 Ibid., 83.

64 Speer cited in Maier, "Systems Connected," 144-145.

65 Segreto, "Stratégies militaires," 81-82.

Table 4.2 – Electricity production in selected European countries, 1939-1945 (in GWh)

	1939	1940	1941	1942	1943	1944	1945
Austria	3,580	3,990	4,429	4,731	5,640	5,877	3,628
Belgium	5,577	4,138	4,773	4,941	5,030	3,647	4,366
Bulgaria	266	295	302	316	342	307	401
Czechoslovakia	-	-	-	-	-	6,805	4,457
Denmark	1,065	873	1,001	1,091	1,133	1,147	1,017
France	20,228	18,833	18,588	17,857	18,228	14,213	18,074
Germany	34,053		39,800		45,200		11,277*
Italy	18,417	19,431	20,761	20,233	18,247	13,545	12,648
Netherlands	3,903	3,624	3,493	3,447	3,414	2,823	1,740
Norway	5,056	4,794	5,520	6,045	7,045	7,387	6,936
Portugal	382	397	416	407	425	447	488
Romania	582	543	606	-	-	647	-
Spain	3,111	3,617	3,890	4,438	4,776	4,720	4,236
Sweden	9,054	8,624	9,117	9,795	11,035	12,427	13,526
Switzerland	5,506	6,267	6,498	6,269	6,960	6,917	7,971

* Only Western Germany.
Source: UNIPEDE annual statistics. For Germany: Stier, *Staat*,15.

dustries led to French laws restricting electricity consumption as early as December 1940. In later war years, many French areas became used to blackouts, not only due to rationing but also to sabotage and bombardments.[66] In general, most European countries experienced a modest growth of their electricity production from 1939 onwards (see Table 4.2). In most occupied countries – Belgium, France, and the Netherlands – this growth turned into a decline in 1943-1944. Exceptions to this trend are Norway and Austria, which were in particular targeted by the National-Socialist regime to supply more hydroelectricity. Still, both countries experienced a decline in 1945, mainly due to destruction related to warfare and damage done by retreating German forces, and scarce energy sources.

Recovery initiatives

Considering their bombing policy, the wartime Allies preferred to keep electricity systems intact. Where they did target them, like in France, the Allies gave restoring electricity supply high priority. There, the repair of damaged plants and lines was a

---

66 Bouneau, "L'Économie," 128-131.

task for U.S. Army engineers. Almost immediately after the landing at Normandy, the engineering division of the *Supreme Headquarters of the Allied Expeditionary Force* (SHAEF) surveyed existing needs and started repair work.[67] These actions resulted in quite a substantial increase in electricity production in France in 1945 (see Table 4.2). Once SHAEF ceased to exist in mid-1945, the so-called *Public Utilities Panel* (PUP) took over its role.[68] PUP was set up in June 1945 on the initiative of British and American Control Authorities in Germany, and reported to the *Emergency Economic Committee for Europe* (EECE, established May 1945).[69]

While SHAEF was only active behind the frontline following the Normandy invasion, the PUP was more of an interim European organization, and thus had a wider range of activities. Belgium, Denmark, France, Italy, Luxembourg, the Netherlands, Norway, Switzerland, the United Kingdom, and the United States were represented at the PUP meetings. Great Britain, France, and the United States also represented Austria and Germany.[70] The PUP was initially concerned with reconstructing and repairing of installations and transmission lines between Germany and its neighboring countries[71]. Thereafter PUP tried to coordinate electricity exports from Germany to Belgium, France, Luxembourg and the Netherlands. Another task was the exchange of information, which in practice consisted of preparing statistical returns on production and consumption, and export and import of electricity and gas.[72]

Both SHAEF and PUP tried to cover acute needs. They were inadequate to supervise a structured reconstruction and modernization of war-torn Europe. In 1947 the EECE, of which the PUP was part, was absorbed by a new organization: the *United Nations Economic Commission for Europe* (UNECE, 1947). The UNECE

---

67 One of the first inventories I found concerned the region around Cherbourg, which saw three weeks of battle after the invasion on June 6, 1944. The purpose of the report was to determine the condition of the electric power (as well as the water supply) facilities in the area. "Report of Inspection. Location: Cherbourg Area," 10-14 July 1944, Record Group 331: Records of Allied Operational and Occupation Headquarters, World War II, file 4.1: Records of the Engineer Division, box 3, National Archives at College Park, Maryland, United States (hereafter: NACP).

68 "Absorption of EECE by the Economic Commission for Europe, 'Emergency Economic Committee for Europe. Paper Submitted by the Acting Secretary-General for the Information of the Economic Commission for Europe'", 26 April 1947, registry fonds GX: Economics, file 12/1, United Nations Organisation in Geneva Archives (hereafter: UNOG).

69 The EECE was one of several European wartime organisations, referred to as the E-organisations. These also included he European Coal Organisation (ECO: officially established in January 1946, but in function since June 1945) and the European Central Inland Transport Organisation (ECITO: September 1945). Their work has not received wide historical attention.

70 "The Work of the Emergency Economic Committee for Europe," n.d., registry fonds GX, file 12/1, UNOG.

71 Ibid.

72 Ibid.

was set up to accelerate reconstruction, "to modernise the structure of industry and to modify the character of the economic system" in Europe.[73] The UNECE was part of the *United Nations* (UN, 1945), an organization that took over the role of the LoN in 1946. The groundwork for the UN was laid during and shortly after WWII. On the whole, the United States, United Kingdom, Soviet Union and China decided upon the structure of the new world organization in 1944, as the basis of a effective system of collective security.[74] The Americans insisted that UN dealt with economic and social affairs as well. This became the task of the *Economic and Social Council* (ECOSOC).[75] In order to accelerate reconstruction ECOSOC set up regional working groups, the ECE being one of them.[76]

ECE was not alone in aiding an ailing Europe. In fact it was outshone by the *European Recovery Program* (ERP). The ERP was the result of an invitation by U.S. Secretary of State George C. Marshall, who in June 1947 spoke of an extensive aid program enabling "the Europeans to help themselves". The foreign ministers of France, Great Britain, and the Soviet Union met that same month. They decided to convene a special conference to discuss the coordination of American aid in July 1947.[77] That conference led to a *Committee of European Economic Co-operation* (CEEC), along with technical committees on Food and Agriculture, Energy, Iron and Steel, and Transport. At a later stage, Timber and Manpower committees were created, as well as a Balance of Payments Committee, and a Committee of Financial Experts. The CEEC's task was to submit a plan for allocating ERP funds for the period 1948-1951. All participating countries were asked to hand in the necessary information to the technical committees. Most information was already submitted in August of the same year.[78] On April 26, 1948 sixteen western European countries signed a convention establishing the organization to handle the ERP, the *Organization for European Economic Cooperation* (OEEC).

---

73 Yves Berthelot and Paul Rayment, "The ECE: A Bridge Between East and West," in *Unity and Diversity in Development Ideas: Perspectives from the UN Regional Commissions*, ed. Yves Berthelot (Bloomington & Indianapolis: Indiana University Press, 2004), 57. Also see Václav Kostelecky, *The United Nations Economic Commission for Europe: The Beginning of a History* (Stockholm: Arbetarrörelsens arkiv och bibliotek, 1989), 16-18.

74 First, in meeting between August and October 1944 at the estate of Dumbarton Oaks near Washington D.C., the Great Powers (the United States, the United Kingdom, the USSR and China) ironed out the main structure of the new world organisation. It should guarantee the basis of a effective system of collective security. The main decisions taken at Dumbarton included a General Assembly composed of all member states with an equal vote, and a Security Council composed of the great (armed) powers, an International Court of Justice, and a Secretariat. Gerbet, Mouton, and Ghébali, *Le rêve*, 139-141.

75 Ibid.

76 Berthelot and Rayment, "The ECE," 56-57.

77 Milward, *The Reconstruction*, 64.

78 OEEC, *The Organisation for European Economic Co-operation: Two Years of Economic Co-Operation* (Paris: OEEC, 1950), 9-10.

This need for new organization was contested by some. At the 1947 Conference, Norway and Sweden pleaded to organize the ERP within the United Nations' framework, and to use the UNECE to administer ERP funds. This Scandinavian initiative did not prevail for several reasons. First of all, not every European country had UN membership.[79] Austria, Bulgaria, Finland, Hungary, Italy, Portugal, and Romania did not join the UN until 1955. The Federal Republic of Germany as well as the German Democratic Republic followed only in 1973 (see Table 4.3). This situation would potentially trouble UN-based decisions on how to allocate and spend the aid. Second of all, with regard to UNECE, the United States was afraid that Soviet political obstruction would stymie its effectiveness.[80] Lastly, the United States wanted more control over the distribution of funds. In particular, it wished to avoid a repetition of the political struggles experienced in an earlier assistance program, the *United Nations Reconstruction and Rehabilitation Administration* (UNRRA, 1943).[81] The U.S. Congress was impressed with UNRRA's results[82] but it also resented the exploitation of its funds, of which 74 per cent came from the United States, by Eastern European communists.[83] The OEEC thus went ahead and, despite their reservations, Sweden and Norway participated.

Matters were different for Central and Eastern European countries, including the Soviet Union. They abstained from becoming OEEC members, despite the fact that Secretary Marshall himself had pointed out that assistance was open to everyone. To Marshall, aid was "directed not against any country or doctrine but against hunger, poverty, desperation and chaos".[84] Initially, the Soviet Union seemed to embrace that idea and sent a mission to Paris, despite having some reservations. Moscow was critical toward aid for Germany and former allies of Hitler, while preferring a "no-strings-attached assistance to the anti-Nazi Allies".[85] The Kremlin was also suspicious of U.S. intentions. On the one hand the Soviets

---

79 Milward hints at it in *The Reconstruction*, note 29. Most of the eastern European countries would join in December 1955.

80 The Soviet Union at least tried to do this at UNECE's first session in May 1947. W.W. Rostow, *The Division of Europe after World War II: 1946* (Austin: University of Texas Press, 1981), 73-74.

81 Robert H. Johnson, "International Politics and the Structure of International Organization: The Case of UNRRA," *World Politics* 3, no. 4 (2006): 520-538. It should be noted that "United Nations" in its title referred to the group of countries providing aid, and not to the "United Nations" as an organization.

82 Milward, *The Reconstruction*, 46; and David W. Ellwood, *Rebuilding Europe: Western Europe, America and Postwar Reconstruction* (London: Longman, 1992), 35-36.

83 This resentment is mentioned in Maier, "Alliance and Autonomy: European Identity and U.S. Foreign Policy Objectives in the Truman Years," in *The Truman Presidency*, ed. Michael J. Lacey (Cambridge: Cambridge University Press, 1989), 277.

84 Excerpt from Marshall's speech, recited in Ellwood, *Rebuilding*, 85. From a geographic point of view one could argue whether Turkey and Greece are really "western".

85 Gerbet, *La construction*, 69; and Vladislav Zubok and Constantine Pleshakov, *Inside the Kremlin's Cold War: From Stalin to Khrushchev* (Cambridge: Harvard University Press, 1996), 104.

Table 4.3 – Membership of the OEEC, CMEA & UN

Country	OEEC/CMEA member	UN-member
Albania	CMEA	1955
Austria	OEEC	1955
Belgium	OEEC	Yes
Bulgaria	CMEA	1955
Czechoslovakia	CMEA	Yes
Denmark	OEEC	Yes
Federal Republic Germany	OEEC	1973
Finland	None	1955
France	OEEC	Yes
Greece	OEEC	Yes
German Democratic Republic	CMEA (1950)	1973
Hungary	CMEA	1955
Iceland	OEEC	Yes
Ireland	OEEC	Yes
Italy	OEEC	1955
Luxembourg	OEEC	Yes
Netherlands	OEEC	Yes
Norway	OEEC	Yes
Poland	CMEA	Yes
Portugal	OEEC	1955
Romania	CMEA	1955
Spain	OEEC (1958; associate)	1955
Sweden	OEEC	Yes
Switzerland	OEEC	2002
Turkey	OEEC	Yes
USSR	CMEA	Yes
United Kingdom	OEEC	Yes
United States	None[†]	Yes
Yugoslavia	None	Yes

*They joined as part of the USSR. † The U.S. did participate as part the Bizone of Germany and the Anglo-American zone of the Free Territory of Trieste. ‡Consultative members did not have the right to vote in the Commission.
Adapted from: Kostelecký, *The United Nations*, 15, figure 1; and Gerbet, Mouton, and Ghébali, *Le rêve*, 426.

desired U.S. credits, but on the other they feared economic blackmail.[86] In 1947 the Soviet ambassador in Washington warned his minister of foreign affairs that "the Marshall Plan [...] is directed toward the establishment of a West European

---

86 This was fed by earlier experiences. A 1945 request for U.S. aid was supposedly "lost". Only six months later the United States spoke of a loan of one billion dollar, but linked to a settlement of various controversial issues. Ibid.

bloc as an instrument of American policy".[87] In addition, Stalin saw the Marshall Plan as a watershed, interpreting it as an attempt to revive German industrial and military potential which threatened Soviet security. It hampered Stalin's vision of a future Europe, and endangered German-Soviet relations.[88] But not only the Soviet Union had reservations about their taking part in the ERP. According to Alan Milward, the U.S. State Department purposely made the ERP incompatible with Soviet wishes.[89] Others have confirmed that view.[90] It was, however, Stalin who decided not to participate, and coerced countries within his sphere of influence to do the same. Thus when the Soviet delegation walked out of the Paris Conference in July 1947, they took the Central and Eastern European states in their wake.[91] The Soviet Union then set up the *Council for Mutual Economic Assistance* (CMEA) in 1949 as a rival organization for regional economic cooperation and development.

This division in Europe between "East" and "West", with a hesitant "North", contributed to a corresponding regional division in the field of electricity. The ERP gave strong incentives to forge a close collaboration between OEEC countries. Over the course of the 1950s, Western European countries strengthened interconnections between their respective systems, and created a power pool. The CMEA over time created its own system, as did Scandinavian countries. In the following section, I will trace these interconnections, focusing mainly on Western European development within the framework of American aid.

U.S. internationalization opposed

The ERP, as described by the European Cooperation Act of 1948 (the U.S. law that called it into being), was based on four main points: 1) the creation of internal financial stability, 2) development of economic co-operation between the countries, and 3) solution of the trade deficit with the U.S. economy. The fourth point was "a strong *production effort* by each of the participating countries, especially in agricul-

87 Recited in Scott D. Parrish and Mikhail M. Narinsky, "New Evidence on the Soviet Rejection of the Marshall Plan, 1947: Two Reports" (Cold War International History Project working paper, Washington, D.C.: Woodrow Wilson International Center for Scholars, 1994), 43.
88 Zubok and Pleshakov, *Inside*, 50-51.
89 Milward, *The Reconstruction*, 64.
90 British and French ministers of foreign affairs Bevin and Bidault sought to strengthen the improbability of Soviet participation, telling the U.S. Ambassador in Paris that "they hoped that the Soviet will refuse to cooperate". Recited in Parrish and Narinsky, "New Evidence," note 105.
91 Zubok and Pleshakov, *Inside*, 51.

ture, fuel and power, transport, and the modernization of equipment".[92] Between 1947 and 1951 the ERP transferred 11.8 billion US$ to Europe.[93] To administer the ERP, the United States set up the *Economic Cooperation Administration* (ECA). ECA had national missions in each participating country to oversee domestic allocation of ERP funds. On the European side, the OEEC coordinated and allocated ERP funds. It was made up of a Council, an Executive Committee, and Technical Committees. In Paris, where the OEEC had its headquarters, was also the *Office of the U.S. Special Representative in Europe* (OSR). The Special Representative was the highest ranking officer responsible for the ERP in Europe. The OSR coordinated the activities of the ECA national missions and worked directly with the OEEC in Paris.[94]

The United States stayed in close proximity to the decision-making process concerning the spending of ERP funds. The ECA tried to exert some leverage on national economic policy in Western Europe through the so-called *counterpart funds*. The equivalent in national currency of all ERP-financed imports had to be deposited in a special account with the national bank. Five per cent of the funds in each account were allocated for the U.S. use for administrative expenditures associated with the ERP, and for the procurements of materials needed by the United States.[95] The remaining counterpart funds had either to be used to retire debt or for investments. To put these funds to use, ECA authorization was required.[96] A stable financial and monetary climate was a first prerequisite for obtaining permission.[97]

The ERP's electricity program was negotiated between the OEEC, ECA and OSR.[98] The overall electricity program, covering the period 1948-1951, had three main aims. First, it should recuperate wartime damage. This included completing

---

92 CEEC, *Committee of European Economic Co-Operation*, vol. 1, *General Report* (Washington, D.C.: U.S Government Printing Office, 1947), 6.

93 Gérard Bossaut, *L'Europe occidentale à l'heure américaine: Le Plan Marshall et l'unité européenne (1945-1952)* (Brussels: Editions Complexe, 1992), 138-139.

94 Hogan, "American Marshall Planners and the Search for a European Neocapitalism," *The American Historical Review* 90, no. 1 (1985): 47 and 54-56. Also see Chiarella Esposito, *America's Feeble weapon: Funding the Marshall Plan in France and Italy, 1948-1950* (Westport: Greenwood Press, 1994), 7.

95 ECA, *Second Report to Congress of the Economic Cooperation Administration*. (Washington, D.C.: U.S. Government Printing Office, 1948), 55.

96 For more on counterpart funds, see Esposito, *America's*, 6-7; Milward, *The Reconstruction*, 107ff; and Bossaut, *L'Europe*, chap. 7.

97 Esposito's study of ERP fund spending in France and Italy elaborately threats the actual implementation of counterpart funds. Often, in the case of these two countries, ECA could not extort absolute control over counterpart spending. National politics and specific economic problems forced ECA to release funds, whereas Paris and Washington not always were eager to do so.

98 The OEEC did also discuss the distribution of available (heavy) electrical equipment. Although related, I will however focus on their activities concerning the construction of international power plants and networks, and international coordination efforts.

Table 4.4 – Planned ECA support for electricity equipment, 1948-1951 (in millions of US$)

	1948	1949	1950	1951	Total
Main national programs	125	100	50	25	300
Supplementary International Program	25	75	75	25	200
Total	150	175	125	50	500

Calculated on basis of: CEEC, *General Report*, 51, table 16.

plants under construction, and overdue maintenance of equipment. A second goal was "to increase [supplies of energy] progressively and thus raise the whole standard of productivity of European workers", which resonated with one of the overall objectives of the ERP.[99] OEEC countries planned to increase electricity by nearly 70,000 million kWh by 1951. This would bring total production to 40 per cent above the 1947 level. In addition, generating capacity would increase by at least 25 GW, approximately two-thirds above the pre-war level. In total, ECA estimated it would need to allocate around 500 million US$ to reconstruct and modernize Western Europe's electricity system, (see Table 4.4 for a breakdown).

Each country identified its national priorities, and presented these to the OEEC. ECA's Industry Division subsequently considered these national plans, and approved them accordingly. Taken together, these plans were known as the National Program. But the Electricity Program had a third aim: stimulating European cooperation. This fitted well with the US's overarching aim of these to have countries pool resources and work together in a close fashion. The CEEC had drafted a number of projects for what became known as the *International Power Program*. CEEC selected nine projects: six hydro plants in Italy, France, and on the frontier separating Austria, Italy and Switzerland, as well as two lignite thermal plants in Western Germany and a geothermal plant in Italy (see Figure 4.1). The CEEC report emphasized that "these projects have been selected without regard to national frontiers".[100] These projects were labeled "international" not only because they supplemented the national plans mentioned above. The idea behind the International Program was to exploit international resources (border rivers, streams of water from mountain ranges on borders) through internationally financed and owned plants and the electricity generated in those plants would be shared among participating countries (see Table 4.5).[101] Economically speaking, the aim of this International Program was to cover electricity shortages during wintertime.[102]

At least according to G.W. Perkins, the International Power Program was

---

99 CEEC, *General Report*, 10.
100 Ibid., 11.
101 CEEC, *Committee of European Economic Co-Operation*, vol. 2, *Technical Reports* (Washington, D.C.: U.S. Government Printing Office, 1947), 132.
102 Ibid, 131.

Figure 4.1 – ECA's international power plants
Source: CEEC, Technical Reports, 164.

"maybe the most important part of the whole Electricity Program".[103] Perkins worked for the Industry Division of ECA, which oversaw the Electricity Program. Its importance in relation to the National Program was reflected in ECA's allocated budget. While ECA reserved 300 million US$ for the National Program, the International Program had a budget of 200 million. While national projects were co-financed by ECA funds, the countries themselves, and counterpart funds, ECA bore the bulk of the costs with regard to the International Program.[104]

In spite of the high hopes, the International Program from the start did not live up to ECA's expectations. In contrast to ECA, the Western European nations gave priority to the National Program. They were not as enthusiastic about the International Program as ECA was. This was reflected in discussions of the

---

103 Arthur S. Griswold (consultant on electricity, Industry Division) to Mr. Perkins (Director, Industry Division), 7 September 1948, RG 469: Records of U.S. Foreign Assistance Agencies, file 2.2: Records of the Office of the United States Special Representative in Europe, subject and country files of the Industry Division, box 1, NACP.
104 Ibid.

Table 4.5 – The International Program in figures

Country		Supplying to	Installed capacity (1,000 kW)	Annual production (million kWh)	Construction time (years)	Cost (million US$)
Adige Noce	Italy	Italy	140	552	4	22
Bouthier		Italy	972	771	4	46
Fessenheim	France (Rhine)	France	120	850	4	67
Goldenberg	Germany	France Benelux Germany	190	1,150	2	18
Larderello	Italy	Italy	75	500	5	6
Piave	Italy	Italy	130	275	5	16
Sarca Molveno	Italy	Italy	180	500	4	30
Upper Inn	Austria Switzerland Italy	Italy Austria	349*	1,407*	4-6*	80*
Weisweiler	Germany	France Benelux	150	1,000	3	30
Total			2,306	6,645		315

* Austrian part only.
Source: CEEC, Technical Reports, 132, table 23.

Electricity Committee of the OEEC. That Committee was composed of national experts on electricity, mostly engineers working for national utilities. According to an internal ECA report, the September 1948 meeting of the Committee saw "inconclusive and at times very heated" discussions on the International Program.[105] Judging by the minutes of the meeting that seems an understatement. The Italian delegate opened the sessions by remarking that none of the five planned power stations in Italy would export electricity. He therefore wanted exclude these plants from the International Program.[106] Subsequently, U.S. officials representing the Bizone in Germany made a similar announcement; the two planned brown coal

---

105 Arthur S. Griswold to Perkins, "Report of O.E.E.C. Electricity Committee Meetings, September 8, 9, 10 and 11, 1948," 15 October 1948, RG 469, file 2.2, NACP. Griswold had been presented at this meeting as ECA observer.
106 "Minutes of the 10th Meeting," 10 September 1948, fonds OEEC, file 1157.3, document EL/M(48) 10, Historical archives of the European Union, Florence (hereafter HAEU). While originally doing my research on-site in Florence, I found several files barely readable from microfilm. I owe many thanks to Jan-Anno Schuur of the OECD Archives in Paris for supplying me several better copies.

plants would supply to German consumers only.[107] This was backed by General Lucius Clay, the Military Governor of the U.S. zone in Germany. He "emphatically opposed" the idea of exploiting Ruhr brown coal fields to the benefit of contiguous countries.[108] He was responsible for making Western Germany self-supporting, a task requiring sufficient energy sources. At the same time Clay felt as if neighboring countries were trying to obtain electricity from Germany as a form of reparations.[109]

The technical and economic soundness of the intentions of the International Program was evidently not in doubt. The British representative stated that it was in the interest of each country to "work a favorable site outside its frontier rather than to work a less favorable site".[110] But implementing the program led to difficulties primarily due to "political and diplomatically uncertainty".[111] According to the United Kingdom the International Program therefore "seriously failed to materialize".[112] Either the definition had to be changed, or a program more thoroughly studied than the 1947 report should be drawn up. Eventually a related suggestion by the chairman, Franz Hintermayer from Austria, was adopted; each country should make a list of "installations which might be of international interest". The definition employed by Hintermayer already reflected an important deviation from the initial American idea, in two ways. First of all, Hintermayer spoke of international *installations*, which included both power stations and transmission lines, which differed from the original emphasis on power plants. Second of all, the definition of "international" seemed to have changed. For ECA, international projects should involve more than one country in terms of resource, finance and electricity supply. By redefining this to installations that "might be of international interest", it came to include power plants and transmission lines that in the first place contributed to the national electricity economy, and only in the second place contributed to other countries. The Committee eventually decided to study obstacles to implementing the International Program, and to submit installations of international interest.

Although the work of the UNECE is reviewed more thoroughly in the next chapter, it is important to note here that they too faced opposition to plans for international ownership of electrical installations. In December 1947 the UNECE discussed the future of Europe with regard to electricity. The meeting had a high profile, considering the presence of the Executive Secretary Gunnar Myrdal, his

---

107 Ibid. "Bizone" was the commonly used name for the merged British and U.S. zones in Germany since 1946.
108 DeForest to Perkins, 13 November 1948, RG 469, file 2.2, box 1, NACP.
109 Ibid.
110 "Minutes of the 10th Meeting", 10 September 1948, fonds OEEC, file 1157.3, document EL/M(48) 10, HAEU.
111 Ibid.
112 Ibid.

special assistant Walt Rostow, and UNECE's chief economist Nicholas Kaldor. At the heart of the discussion was a paper by the Director of the Electric Power section, James Houston Angus.[113] Angus proposed a formal resolution, a "European Power Charter", in which each member state would promise to develop its indigenous power resources to the maximum economic benefit of all signatories. Furthermore, he wanted to compile an overall program according to jointly determined priorities. But his most ambitious suggestion was the European Power Board, that would "[market] surplus national power production" as well as *own* and operate HV-interconnections. The Board would also act as a finance corporation, and consider international questions of system operation and load control.[114]

Kaldor was very open to the suggestion, and in addition he recognized the need to think about the relation between this project and the ERP.[115] In an earlier response Walt Rostow[116] expressed mixed feelings. On the one hand he strongly agreed with the timing for implementing a long-term scheme for Europe's electricity supply. On the other, he doubted whether nations desired such a charter.[117] French expert Pierre Ailleret, also present at the meeting, immediately renounced the idea of the Board. He considered bilateral agreements a better option, and the ownership of transmission lines "was out of the question".[118] The only possible option for such a board was to attract finance for developing new projects. After some discussion it was agreed that no specific project of such a board would be laid before the Committee on Electric Power at this stage.

The withdrawal of Angus' proposal was also the end of the European Power Board, and similar suggestions. No consensus could be found within the ECE for a formal body for international, or supranational, cooperation and ownership. This

---

113 The director was part of the ECE's Secretariat.

114 Draft note by James Angus Houston, "Electric Power. European Power Board," 13 December 1947, registry fonds GX, file 12/1/1, UNOG.

115 Note of meeting held in the Executive Secretary's office to discuss the proposal that the Power Committee be asked to consider the formation of a European Power Board, 19 December 1947, registry fonds GX, file 12/1/1, UNOG.

116 Walt Whitman Rostow was born as a son of Russian-Jewish parents on October 7, 1916 in New York City. Rostow received a PhD in economics from Yale in 1940, and spend his wartime service in the Office of Strategic Services. After the war he worked in the German-Austrian Affairs Unit, under Charles P. Kindleberger, in the economic section of the State Department, which was headed at that time by Under-Secretary of State for Economic Affairs, William L. Clayton. After his two-year employment in Geneva as special assistant to Myrdal, he became professor of economic history at MIT, although still being active in Washington. He became a policy advisor to Kennedy in 1958. Shortly after publishing his acclaimed *The Stages of Economic Growth: A Non-Communist Manifesto* he was promoted to Kennedy's deputy special assistant for national security affairs. Under president Johnson he was national security advisor and a relentless supporter of military intervention. He died on February 13, 2003.

117 W.W. Rostow to Angus Houston, 16 December 1947, registry fonds GX, file 19/13/1, UNOG.

118 Note of meeting, 19 December 1947, UNOG.

did not imply that other forms of collaboration were undesired. Hintermayer, also active in the UNECE Committee on Electric Power, proposed "an informal international group to exchange ideas with a view to closer co-operation [and providing] valuable data for any European grid system which might be established in the future".[119] He saw his suggestion supported. Clearly Western European engineers were in favor of international cooperation, but both within the OEEC and UNECE, they opposed plans for international or European ownership of power plants and transmission lines.

The TECAID mission

ECA was not happy with the lack of progress of the International Program after the September 1948 meeting of the OEEC Electricity Committee. One month later, Perkins wrote Special Representative Harriman that

> [t]he international program could and should be one of the important elements in the general European recovery and in European economic cooperation. As matters stand, it is not.[120]

The Electricity Committee did not take up the International Program again before the end of 1949. ECA, however, did. Its December 1948 report reckoned that the International Program was "a controversial matter" from the start, which had "continued to remain unsettled".[121] ECA underlined its definition of international projects as "those plants requiring an international agreement for their financing, construction, or for the utilization of the power they produce".[122] According to the report, many of the plants included in the initial program had no international aspect whatsoever, and the Bizone authorities had not been consulted about the two German plants.

But this was not the only problem for ECA. Whereas the Paris Report assumed an expansion of generation capacity by 21,203 MW through the National Program, recalculations in 1949 indicated that an increase of only 14,867 MW would be

119 UNECE, *Committee on Electric Power, First Session, Fifth Meeting, October 14, 1947*, UN doc, ser., E/ECE/EP/SR.1/5 (Geneva: UNECE, 1947), 7.
120 G.W Perkins to A.W. Harriman, 7 October 1948, RG 469, file 2.2, box 1, NACP.
121 C.W. DeForest, A.S. Griswold and S.F. Neville, "The Electricity Programs, Long-Term and 1949/50," Annual Report prepared for Electric Power Branch, Industry Division, Office of Special Representative (Paris: ECA, 1948), 14. Found in RG 469, file 2.2, box 1, NACP.
122 Ibid.

possible.[123] This considerable gap was due in part to inaccurate estimates in 1947, but mostly to the unavailability of materials and financial means. ECA wanted to make up for this deficit, as the planned growth of industrial activities of Western European countries was based on the initial calculation.[124] It also wanted to tackle the lack of reserve capacity. It therefore suggested initiating a Complementary Program, which would aim to meet the deficit. The report provided an extensive list of 74 plants, both thermal and hydroelectric, representing a capacity of 7,865 MW.[125] The list contained national plants not part of the National Program, as well as most of the plants of the original International Program. In addition, ECA indicated that surplus capacity was not always and sometimes could not be offered to contiguous countries during peak times. To a large extent this was caused by a lack of interconnections, ECA argued, which prevented a more effective pooling of resources.[126] This was in contrast to the United States, where interconnected systems often formed voluntary operating committees. Such forms of collaboration enabled more economic operation and made more effective use of available equipment, assuring "the greatest benefit to all concerned".[127]

This apparent lack of international coordination was earlier pointed out by ECA's most important consultant concerning electricity, Walker Cisler (see Figure 4.2). Cisler was a prominent American engineer who had already worked on electricity systems in Europe through SHAEF and PUP.[128] In October 1948 he pointed out to Perkins that little coordination of operation of electricity systems existed between countries in North-Western Europe.[129] More coordination had several advantages, argued Cisler. First, participating countries would be able to schedule

---

123 Ibid., 10.
124 Ibid., 8.
125 Ibid., 16-19.
126 Samuel F. Neville (Assistent Chief, Electric Power Section) to Huntington Gilchrist (Director, Industry Division), 11 September 1950, RG 469, 2.2, box 5, NACP.
127 C.W. DeForest, A.S. Griswold and S.F. Neville, " The Electricity Programs, Long-Term and 1949/50," Annual Report prepared for Electric Power Branch, Industry Division, Office of Special Representative (Paris: ECA, 1948), 22-23. Found in RG 469, file 2.2, box 1, NACP.
128 Walker Lee Cisler (1897-1994) graduated from Cornell University with a degree in mechanical engineering, after serving in WWI. He began to work for the Public Serve and Electric Gas in New Jersey. He would be employed by the Office of Production Management (later named War Production Board) in 1941. In mid-1943 he shortly joined Detroit Edison Company, but was asked by Eisenhower to become chief of the public utilities headquarter of SHAEF (Supreme Headquarters Allied Expeditionary Force). Cisler's main task was to restore power plants across war-torn Europe. He was for example part of the restoring power and gas service in Paris in 1945. After WWII he would join the board of Detroit Edison, and Walker Cisler was also asked by Paul G. Hoffman to become the head of ECA's Power Branch. Cisler became the first U.S. chairman of the World Energy Conference in 1968. He further dedicated his efforts to promote peaceful use of nuclear power, and was a frequently consulted advisor for many national and international organisations.
129 Walter Cisler and C.W. DeForest to George Perkins (Director Industry Division), 26 October 1948, RG 469, file 2.2, box 1, NACP.

power plant outages for maintenance and help cover each other's electricity shortages during such periods. Second, since it would enable mutual assistance, each
country could reduce the margin of reserve requirements. Third, because closer
coordination enables better use of existing capacity, the total amount of available
electricity would increase.[130] According to Cisler, collaboration between utilities
had proven to be very effective in the United States.[131] He therefore recommended
having Western European network operators exchange experiences with their
American counterparts, under the sponsorship of ECA Such a visit would also
"be very helpful in furthering the aims and purposes of ECA from the standpoint
of electric power".[132] Cisler preferred that this visit take place as soon as possible.
Perkins took over Cisler's suggestion and subsequently informed Robert Majorlin,
the Secretary-General (1948-1954) of the OEEC.[133]

Between April and May 1949, a group of twenty-five electrical engineers from
Western Europe visited the United States for a period of six weeks. Several of these
men were Electricity Committee members, and in general all were involved with
load dispatching in their respective countries. A number of people on the mission had already worked together. For example Louis de Heem (Belgium) was
acquainted with Walker Cisler through PUP. Through the first ECE Electricity
Committee meeting in 1947, De Heem also knew Dutchman G. J. Th. Bakker,
Frenchman Crescent, and Swiss René Hochreutiner as well as the chairman of the
group, Franz Hintermayer.

OEEC Technical Assistance Project No. 1, or the TECAID mission as it became known, had an extensive program. Steam and water power stations – including plants of the Tennessee Valley Authority and Niagara Hudson Power Co.
– plant manufacturing works of Westinghouse, research installations, and central
control rooms were all part of the tour across the United States.[134] In particular,
much attention was devoted to a number of large interconnected groups, or power
pools. This was reflected in the TECAID report, which consisted of two parts.
The first dealt with American practices, the second reviewed existing interconnections in Western Europe. In the first part, the report focused upon the *South
Atlantic & Central Areas Group* (SA & CA Group) and the *Pennsylvania-New Jersey*

---

130 Ibid.
131 Ibid.
132 Ibid.
133 William Foster to Robert Marjolin, 26 November 1948, RG 469, file 2.2, NACP. The letter was send
under the name of Foster, at the time Deputy Special Representative in Europe, but was drafted by Perkins.
134 A complete list is printed as Appendix B of the official report. See OEEC, *Interconnected Power
Systems in the USA and Western Europe: The Report of the Tecaid Mission, the Report of the Electricity Committee* (Paris, 1950), 29ff.

Interconnection (PNJ) as examples of a *loosely-knit* system and a *closely-knit* system, respectively.[135] The PNJ was planned from the start to be an interconnection between companies. Founded by three utilities in 1927, they decided to construct a 220 kV ring between the utilities to their mutual benefit.[136] Utilizing this ring structure, a central control organization in Philadelphia allocated the total load to the most economical plant available in the whole interconnected system. The PNJ did not see the need for automated control of frequencies. The overall transmission capacity was large and the frequency was centrally monitored by control staff in Philadelphia.

The SA & CA Group represented a loosely-knit system. At the time it was the largest interconnected system in the world, stretching from the Great Lakes to the Gulf of Mexico. As to geographical size, according to the Report, it was quite comparable to the surface of Western Europe including Italy. The Group was established in 1928 as a voluntary association and gradually came to include over eighty public utilities, both private and public. These were connected through *tie-lines*, which are defined as interconnections between different control areas or utilities.[137] As the interconnected system grew, manual control of frequency and exchanges between utilities became insufficient. The Group therefore changed to automated control of frequency and tie-line loading.[138] Crucially, however, the Group did not have a centralized system of control. Each participating utility took responsibility for their own system conditions. Once a year, representatives of all utilities met, mainly to coordinate maintenance programs. Regional committees met twice a year. The most frequent contact between utilities was telephone calls between load dispatchers of neighboring utilities. Contact with load dispatchers other than from neighboring areas was rare. According to the TECAID report, a closer organization was not economically justified. American engineers argued that allocating load to the cheapest available units in the Group resulted in between 80 to 90 per cent of total possible savings.[139] Relatively little attention was devoted to allocation of load to utilities further than the adjacent areas.

The resultant report, presented to the OEEC in June 1949, also reflected on the applications of American practices in Western European countries. The European engineers were particularly fond of the loosely-knit system of the SA & CA Group,

---

135 Ibid., 14ff.
136 The history of the Pennsylvania-New Jersey Interconnection is by Hughes as an example of a planned system. See his *Networks*, 325-332.
137 See Steven L. Rueckert, "Transferring Electrical Power between Utilities: Economics and Reliability Tie Energy Suppliers Together," *IEEE Potentials* 7, no. 4 (1988): 13-14.
138 OEEC, *Interconnected*, 15.
139 Ibid., 16.

Table 4.6 – Interconnections between TECAID countries, 1949

From/to	Austria	Belgium	Denmark	France	Netherlands	Norway	Switzerland
France		1 x 65 kV 1 x 70 kV					2 x 60 kV 1 x 70 kV 1 x 125 kV 4 x 150 kV
Italy	1 x 130 kV			1 x 70 kV 1 x 150 kV			1 x 130 kV 1 x 140 kV 1 x 150 kV
Netherlands		1 x 220 kV					
Sweden			1 x 50 kV			1 x 80 kV	
FRG	2 x 220 kV 9 x 110 kV	1 x 220 kV		1 x 110 kV 1 x 150 kV 2 x 220 kV	1 x 220 kV		3 x 110 kV 1 x 220 kV

Source: OEEC, *Interconnected*, 52-55.

which showed that interconnecting relatively small systems was economically advantageous. Recognizing that interconnected operation was already in place in some Western European countries, the TECAID mission nevertheless thought that further efficiency could be attained by expanding this interconnection. The report stated that at this point that "the major advantages are to be gained *within* national frontiers".[140]

But the report also stressed the possible advantages of interconnected operation *between* countries in Western Europe. There, however, the lessons to be drawn from the TECAID mission were less clear. Contrary to power pools in the United States, interconnections between Western European countries often involved "national interests" and sometimes currency exchange issues.[141] But even with that being the case, a considerable number of international interconnections did already exist between the FRG and France, Switzerland and France, and Switzerland and the FRG (see Table 4.6), and were used for electricity imports and exports (see Table 4.7). The report stressed that these cross-border connections were the result of negotiations between individual parties, without substantial interference of authorities or international organizations. According to the report, organizations like UNIPEDE, OEEC or UNECE could play a role in preparing surveys of economic possibilities of electricity exchanges, but the Mission nevertheless recommended that "discussions of possible interchanges be left to the free negotiation of the utilities concerned [...]".[142]

---

140 Ibid., 24. My emphasis.
141 Ibid.
142 Ibid.

Table 4.7 – Imports and exports in TECAID region in 1949, in GWh

Import by → / Export by ↓	FRG	Austria	Belgium	Luxembourg	Netherlands	Denmark	France	Italy	Switzerland	Total imports
FRG		565	40	0	14,7	0.06	2.5	0	66	707.26
Austria	141		0	0	0	0	0	0	0	141
Belgium	40	0		0	21	0	22.8	0	0	83.8
Luxembourg	0	0	0		0	0	10	0	0	10
Netherlands	0.8	0	1	0		0	0	0	0	1.8
Denmark	0	0	0	0	0		0	0	0	0
France	520	0	13.6	4.9	0	0		8.1	241.5	1,023.6*
Italy	0	0	0	0	0	0	80.4		0	182.4
Switzerland	35	0	0	0	0	0	91.3	45		171.3
Total exports	776.8	610	54.6	4.9	35.7	150.06	220	53.1	409.5	2,569.16

*Including 235,5 GWh from the Saar.
Totals in general may vary from the figures given due to the exclusion of Sweden, Yugoslavia, Lichtenstein, Monaco, Andorra, Saar, and Czechoslovakia.
Source: OEEC, *Interconnected*, 61.

In addition, the report gave several recommendations. First, it advised setting up international regional committees to enable regular electricity exchange with or without formal contracts.[143] The utilities themselves should elect the committee members. This was quite similar to Hintermayer's proposal within the ECE, which also spoke of forming an informal group. In addition, the report stated, these regional committees could only work effectively within "a spirit of mutual trust".[144] It was thus desired that committee members would be appointed as private persons, and would be people who would get along well. Second, the Mission named obstacles to interconnected operation in Europe. Of particular concern were foreign currencies, which at the time were not convertible. Another obstacle was posed by difficulties of a political and administrative nature, which restricted the increase of cross-border transmission – an issue already recognised during the interwar period. These difficulties were reported to OEEC's Electricity Committee, and became the object of study.

143 Ibid., 49.
144 Ibid.

Figure 4.2 – Europe's electrical engineers
From left to right: P. Smits (Belgium), S. Tuonioja (ECE Executive Secretary), René Hochreutiner,
Pierre Sevette (ECE director of Energy Sections), Walker Cisler (USA), and Pierre Ailleret
(France).
Source: UN Photo archive, Geneva, UN no.13113, "ECE's Committee on Electric Power celebrates
10th anniversary", Geneva, October 10, 1957. Used by courtesy of United Nations Office, United
Nations Library, Geneva.

European ideas on international operation

But outside of intergovernmental organisations plans were also being made for
electricity systems in Europe. Only a few months after the TECAID mission,
UNIPEDE held its first postwar meeting in Brussels. For the first time a Study
Committee on International Interconnections held a session and presented ideas
for international network operation in Europe. Although this Committee was
new, most of the members already knew each other. They included G.R. Peterson,
the vice-chairman of the TECAID mission, Louis de Heem, J, van Dam van Isselt
(Netherlands) and Jan Latour (Poland) who knew each other through the UNECE's
work on electricity. Although they were not members of the UNIPEDE Committee

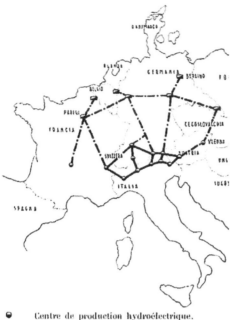

Figure 4.3 – *Berni's plan for a European net-*
work (1949)
Source: Berni, "La construction," 10. Used
with kind permission of Union of the
Electricity Industry/EURELECTRIC.

●   Centre de production hydroélectrique.
▣   —   —   thermoélectrique.
▪—▪. Réseau à 380 kV.
▬   —   220 kV.

itself, Pierre Ailleret, René Hochreutiner (see Figure 4.2), and G. Bardon (a French TECAID member) took part actively in the first meeting. The papers presented at the conference all reflected on collaboration and interconnection in Europe. Many engineers present reiterated the recommendations made in the TECAID report. In addition, several papers sent to the UNIPEDE committee showed remnants of the interwar planned European networks.

One of the papers was from Italian engineer Amilcare Berni. He noted that during the 1930s, continuous struggles between European countries had prevented plans like Viel's and Oliven's to become reality. Now, in the spirit of reconstruction and collaboration similar schemes should again be studied.[145] Like the plans of Viel and Oliven, Berni envisaged an interconnected European network of a number of main lines, resulting in a better economic mix between hydro and thermal energy sources (see Figure 4.3). He proposed to use 380 kV transmission lines, but seemed to ignore existing networks. In addition, Berni's paper lacked sufficient detail on *how* such a European network should be built. For one, based

---

145 Amicare Berni, "La construction d'un réseau d'interconnexion européen au point de vue technique et économique (report no. 2.)," in *Compte rendu des travaux du huitième congrès international tenu à Bruxelles en septembre 1949*, vol. 2, *Rapports des Comités d'Études IV à IX* (Paris: Imprimerie Chaix, 1949), 2.

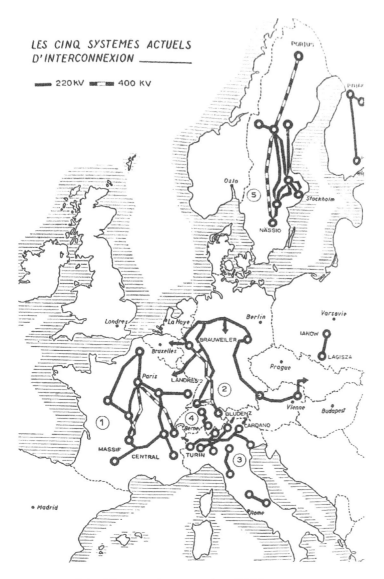

Figure 4.4 – Selmo's European interconnections (1949)
Source: Selmo, "Les interconnexions." Used with kind permission of Union of the Electricity
Industry/EURELECTRIC.

on their calculations French engineers François Cahen and René Pélissier deemed such an extensive AC network with north-south and east-west axes as economically unjustifiable.[146]

---

146 François Cahen and Réne Pélisser, "La compensation des pointes de puissance par l'interconnexion internationale (report no.3)," in UNIPEDE, *Compte rendu des travaux du huitième congrès*, vol. 2, vol. 2.

Others, however, were more specific than Berni. Italian engineer Luigi Selmo started by examining existing interconnected networks at 220 kV and above. By linking these, what Selmo called a "dynamic balance" could be established between thermal and hydroelectric energy (see Figure 4.4).[147] In particular he stressed the potential to use hydroelectricity to the largest extent possible. Interconnecting these five systems would enable utilities to take advantage of seasonal differences in water availability, resulting in savings in terms of mineral fuels.[148] But Selmo did not specifically think of using AC transmission lines. He argued that DC technology was better suited to transmit electricity over longer distances. He referred to a French plan that envisioned interconnecting resources in Poland, Scandinavia, the Alpine region, and the Atlas in Morocco by very high voltage DC lines – yet without giving specific details.[149] DC was also seen as a viable alternative to AC by Italian engineer Leonardo Maggi.[150] When interconnecting AC networks in synchronous operation, issues of frequency and tension stabilisation had to be solved. This was not the case with DC technology.

Another paper argued for a more practical approach than planning vast axes and grids. According to Swiss engineer René Hochreutiner two tendencies characterised existing networks in Europe.[151] First of all, networks of 150 kV to 220 kV were currently sufficient for densely populated countries, or in countries were electricity generation was close to areas of consumption. Hochreutiner identified France, the Netherlands, Belgium, Italy, and the FRG as examples. Second of all, longer transmission lines with higher voltages were built in countries that were less densely populated, or had distant centres of production. Hochreutiner named Sweden as an example, where at the time 380 kV lines were under construction.[152] Generally speaking, each country used its thermal and hydraulic resources for its own needs. With exception of Switzerland and Austria, no other European countries produced substantial amounts of electricity apart in excess of domestic needs.[153] His claim was indeed demonstrated by Figure 3.5. But even in Switzerland, electricity export was relatively small and was facilitated primarily by 150 kV transmission lines.

---

147 Luigi Selmo, "Les interconnexions européennes (report no. 4)," in UNIPEDE, *Compte rendu des travaux du huitième congrès*, vol. 2, 2.
148 Ibid., 11.
149 Ibid., 13.
150 Leonardo Maggi, "Considérations générales sur les interconnexions (report no. 13)," in UNIPEDE, *Compte rendu des travaux du huitième congrès*, vol. 2, 4.
151 René Hochreutiner (1908-1991) received a diploma from the l'Ecole polytechnique fédérale de Zurich and later studied law at the University of Geneva. He became employed at a company making electricity meters, but later came to work for the utility at Laufenburg. He became director there in 1946.
152 René Hochreutiner, "L'Interconnexion au service des échanges d'énergie en Europe occidentale (report no. 9)," in UNIPEDE, *Compte rendu des travaux du huitième congrès*, vol. 2, 3.
153 Ibid.

Extrapolating these examples to the European level, Hochreutiner constructed a hypothetical case whereby Austria wanted to exchange hydropower with thermal power in the eastern France. Rather than building new HV lines, Hochreutiner proposed to transmit Austrian electricity to the eastern part of Switzerland. This freed resources in the west of Switzerland, which were then exported to eastern France. In general, he thought international *load shifting* along existing networks enabled the transport of electricity over considerable distances, without having to construct new lines. Yet to be able to exchange between utilities and countries, networks should operate at a similar frequency, 50 Hz.[154] Eventually, Hochreutiner thought the construction of a 400 kV network would be ideal. At this stage, however, European countries should use their existing electrical installations to a maximum extent, and only construct new lines of the highest priority. 150 and 220 kV offered enough possibilities to utilize untapped potential, while creating "a favorable climate for regional ententes".[155]

This approach of gradually interconnecting national systems was endorsed by others as well. Briton G.R. Peterson underlined how currently existing interconnections were negotiated between individual utilities. He therefore argued against the establishment of a "super-dispatching" office, in favor of continuing current practices. He felt proper methods for regulating tension and frequency should be negotiated, however.[156] Peterson's view was supported by Dutch engineer Zuidweg. He stressed that the autonomy of individual countries should remain untouched. To him only a complete and revolutionary change of regime would be grounds to change that, like for example the creation of "d'une Féderation des Etats-Unies d'Europe".[157] In line with TECAID recommendations Zuidweg too stressed that any mode of collaboration should be based on by free negotiation between interested network operators. "Mutual confidence" between them was a prerequisite to establish permanent cooperation.[158] Like they had at OEEC and UNECE earlier, engineers again pleaded for an informal and independent forum where European network operators could meet. In Brussels, this idea was put forward by Peterson. He thought a voluntary committee of network operators would be highly useful.[159] Such a committee could meet two to three times per year to discuss issues like maintenance schedules, network extension, and exchange of electricity.

---

154 Ibid., 4.
155 Ibid., 6-7.
156 Peterson's address in "Minutes of the 'Comité d'Études des Interconnexions Internationales'," in UNI-PEDE, *Compte rendu des travaux du huitième congrès*, vol. 2, 115.
157 Zuidweg in "Minutes of the 'Comité d'Études'," 115.
158 Ibid., 116.
159 Peterson in "Minutes of the 'Comité d'Études'," 114.

While Hochreutiner and others stressed mainly technical-economic reasons, the Study Committee's president paid attention to more ideological aspects of European cooperation. Professor Giovanni Silva brought into remembrance how after WWI three engineers – Viel, Schönholzer, Oliven – proposed to build a tight link between European countries in the field of electricity.[160] These ideas for a European network were based upon technical-economic aims and possibilities well-known by engineers. But they also found justification in creating solidarity between countries as well. Perhaps, argued Silva, these ideas had been premature. Now, after another disastrous war, Silva told his fellow engineers that "[w]e Europeans of today, we must be optimists".[161] But to Silva optimism alone would not suffice. It should be accompanied by a firm will to create solid agreements between European countries. Silva saw *solidarity* between European countries as a way of preventing recurring tragedies on European soil, and saw the creation of such a sentiment as a duty of the electricity sector. This solidarity would be a reality, Silva proposed, on the day that a country in need of electricity will see neighboring countries running to help it. He added in 1955 that "[w]ell beyond the cold technical considerations, our work will be always directed, as silently as indefatigably, towards the realization of a future of happiness and peace".[162]

In other words, Silva's thoughts reflected interwar ideas. Not only technical-economic considerations should lie at the heart of cooperation across borders, ideological arguments had to be taken into account as well. The interwar consensus regarding the organization of a European network did not change either. Again, planned large-scale European networks met significant opposition. Many engineers, including Silva, opted to gradually construct a European system by interconnecting utilities across borders.[163] In the months following the UNIPEDE meeting, the idea of organizing permanent collaboration between Western European countries on such a basis took more serious form.

---

160 Silva was the Director General of the *Compagnia Nazionale Imprese Elettriche*.
161 "Nous, les Européens d'aujourd'hui, nous nous devons d'être optimistes." Silva's opening in Ibid., 108.
162 "Bien au delà des froides considérations techniques, notre travail sera toujours dirigé, aussi silencieusement qu'inlassablement, vers la réalisation d'un avenir de bonheur et de paix." "Minutes of the 'International Interconnections Study Committee'," in *Tenth Congress of UNIPEDE, London, 1955*, vol. 1 (Paris: Imprimerie Chaix, 1955), 126-127.
163 "En conclusion, le rapport général préconise une organisation progressive du réseau européen obtenue par le raccordement toujours plus complet entre les réseaux nationaux." Ibid. This was acknowledged by several others including Hochreutiner in "Minutes of the 'Comité d'Études'," 115.

Table 4.8 – The Emergency Program in figures

Country	Capacity in MW	Cost per installed KW in US$	Total cost in million US$
W. Germany	325	121	39
France	250	175	43.5
Italy	250	160	42
Greece	60	200	12
Austria	80	180	15
Benelux	70	165	12
Total	1,035 MW		163.5

Source: see note 166.

Towards a Western European power pool

After the TECAID mission in May-June 1949, both ECA and the OEEC Electricity Committee re-examined the International Program. While the "international" aspect of the program was already redefined in 1948, now the character of the program as a whole was changed. The idea that European countries should share resources and co-own power plants was given up from the American side. At the same time, the notion of a Western European power pool was tied to the International Program. Both changes were related to solving the deficit left by the National Program.

That deficit ranked high on the priority list of the OEEC Electricity Committee. In October 1949, the Electricity Committee reformulated its electricity policy in order to make more electricity available. Three main tasks were identified: 1) drawing up a long-term program for power plants, 2) proposing measures to intensify the use of resources, and 3) taking away barriers to the exchange of surplus electricity.[164] In addition, the Committee prioritized those areas still facing electricity deficits after the National Program was completed.[165] The aim was to provide "a maximum amount of kWh during the critical period for a minimum investment within the shortest possible building time".[166] The "critical period" primarily referred to the winter months, when electricity demand was relatively high but hydroelectricity production is lower than during spring and summer. This led the Electricity Committee to believe that the initial emphasis should be on building

---

164 "Minutes of the 29th, 30th and 31st Meetings," 26-28 October 1949, fonds OEEC, file 1157.4, document EL/M(4) 4, HAEU.
165 Ibid.
166 "Report by the Electricity Committee for an Emergency Programme," n.d. (likely November or December 1949), OEEC document EL (49) 19. Found in RG 469, file 3.2: Records of the Office of the United States Special Representative in Europe, Records relating to West Germany, box 8, NACP.

new thermal power stations. Hydroelectric plants had two disadvantages; river-run plants produce less electricity during wintertime, and storage plants are costly and have a long construction-time.[167]

The Emergency Program, as this first phase would be called, involved an expansion of generation capacity by 1,035 MW, divided over the neediest countries (See Table 4.8). The largest deficits would remain in Western Germany, France and Italy, whereas Austria and the Benelux countries had relatively small ones.[168] Ten per cent of the financial burden would be carried by countries themselves, 25 per cent by ECA, and 65 per cent by private finance or the International Bank for Reconstruction and Development (IBRD). In November, the OEEC Executive Committee endorsed this new policy.[169] According to Huntington Gilchrist – Perkins' successor as Chief of the Industry Division – the Emergency Program differed from the International Program in terms of finance and operation. Within the original program, these two aspects were arranged internationally. Now, plants were financed within a single country, and therefore the financing country "naturally" maintained complete control of the produced electricity.[170]

This change did not please the OSR, who still hoped to see some form of supranationality in European electricity systems. In January 1950 the director of the Industry Division wrote to Harriman's successor Milton Katz about the combined proposal by Denmark, Norway and Sweden. This project encompassed the construction of new generation capacity in Norway (122 MW), which would subsequently be exported to Denmark via Sweden. Denmark, which was having trouble in covering their peak load on the islands Seeland and Lolland-Falster, would import 600 GWh per year.[171] Eventually the Danish government did not approve the proposal in 1950.[172] Director Gilchrist complained with Katz that

> [i]t as been my feeling that to be truly genuine, an international project should [...] place final authority, in case of the inability of the cooperating countries to reach agreement, in some one person or group. [...] None of

---

167 Ibid.
168 Ibid.
169 "Executive Committee Decision Concerning the Implementation of the an Emergency Programme for the Building of Electrical Power Plants," 22 November 1949, OEEC document EL (49) 19. Found in RG 469, file 3.2, box 8, NACP.
170 Everett Eslick (Acting Chief, Electric Power Branch, Industry Division) to Huntington Gilchrist (Chief, Industry Division), 27 November 1949, RG 469, file 2.2, box 6, NACP. Gilchrist became Chief of the Industry Division in 1949, succeeding Perkins.
171 "Memorandum Prepared by the Secretariat on the Scandinavian Power Project," 25 January 1950, fonds OEEC, file 1156.1, document EL(50) 6, HAEU.
172 The Scandinavian proposal made in the framework of the ERP resembled earlier schemes for electricity exports from Scandinavia. Kaijser, "Trans-Border," 7ff.

the governments would appear to be giving away here one iota of so-called sovereign rights and to this extent the Scandinavian project is weak as an international one.[173]

But ECA in Washington rejected a suggestion by the OSR to provide more funds for international projects in order to stimulate integration and cooperation. According to the Washington bureau, "Congressmen [were] in such a bitter mood over the failure of European Nations to integrate that they would 'explode' if told that we used some few millions of dollars to induce them to integrate their power investment".[174] Harlan Cleveland, the Assistant Director for Europe at ECA, wrote Paris that the whole notion of international projects was under revision, and strongly advised not to make any commitments regarding U.S. support international electricity projects.[175] In fact, ECA dropped the International Program as of October 1950, only allocating funds to meet urgent economic objectives.[176] Eventually only the hydroelectric plant at Braunau on the Inn river between Germany and Austria was financed.[177]

While the OSR regretted the apparent lack of integrated international projects, it stressed the importance of expanding generation capacity in a telegram to all national ECA missions.[178] It underlined that the shortage of electricity increasingly starting to limit the expansion of industrial production. Therefore, with regard to national and international projects, the OSR did not see the necessity to "make any distinction as to the relative urgency of power needs".[179] But while ECA gave up on integrating Europe's electricity systems, the OEEC undertook steps toward closer cooperation. Following the proposal of the Belgian Delegation, several members of the Electricity Committee agreed to consider the 1,035 MW program as if it were "a hypothetical international power station".[180] In other words, these OEEC

---

173 Huntington Gilchrist to Milton Katz, 12 January 1950, RG 469, file 2.2, box 6, NACP. Katz at this moment was U.S. Special Representative in Europe, with the rank of ambassador extraordinary and plenipotentiary (1950-1951). He also acted as chief of the U.S. delegation to the ECE, and was the Chairman of the Defense and Economic Committee of NATO.

174 F. Taylor Ostrander to Lincoln Gordon, 23 February 23 1950, RG 469, file 2.2: Subject and geographic files of the Office of the Director of Administration, box 39, NACP.

175 Taylor Ostrander to Gordon, 27 April 1950, RG 469, file 2.2, box 39, NACP. Ostrander report about a phone call with Cleveland.

176 Telegram from OSR to all missions and Washington, 19 October 1950, RG 469, file 2.2: Office of the Deputy for Defense Affairs, box 5, NACP.

177 ECA, *Thirteenth Report to Congress of the Economic Cooperation Agency* (Washington, D.C.: U.S. Government Printing Office, 1951), table B-9, 120-121.

178 Telegram from OSR to all ECA missions, 28 December 1949, RG 469, file 2.2: Office of the General Counsel, box 36, NACP.

179 Ibid.

180 "Declarations Made to the Electricity Committee with Regard to the International Character of the Emergency Programme in the Course of the 34th Meeting", n.d. (likely November or December 1949, OEEC document EL (49) 19, p.47. Found in RG 469, file 2.2, box , NACP.

members were willing to regard the capacity as an international resource. Though closer international cooperation became a cornerstone of the Emergency Program, it nevertheless had to respect that "the semi-autonomous development of power systems enclosed within national frontiers proceeds along the lines which by stages will lead to greater organization of European electrical economy".[181]

In February 1950 a concrete proposal for the power pool was presented by the Electricity Committee.[182] After completing the Emergency Program, some 950 MW[183] was made available to the pool. Although the output of new power stations was destined primarily for domestic use, the countries in the Emergency Program would "pool" electricity in response to requests for assistance.[184] Although the construction of more cross-border connections was envisaged, such assistance was already possible over existing interconnections. The Electricity Committee assumed that the pool should be controlled by joint operation of national utilities.[185] Electricity exchanges within the framework of the power pool would be arranged bilaterally, in line with common practice.[186]

The UCPTE

The idea of a Western European power pool was endorsed by the OEEC Council in March 1950.[187] A draft agreement to establish the *Union of Electricity Producers of Western Europe* drawn up accordingly.[188] This agreement was initially limited to the countries participating in the Emergency Program, and only for the new capacity arising from that Program. The OSR however believed that "power pooling should not wait on or be exclusively associated with new capacity financed by

---

181 "Memorandum by the Secretary General: Suggestions for a Complementary Equipment Programme," n.d. (likely late January or early February 1950), fonds OEEC, file 1156.1, document EL(50)7, HAEU.
182 "Memorandum by the Special Study Group on the 1.035 MW Thermal Programme," 2 February 1950, fonds OEEC, file 1156.1, document EL(50)11, HAEU.
183 As an exception, additional capacity of 60 MW for Greece as well as 25 MW for Portugal was included into the Program. Both countries were not connected with the other Program countries and thus not part of the power pool. For the situation of Greece, see the next chapter and "Declarations made to the Electricity Committee," n.d. (likely November or December 1949), OEEC document EL(49)19, Found in RG 469, file 2.2, box 8, NACP.
184 "Memorandum by the Special Study Group, " 2 February 1950, HAEU.
185 "National organizations" does not imply that every country had just one system operator, nor that this in all cases was a government-related organisation. In many countries, like Switzerland, Germany and the Netherlands, various utilities were represented by a national union of utilities.
186 Ibid.
187 "Council Recommendation Concerning the Working of the International Power Pool," 26 March 1950, fonds OEEC, file 1156.1, document EL(50)16, HAEU.
188 "Draft Agreement between the Countries of Western Europe for the Joint Operation of Electric Power Resources," 20 May 1950, fonds OEEC, file 1156.1, document EL(50)22, HAEU.

ECA".[189] The OEEC Electricity Committee took this advice to heart. In November 1950, it initiated a discussion on how to coordinate and develop electricity production in Europe.[190] The main questions were as to how to plan new generation capacity, how to geographically distribute its output, and how each energy source should be used to make "a regime of optimal operating efficiency". An additional question was how and when a "European high-tension network" should be developed to ensure the best use of electricity sources.[191]

The framework in which these questions would be addressed had already been determined. The recommendations of the TECAID mission suggested setting up regional committees. Similar thoughts were expressed during the meeting of UNIPEDE's Study Committee on International Interconnections. Already in mid-November 1950 the Electricity Committee unanimously approved the recommendation to establish such a coordinating body, now renamed to *Union pour la Coordination de la Production et du Transport de l'Électricité* (UCPTE).[192]

The discussion as to how this new body should function continued at a meeting in April 1951.[193] The focus was on how the UCPTE could contribute to meeting electricity demand. Two strategies were envisaged, which should be followed simultaneously.[194] In the first place, the national programs should more or less result in a balance between production and consumption. International electricity exchanges would then only be of a marginal character. The second strategy was focused on the regional level, and envisioned using the advantages of interconnections between countries. From "the angle of regional integration", these electricity exchanges would then ensure the balance and economic operation of the participating national systems.[195] Both aims required a certain "degree of solidarity" between countries, argued the Electricity Committee.[196]

In May 1951, the UCPTE was officially founded. It was established by representatives of utilities from eight countries (Belgium, Germany, France, Italy, Luxemburg, the Netherlands, Austria and Switzerland) on a basis of voluntary cooperation. The Union consists of a *Comité Restreint* (Restricted committee), which

---

189 Telegram from OSR to all missions and Washington, 19 October 1950, RG 469, file 2.2, box 5, NACP.
190 "Notes on the Preparation of a Scheme for Co-Ordinating the Development of Electricity Production in Europe," 8 November 1950, fonds OEEC, file 1156.1, document EL(50)25, HAEU.
191 Ibid.
192 "Recommendation for Co-Ordinated Use of the Power Resources," 17 November 1950, fonds OEEC, file 1156.1, document EL(50)26, HAEU.
193 "Esquisse d'un plan de developpement de l'economie electrique des pays interconnectes," 6 April 1951, fonds OEEC, file 1156.2, document EL(51)4, HAEU.
194 Ibid.
195 Ibid.
196 Esquisse d'un plan," 6 April 1951, HAEU.

meets three to four time per annum to prepare the Assembly meetings, and the Assembly, in which all Union members are represented, which meets bi-annually. The Union elects a President and a Vice-President yearly, with the possibility of one renewal of term. The Union has no budget; the President's utility provided for the Secretariat. From a commercial point of view, the Union is neutral and cannot intermingle in the preparation or execution of commercial contracts between its members.[197]

The UCPTE was set up in accordance with two important conditions for regional collaboration determined by the TECAID mission; first, it worked independently of international organizations, and second, the UCPTE stimulated a "spirit of mutual trust". With regard to the first, although the idea behind the UCPTE stemmed from OEEC and UNECE, and was supported by UNIPEDE, the organization was not linked to any of these. Several of its members were, however. Many members also sat on the electricity committees of both OEEC and ECE, and took part in UNIPEDE; the first members included Ailleret, Bardon, Hintermayer, Hochreutiner, De Heem, and Crescent. With regard to the second condition, the UCPTE had an informal structure. The founding members therefore set out to create an atmosphere where utility managers from Western Europe could frequently meet to study the best possible utilization of means of production and transmission. This informal nature was reflected in the first article of its statutes; the Union was made up of people, and not the companies they represented.[198] Yet although membership was based on personal capacity, one had to be associated to production and transmission of electricity.[199] The Union's members were both representatives of production and transmission enterprises, as well as delegates of public administrations charged with electricity affairs. The presence of the latter was crucial for some enterprises to obtain government permission necessary for cross-border electricity exchanges.

The UCPTE had five main objectives. First, it sought to improve the possibilities for short-term energy exchanges between countries. This required not only more interconnections, but also an improvement in the means of communication between network operators. In addition, a standardized form was drawn up, on which each utility announced in advance their intention to either export or import electricity the coming trimester. These forms included the actual exchanges recorded during the previous trimester. The goal behind this was to identify a pattern of exchange, and to document the availability of hydroelectricity in order

197 UCPTE, *Rapport Annuel 1951-1952* (Paris: UCPTE, 1952), 6-7.
198 Ibid., 5.
199 Ibid., 9. Also see UCPTE, *1951-1976: 25 jaar UCPTE* (Arnhem: UCPTE, 1976), 159-160.

to increase exchange.[200] Second, the UCPTE coordinated the maintenance of thermal plants among members. Often repair or maintenance work required plants to be taken out of operation temporarily, resulting in a lower domestic electricity production. Through the UCPTE, members informed their colleagues of the timing and period of plant maintenance, so that available electricity could be increased through international assistance.[201] The third, and arguably the most important, aim of the UCPTE concerned parallel operation between the utilities in the Union. This was already pointed out by Hochreutiner at the UNIPEDE congress in 1949. Synchronous operation made it possible to determine the necessary installed reserve capacity for the collective network. Within seven years, starting in April 1958, the electricity networks within the UCPTE were in synchronous operation.[202] From this point in time all UCPTE-countries had their respective networks operating at 50 Hz. With the achievement of this technical integration, control of the intermeshed networks nevertheless remained a matter of national utilities, and regional utilities within countries themselves.

A fourth aim was linked to operating of international connections, and concerned UCPTE's efforts for liberalizing electricity exchanges.[203] This had already been seen during the interwar period as an indispensable precondition to improve electricity exchanges After WWII, occasional or incidental exchanges were still subject to administrative and financial stipulations, a situation which UNIPEDE's Study Committee had already returned attention to in 1949.[204] The UCPTE placed this issue before the OEEC Electricity Committee, and also gained the support of the UNECE. The latter organization stated in 1951 that "national legislations concerning the supply and exchange of electric power were for the most part of long standing, complex and not sufficiently well-suited to the present grid operation system".[205] By means of a letter to all European ministers of foreign affairs, ECE urged countries to simplify their regulations in able to guarantee exchanges and accidental assistance.[206] In March 1953 the OEEC issued a recommendation to liberalize incidental exchanges of electricity. This exempted exchanges in order

---

200 UCPTE, *R.A. '51-'52*, 7.

201 Ibid.

202 UCPTE, *Rapport Annuel 1976-1977* (Arnhem: UCPTE, 1978), 103.

203 UCPTE, *R.A. '51-'52*, 7.

204 E. Fehr, "Conditions juridiques et économiques de l'exportation hors de Suisse de l'énergie électrique (report no. 12)," in *Compte rendu des travaux du huitième congrès international tenu à Bruxelles en septembre 1949*, vol. 2, *Rapports des Comités d'Études IV à IX* (Paris: Imprimerie Chaix, 1949).

205 ECE, *Report of the Committee on Electric Power to the Economic Commission for Europe*, UN doc, ser., E/ECE/127-C 24 (Geneva: UNECE, 1951), 3.

206 Letter of Myrdal sent to European ministers of foreign affairs and relevant international organisations, 30 October 1951, registry fonds GX, file 19/6/1/4-3815, UNOG.

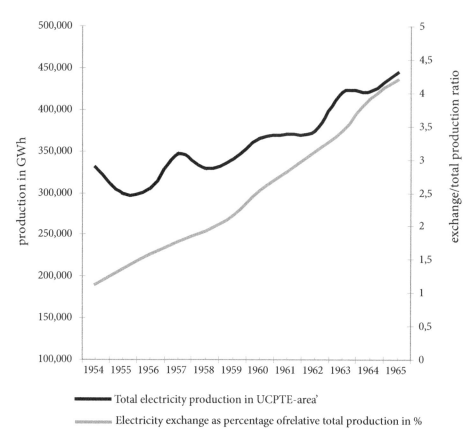

Figure 4.5 – Total electricity production and electricity exchange relative to total production in the UCPTE zone, 1953-1965
Source: Calculated on basis of UCPTE Rapports Annuel.

to avoid wasting available hydroelectricity and immediate emergency supply.[207] In 1956 restrictions applying to seasonal exchanges of electricity were lifted. Three years later all other forms of international electricity transmission was liberalized.[208] This enabled the ratio of electricity exports relative to national production to grow after 1956 (see Figure 4.5).

207 UCPTE, *1951-1976*, 166.
208 Ibid.

Further regional grouping

As stated at the start of this chapter, the UCPTE was not the only regional group that formed during this period. When discussing a Western European power pool in February 1951, the Electricity Committee had the intention to form regional *groups* rather than a single group.[209] Several organizations similar to UCPTE were set up in subsequent years. Discussions for a form of cooperation between Spain, Portugal, and France had been ongoing since 1950, which led to the founding of the *Union Franco-Ibérique pour la Coordination de la Production et du Transport d'Électricité* (UFIPTE) in 1962.[210] Its statutes were very similar to those of the UCPTE, and here, too, collaboration was based upon personal contacts.[211]

Another regional grouping was formed in Scandinavia. Also here regional collaboration was anticipated earlier, and in fact the earliest ideas dated back to the interwar period.[212] One of the ERP International Projects concerned the transmission of electricity from Norway to Denmark via Sweden. According to the Electricity Committee, the merits of the project lay mainly "in the progress made towards the pooling of nearly all the Scandinavian sources of energy, thus enabling closer interconnection to be established between the distribution network if these three countries".[213] In 1954, when the OEEC Electricity Committee examined obstacles to the transfer of electricity between countries, it noted that Scandinavian cooperation in the field of electricity was prominently on the agenda of the August meeting of the Nordic Council.[214] But due to differences of opinion between Scandinavian countries, negotiations stalled.[215] It was not until the early 1960s that

---

209 "Report on the Regional Operating Groups," 21 February 1951, fonds OEEC, file 1156.2, document (51)1, HAEU.
210 "Report to the Executive Committee on the Final Emergency Programme," 6 March 1950, fonds OEEC, file 1156.1, document EL(50)12, HAEU.
211 "Note sur la constitution de l'Union Franco-Ibérique pour la coordination de la production et du transport de l'électricité," 4 April 1963, fonds OECD, file 1157.8, EL/M (63) 1, Annex II, HAEU.
212 Maier has referred to so-called Inter-Scandinavian Superpower Project of 1921. See Maier, *Erwin Marx*, 77; and Fridlund and Maier, "The Second," 4-5.
213 "Report to the Executive Committee on the Final Emergency Programme," 6 March 1950, HAEU.
214 Ibid.
215 Kaijser explains the postponement by pointing to the Danish government who did not support in 1950. "Trans-Border," 10. A 1952 letter from a Danish UN official to the Executive Secretary of the ECE seem to suggest that there was some difference of opinion between Denmark and Sweden on the one hand, and Norway on the other. The Danish official reckoned that talks were still going on, "but in order not to interrupt the discussions on a political policy level, they have been reticent for some time". Viggo A. Christensen to Gunnar Myrdal, 4 October 1952, registry fond GX, file 19/6/1/4-3815, UNOG. Also Sven Lalander (acting as a Secretary member of the ECE) seemed to suggest that political reasons in Norway prevented the International Project in Scandinavia. Interoffice memorandum from Sven Lalander to Gunnar Myrdal, 7 October 1952, Accession of Retired Records (ARR) 14, number 1360: Files of Office of Executive Secretary Gunnar Myrdal (1947-1957), box 78, UNOG.

Centrala Driftledningen, the Swedish body for electricity exchanges, took the issue up again. Despite some reservations from the Norwegian side, *Nordel* was set up in 1963.[216] Nordel coordinated its work with the UCPTE, and gained the right of representation in the UCPTE's Extended *Comité Restreint*, as well as its Working Group for Load management.[217] It could not vote or participate in the plenary session. One year later, utilities from Austria, Italy, and Yugoslavia established another similar body. SUDEL, as it was called, resembled the UCPTE in its manner of working. Franz Hintermayer was one of its founding members and acted as SUDEL's president between 1966 and 1968.[218] With regard to relations with the UCPTE, SUDEL and UFIPTE members had rights similar to Nordel. In addition, they could send representatives to all working groups.[219]

Whereas the regional organizations in Southern, Northern and Western Europe worked together, the same cannot be said of Central and Eastern Europe, which remained isolated from these initiatives. As a response to the OEEC and the subsequent plans for European (economic) integration, the Eastern block instituted an organization for economic cooperation in the region as well. Although CMEA was established in 1949, very few conferences were actually held. The organization was hardly ever mentioned by politicians or in the press. It was not represented at the International Economic Conference, held in Moscow in 1952. As an illustration of its slow start, CMEA's juridical status was only fixed in 1959, followed by ratification of its Charter in 1960.[220] It was only in the early 1960s that some progress was made in the field of electric power, which according to the CMEA Secretary had high priority. In 1965 he wrote that electrification was the essential part for expanding the Communistic economy. Interconnecting the Soviet electricity system with that of neighboring Socialistic countries was an important step to creating a "material-technical basis for Communism".[221]

In accordance with these intentions the *Central Dispatch Organization* (CDO) was established in 1963. CDO was an independent international organ that coordinated the activities of the national dispatch organizations – quite similar to

216 Arne Kaijser, "Trans-Border," 13-14.
217 UCPTE, *1951-1976*, 186-187.
218 UCPTE, *SUDEL* (n.p.: UCPTE, 1970), 3.
219 UCPTE, *U.C.P.T.E. 1951-1971: 20 ans d'activitè* (Rome: UCPTE, 1971), 27.
220 Michael Kaser, *COMECON: Integrated Problems of the Planned Economies* (London: Oxford University Press, 1965), 42-43.
221 "Die Schaffung des Einheitlichen Energiesystems de UdSSR, das mit den Energiesystemen anderer sozialistischer Länder verbunden ist, ist eine wichtige Etappe auf dem Wege zur Schaffung der materiell-technischen Basis der Kommunismus." N.W. Faddeev, *Der Rat für Gegenseitige Wirtschaftshilfe* (Berlin: Staatsverlag der Deutschen Demokratischen Republik, 1965), 102. Faddeev was a long-time secretary of CMEA.

Table 4.9 – Electricity production in selected European countries, in GWh (1938-1951)

	1938	1939	1947	1948	1949	1950	1951
Austria	3,197	3,580	3,902	5,326	5,517	6,365	7,376
Belgium	5,266	5,577	7,212	7,903	8,163	8,481	9,250
Czechoslovakia	4,052	-	6,662	-	-	-	10,296
Denmark	1,142	1,065	1,679	1,843	1,983	2,218	2,541
France	18,770	20,228	26,098	29,117	30,224	33,319	38,350
Italy	15,544	18,417	20,574	22,694	20,782	24,681	29,223
Netherlands	3,540	3,903	4,374	5,265	5,900	6,932	7,481
Norway	4,877	5,056	11,598	12,818	15,563	17,761	17,750
Portugal	354	382	722	812	836	942	-
Spain	2,748	3,111	6,005	6,165	5,629	6,915	8,299
Sweden	8,162	9,054	13,409	14,084	16,042	19,348	20,545
Switzerland	5,448	5,506	9,770	10,426	9,745	-	12,247

Source: The years 1931-1939 is based on UNIPEDE annual statistics, the other years are from ECE Annual Bulletins of Electricity Statistics.

UCPTE. It controlled and regulated the so-called *Interconnected Power Systems* (IPS), a regional network of interconnected electricity systems including Bulgaria, Czechoslovakia, the German Democratic Republic, Hungary, Poland, and Romania.[222] At the core of this system were interconnections between the GDR, Poland, Czechoslovakia, Hungary, and the Ukrainian SSR. Romania and Bulgaria joined in 1963 and 1964 respectively. CDO's main difference with the UCPTE was that it had a centralized dispatch centre. Member-countries coordinated the work of CDO through a representative Council, which met several times per year. The Council discussed the activities of CDO and also named CDO's director for a period of three years.[223]

---

222 Ibid.,100-103.
223 Ibid.,100.

Table 4.10 – ECA Industrial projects expenditure for power facilities, 1947-1951 (in millions of US$)

	Overall costs	ECA funds	% ECA
Austria	–	–	–
Belgium	–	–	–
Denmark	9.5	5.1	53.2
France	59.3	20.9	35.3
FRG)	–	–	–
Greece	86.9	22.4	25.7
Iceland	11.2	5.1	45.2
Italy	105.6	62.7	59.3
Netherlands	21.0	3.4	16.1
Norway	–	–	–
Portugal	–	–	–
Turkey	56.1	15.0	26.8
United Kingdom	–	–	–
International projects	28.6	0.5	1.9
Total	378.3	135.0	35.7 %

Extracted from: ECA, *Twelfth Report to Congress*, Table B-11, 130-133.

Conclusions

1951 was an important year for the electricity industry in Europe for three reasons. First of all, according to the OEEC Electricity Committee, this was the year when an "almost-normal" period started, resembling the period of 1938-1939.[224] This meant that electricity systems again functioned without frequent outages due to lack of reserve capacity and fuel. This operational achievement is not visible in production statistics. Yet as we can see in Table 4.9, electricity production in 1951 had at least doubled in most countries. For some countries, like Spain and Norway this growth was even bigger. As population between 1938 and 1951 had not come close to doubling, this implied that electricity per capita had substantially risen. Overall, perspectives on electricity had changed. While during the interwar period electricity networks were seen as spiritual bond, and an object of fascination, by the 1950s they had become a cornerstone of economies and societies. This change could be witnessed in the course of 1930s. Electricity networks then were being built to support economic and military defense, and to prevent potential warfare. In addition, we have seen that electricity networks in France were a popular object

---

224 "Memorandum by the Secretary of the Electricity Committee. First Results of the Enquiry on the Electricity Position in the Member Countries," 8 March 1950, fonds OEEC, file 1156.1, document EL(50)13, HAEU.

Table 4.11 - ECA approvals for withdrawals of Counterpart funds, 1948-1951 (in millions of US$)

	Electric, gas, & power facilities	Total	% of total
Austria	50.6	310.8	16.3
Belgium & Luxembourg	–	2.2	–
Denmark	–	118.9	–
France	555.1	1.965.2	28.2
FRG	166.6	842.5	19.8
Greece	2.7	330.4	0.8
Iceland	0.9	0.9	100.0
Italy	–	618.5	–
Netherlands	–	270.9	–
Norway	–	200.9	–
Portugal	10.4	15.4	67.5
Trieste	–	26.4	–
Turkey	0.3	34.2	0.9
United Kingdom	–	1,546.8	–
Total	786.6	6,284	12.5 %

Extracted from: ECA, *Thirteenth Report*, Table C-3, 128.

of wartime sabotage. The Allied forces consciously chose to spare electricity facilities in both Germany and Italy. Where electricity systems were targeted, like in France, reconstruction was started almost immediately behind front lines.

In light of this growing recognition of electricity as a central part of economic and social life, electricity was a priority sector within the ERP's overall economic reconstruction program. This leads us to the second reason why 1951 was a significant year: in June of that year the ERP ended. The increase in available electricity had illustrated the relative success of its National Program. This can be seen in Tables 4.10 and 4.11. Domestic electrification programs received most investments, whereas international projects received only half a million from a total of 135 million U.S. dollars.[225] But investment was not the only source of funding in this sector. To a large extent counterpart funds were also utilized for infrastructure in Western Europe. Between April 1948 and June 1951, 786.6 million of a total 6,284 million US$ counterpart funds were spent on electricity, gas and power facilities (amounting to nearly 12.5 per cent, see Table 4.11). The National Program

---

225 Missing from this list are Western Germany and Austria. These latter two were not only financed through the ERP. Much of their aid came through the Government Appropriations for Relief in Occupied Areas (GARIOA). Western Germany received some 1,793 million US$ through GARIOA between 1945 and 1952 (on top of 1,678 million by the ERP). See Helge Berger and Albrecht Ritschl, "Germany and the Political Economy of the Marshall Plan, 1947-1952: A Re-Revisionist View," in *Europe's Postwar Recovery*, ed. Eichengreen (Cambridge: Cambridge University Press, 1995), 205.

was thus rather successful, and led an expansion of generation capacity. Yet at the same time, we have seen ECA's frustrations with a lack of International Projects. Their hopes of bringing about an integrated European electricity network, where plants would be financed, built and operated internationally rather bilaterally, did not materialize.

This brings me to the third reason to highlight 1951. This was the year when the first regional power pool – the UCPTE – was inaugurated. Several others were set up in the following decade and a half. The notion of a power pool stemmed partly from ECA, and partly from European engineers themselves, though these parties had diverging opinions on how European collaboration should function in the electricity sector. The outcome of this process showed both the influence of the United States, as well as continuity from the European plans of the interwar period. From the start, ECA tried to introduce a degree of supranationality with regard to financing and operating new power plants. From side of European countries, they gave higher priorities to their domestic electricity balance. In addition, European engineers underlined that attempts at supranationality would be hampered by what they called "political uncertainties".

But while ECA did not succeed in having European countries to co-construct and co-own power plants, it played a role in having them cooperate across borders. One important event was the TECAID mission of 1949. European engineers were clearly inspired by the loosely knitted system of the South Atlantic & Central Areas Group. This type of organization in the European context enabled collaboration by tying together national networks, to gain significantly greater efficiency. Such an approach to building a European system was close to ideas from the interwar period, which stressed the gradual growth of such a system. Another element also reflected interwar thinking. Although electricity was now regarded as indispensable for modern economies, again after WWII non-technical-economic arguments for collaboration continued to play a role. It was in this context that plans like that of Oliven and Viel were referred to shortly after WWII. Furthermore, at the UNIPEDE Congress, but also in the discussion leading to the UCPTE, engineers saw collaboration leading to more "solidarity" between countries, and as a way of preventing future tragedies.

Chapter 5
Securing European cooperation, 1951-2001

In 1963 the *North Atlantic Treaty Organization* (NATO, 1949) commissioned a temporary working group of experts to study electricity production and distribution of electricity in wartime situations. The working group consisted of internationally distinguished electricity experts, including former TECAID-ers R. Marin (Italy) and G. Bardon (France), as well as founding members of the UCPTE W. Fleischer (FRG) and chairman J.C, van Staveren (Netherlands).[1] After meeting five times between 1963 and 1964, the group drew two conclusions. First, they insisted they should rely upon existing forms of collaboration, and did not regard a "supranational coordinating body" as useful.[2] Second, the group's final report concluded that there was one matter "of fundamental importance for the use of electrical power in wartime: <u>interconnections</u>".[3] Overall, it advised that the number of interconnections should increase, both at high and low voltages.[4]

Existing cooperation and networks thus not only served economic interests and the pursuit of a "happy and peaceful future",[5] they were also meant to face the threat of a new conflict during the Cold War. This gave a powerful strategic and ideological twist to the potential advantages of an international interconnected network. Historian Michael Hogan has claimed that integration "was the interlocking concept in the American plan for Western Europe, the key to a large single market, a workable balance of power among the Western states, and a favorable correlation of forces on the Continent".[6] Although the aim of security and political stability gained prominence in the 1950s, the ERP had already endeavored in that direction.[7] These ideals fitted with another part of U.S. strategy – that of *containment*– which sought to halt the spread of oppressive communist regimes. Several

---

1 The group was completed by Mr. H, de Wasseige (Belgium).
2 Report by the Special Working Group, "The Production and Distribution of Electricity in Wartime," 4 December 1964, file AC/143: Industrial Planning Committee, document D/113, North Atlantic Treaty Organisation Archives, Brussels (hereafter: NATO).
3 Ibid. Emphasis is from the original document.
4 Ibid, p.6.
5 Quoted in Chapter 4, note 162.
6 Hogan, *The Marshall Plan*, 294.
7 Winand, *Eisenhower*, 10.

examples show how this was already the case with the ERP. Western European economic strength was, according to U.S. policymakers, intertwined with defensive strength and the construction and expansion of electricity networks was seen as an integral part of that strength. But internal development in Western European was not all that mattered. NATO strategy also aimed to deny electrical equipment to the Eastern block, as well as to prevent close relations between East and West in the field of electricity.

This latter policy line was contested. The UNECE was the main driver, with increasing support from engineers and network-operators on both sides, toward creating electrical links across the Iron Curtain. Idealistic and ideological arguments also played a key role here: UNECE saw East-West cooperation in the field of electricity not only as an economic necessity, but also as potentially contributing to more peaceful relations in Europe. As part of their efforts, several options concerning electricity deliveries from Central and Eastern Europe came under scrutiny. These included Poland, Czechoslovakia, and Yugoslavia as main electricity supplying countries, and Austria as the prime transit country.

This chapter shows how considerations of Europe's ability to resist a possible Soviet-led attack were interwoven into efforts to develop electricity networks. Whereas there was widespread support for cooperation between network operators within regions, cross-regional cooperation were not always stimulated. In particular East-West linkages were only approved by the NATO Alliance if they complied with their strategic interests. The strategies of détente after 1966 opened up more possibilities for East-West interconnections. Yet strategic interests continued to play a role. The East-West collaboration that did come about included primarily non-NATO countries in Western Europe. Only after the political upheaval in 1989 a quick multilateral process led to the establishment of a synchronized grid ranging from Poland to Portugal. In addition, it was only then that the European Union made itself felt to the electricity sector.

U.S. containment strategy

In the preceding chapter, we saw how the ERP aimed to increase stability and stimulate economic recovery. It also served other American interests. While emphasizing increased productivity and the improvement in standards of living, it aimed to strengthen Europe's capability to defend itself as well. U.S. President Truman stated in March 1947 that "totalitarian regimes imposed on free peoples, by direct or indirect aggression, undermine the foundations of international peace and hence the security of the United States".[8] This line of policy became known as the Truman Doctrine, which sought to contain communism's expansion. Cold War historian John Gaddis Lewis stresses how "American partners assumed a direct correlation between economic health, psychological self-confidence, and the capacity for defense".[9]

Similar assertions were part of U.S. intentions with Europe's electricity systems. When receiving the TECAID engineers in 1949, ERP-administrator Hoffman argued that the mission was also about promoting better understanding between Western European countries and the United States. "[T]he quicker we can get free understanding between the free countries of this world", Hoffman argued, "the surer we are there will remain free countries on earth".[10] In 1955 ERP Electricity consultant Walker Cisler concluded that

> by working with our neighbor countries and allies our common interests have been advanced and our bonds of friendship strengthened. We know we are all stronger – and that Russia's Iron Curtain has not advanced.[11]

Whereas this strategic aspect did not substantially influence Western European collaboration between system-builders, it did affect fund allocation in individual countries. Greece was a case-in-point, albeit an extreme one. Wartime agreements between Churchill and Stalin placed Greece in the Western zone of influence.[12] WWII and civil strife between 1943 and 1949 ravaged the relatively underdeveloped country, and the Western Allies feared that communist insurgents might reorient Greece towards Moscow.[13] When Britain stopped economic and military aid to Greece, the United States took over.[14] Along with Turkey, Greece became the first country to receive U.S. military and economic aid immediately following the Truman Doctrine in March 1947. Greece continued to receive assistance to develop and strengthen the country through the ERP. Milton Katz, ECA's Special

---

8 "Address of President of the United States: Recommendation for Assistance to Greece and Turkey" (Washington, D.C., March 12, 1947), http://www.trumanlibrary.org/whistlestop/study_collections/doctrine/large/documents/index.php?documentdate=1947-03-12&documentid=31&studycollectionid=TDoctrine&pagenumber=1.

9 John Lewis Gaddis, 'The Insecurities of Victory: The United States and the Perception of the Soviet Threat after World War II," in ed. Lacey, *The Truman Presidency*, 265.

10 "Address of Welcome to European Electric Systems Operators Group and Press Conference," 22 April 1949, Paul. G. Hoffman papers

11 Walker L. Cisler, *Partners in Electric Power: Development under the Marshall Plan* (New York: The Newcomen Society in North America, 1955), 12.

12 Marc Trachtenberg, *A Constructed Peace: The Making of the European settlement, 1945-1963* (Princeton: Princeton University Press, 1999), 5-6.

13 For more on the Greek civil war and foreign assistance see Amikam Nachmani, "Civil War and Foreign Intervention in Greece: 1946-49," *Journal of Contemporary History* 25, no. 4 (1990): 489-522.

14 Ellwood, *Rebuilding*, 68.

Representative in Paris, told national Mission Chiefs in 1950 that in Greece "ECA actually has a role to go beyond our own Statute". In situation as in Greece, he continued, "we are carrying on other aspects of American policy".[15]

American influence on Greek affairs was huge, and much larger than in other European countries.[16] According to historian Geir Lundestad, Americans themselves even wrote the Greek application for aid, as well as the subsequent "thankyou note".[17] In the same way, the execution of the electricity program was not left to Greek engineers, like it had been in other ERP-countries. In Greece the studies and actual construction work were entrusted to the American Ebasco Company.[18] Ebasco advised ECA that not just new plants needed to be built, but also a modern integrated electricity system.[19] This electrification project was not only a program "for the efficient utilization of the country's indigenous resources"; it also would help to maintain "[s]ecurity and peace, attained in 1949".[20] The project was also part of the International Emergency Program of the OEEC in 1950. Although for obvious geographical reasons Greece did not take part in the power pool, it was given priority by the OEEC because of the "exceptionally serious situation in the country".[21]

Another example was West Berlin. When Britain, France and the United States decided to eventually create a West German state in June 1948, Stalin responded by blocking road and rail access to the Western zones of the city. West Berlin, the amalgam of the British, French and U.S. zone, was thereby turned into a mere island, 150 kilometers into the Soviet occupation zone of Germany.[22] Similarly, on June 23, 1948 the Soviet Military Government ended quadripartite operation of

---

15 Extract from Mission Chief's Conference Transcript, covering "New Role of Technical Assistance," 28 June 1950, RG 469, file 2.2: Subject files and issuances of the Organization and Management Division, box 5, NACP.

16 Whereas the larger countries had between 8 to 11 Division Chiefs, Greece had 18. By 1952 the American mission in Greece had 185 members, along with approximately 1,000 Greek employees. See Bossaut, L'Europe, 177-178.

17 Lundestad, "Empire," 267.

18 Ebasco, or the Electric Bond and Share Company, formed in 1905 by Thomas Edison's General Electric Company. It was intended as a holding company to manage General Electric's investments, as well as to service as a consultancy firm with experienced utility executives and specialists. By May 1986, EBASCO had built 220 hydro, 700 fossil and 35 nuclear plants all throughout the world. See William Wallace III and Russel J. Christesen, Ebasco Services Incorporated: The Saga of Electric Power: Meeting the Challenge of Change (New York: The Newcomen Society of the United States, 1986).

19 Ebasco Services Incorporated, Electric Power Program, Kingdom of Greece (New York: Economic Cooperation Administration, 1950), 1.

20 Ibid., 4.

21 "Report to the Executive Committee on the Final Emergency Programme," 6 March 1950, HAEU

22 Trachtenberg, A Constructed Peace, 78-80. Also see William Stivers, "The Incomplete Blockade: Soviet Zone Supply of West Berlin, 1948-49," Diplomatic History 21, no. 4 (1997): 569-602. Stivers' study encompasses a revisionist view of the blockade. He forcefully argues that the blockade was far from a complete lock down of the Western sectors.

Berlin's public utilities. Imported electricity was no longer transmitted beyond the Soviet sector, and current generated within that sector ceased to be distributed to the Western sectors.[23] The immediate response to the Soviet blockade was an airlift. Between June 1948 and May 1949 West-Berlin was supplied around-the-clock through the air in an allied effort of the British, French, and Americans.

In West Berlin electricity was seen as a vital sector, for both industry and morale. Even before the Soviet blockade, electricity shortages left the Western zones of Berlin practically at the mercy of Soviet authorities to grant them sufficient energy. The reinstatement of the power plant Berlin West in the British zone, which would mitigate dependency on Soviet electricity deliveries, proved to be a bone of contention with Soviet officials in Berlin. [24] Power station Berlin West used to be the capital's most modern power plant but it had to be taken out of operation completely in the first months after the war. It had suffered severely from warfare and from Soviets dismantling and seizure of equipment.[25] Of its 740 MW output in 1939, only 271.5 MW remained in December 1945.

The blockade provided a pretext for the U.S. to act unilaterally. Therefore amongst the expected cargo, like coal, food, and other essentials for survival, there was equipment for the reconstruction of Berlin West. Since August 1948 U.S. Army engineers planned the airlift of boiler equipment, while lighter material was already flown into Berlin.[26] It was due to these efforts that the repair work of Berlin West continued. Immediately after the Soviets ended their blockade in May 1949, all available material for Berlin West was loaded onto rail cars for immediate shipment to Berlin.[27] In December 1949 Berlin West was officially inaugurated, in the presence of U.S. High Commissioner for Germany, John McCloy. The next year, an ECA report concluded that "[t]he electricity flowing from this rebuilt plant not only defeated the Russian move to destroy the morale of the people of West Berlin, but also gave them renewed confidence in their ability to rebuild their crippled city".[28]

---

23 Office of Military Government U.S. Sector Berlin, *A Four Year Report: July 1, 1945 - September 1, 1949* (Berlin: Office of Military Government U.S. Sector Berlin, 1949), 108.
24 Rohrbaugh to the Deputy director, "Unilateral Action of the Soviets on Matters of City-Wide Importance," 8 April 1948, RG 260: Records of United States Occupation Headquarters World War II, file 7.5: Records of the Office of Military Government, Berlin Sector, Records of the Public Works and Utilities Branch, box 879, NACP.
25 City of Berlin Electricity Supply, "Brief Description of System, " September 1945, RG 260, file 7.5, box 878, NACP.
26 "List of Actions till Now Taken for Air Lift of Parts Required at the Beginning of the Boiler Assembly at Power Station West (scheduled for 1. Nov. 48)," n.d., RG 260, file 7.5, box 879, NACP.
27 ECA, *Tenth Report to Congress of the Economic Cooperation Administration* (Washington, D.C.: U.S. Government Printing Office, 1955), 55-56.
28 Ibid.

A more general consequence of the Berlin blockade was that U.S. and Western European political leaders demonstrated their determination to resist Soviet expansion.[29] This resistance was molded into permanent military cooperation. Even before the blockade, in March 1948 the Treaty of Brussels had been signed to set up a joint defensive system in North-western Europe.[30] The blockade showed that a confrontation over Germany was a serious possibility, and that Western defense had to be properly organized. In April 1949 the North Atlantic Treaty was signed that brought NATO into being.[31]

After the Korean War started U.S. assistance to Europe come to emphasize defense-related and strategic intentions. The 10th ECA Report to the U.S. Congress underlined this change:

> The international developments set off by the open aggression of Communist forces in Korea have altered the direction of the European Recovery Program. [...] Most participating countries will be diverting to military production or the maintenance of military strength, resources that would otherwise be available to augment civil consumption and investment to promote viability and raise the standard of living. [...] The impact of the war in Korea and enlarged defense programs, will undoubtedly stimulate the growth of European production.[32]

Although Berlin and Greece might have been exceptional situations, the policy shift also affected ERP's general electricity activities. After the International Program was terminated in 1950, only economically urgent projects would be funded according to ECA. Qualifying projects should preferably "primarily relate to defense".[33] Yet ECA also affirmed that "[c]loser integration of the economies of the countries of Western Europe was never more vital".[34] One project that met the twin aims of defense and integration was the hydroelectric plant at Braunau on the Inn bordering the FRG and Austria. In late 1950 it was not only earmarked for extra financial support as an international project that promoted integration, but as the supplier of electricity to a nearby aluminum factory in Ranshofen, which thereby increased its production of this "critical material" to 250 per cent of the

---

29 Lewis Gaddis, *We Now Know: Rethinking Cold War History* (Oxford: Clarendon Press, 1997), 68.
30 This so-called Western European Union was signed by Belgium, France, Luxembourg, the Netherlands, and the United Kingdom. The Brussels Treaty Organisation existed of a Consultative Council, encompassing the five foreign ministers. A Western Defence Committee was composed of the five defence ministers. Lord Ismay, *NATO. The First Five Years, 1949-1954* (Paris: NATO, 1954), 8-9.
31 Trachtenberg, *A Constructed Peace*, 86.
32 ECA, *Tenth Report*, 3.
33 Telegram from OSR to all missions and Washington, 19 October 1950, RG 469, file 2.2, NACP.
34 ECA, *Tenth Report*, p.22.

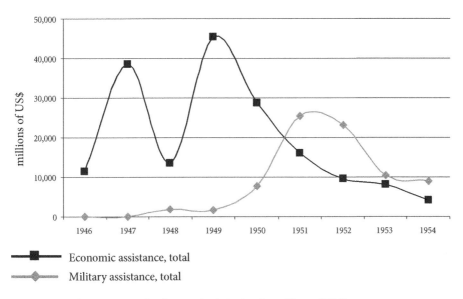

Figure 5.1 – U.S. economic and military aid, 1948-1954 (in millions of US$)
Based on: U.S. Agency for International Development, U.S. Overseas Loans and Grants.

current level.[35] The Ranshofen plant was completed during WWII, and by far the largest producer of aluminum in Austria. Much of postwar output was destined for export.[36] Katz wrote to Washington that "defense developments have led us give highest priority to expansion [of] aluminum production [at] Ranshofen in Austria, for which one-half Braunau power supply is essential".[37]

This development became institutionalized when the ERP was terminated in mid-June 1951, but aid continued to flow to Western Europe. That shift is visually represented in Figure 5.1. The Economic Cooperation Administration was replaced by the *Mutual Security Administration* starting January 1952. The change of name signified the change of heart; strategic interests now had highest priority. In the course of the 1950s, the OEEC subsequently lost ground to NATO.[38] OEEC transformed into the *Organization for Economic Cooperation and Development* (OECD) in 1957, and its mandate went beyond the European economy. Canada and the United States gained full membership, and Japan joined in 1964.[39] With

---

35 Telegram King (Vienna) to ECA Administration, 2 November 1950, RG 469, file 2.2, box 14, NACP.
36 George W. Hoffman, "The Survival of an Independent Austria," *Geographical Review* 41, no. 4 (1951): 612-613. Hoffman writes that Ranshofen at full capacity consumed as much electricity as the entire city of Vienna.
37 Milton Katz (Paris) to ECA Administration, 7 December 1950, RG 46, file 2.2, box 14, NACP.
38 Bossaut, *L'Europe*, 218-224; and Hogan, *The Marshall*, 312 and 334-335.
39 Derek W. Urwin, *The Community of Europe* (London: Longman, 1991), 22.

NATO playing a more influential role in economic affairs, strategic and defensive objectives – and objections – started to surface more often within its discussions.[40]

The U.S. work toward the economic and defensive strengthening of Western Europe is generally well-known, but it was only one side of the coin. What is less known is how the United States and its Cold War allies tried to *prevent* any possible Western European assistance from increasing defensive capabilities on the other side of the Iron Curtain. In the previous chapter we have seen how regional groupings were brought about through the negotiations between American administrators and European engineers. Although this division in regions was analogous with the progress of electrification, it corresponded with the Cold War division within Europe as well. The East-West division ran like a river through the reconstruction and modernization efforts, and affected strongly the way electricity networks and electricity collaborations were shaped.

An all-European approach: the ECE

Crucially, cooperation between regions, and in particular between East and West, was never ruled out from the start. In particular, the ECE made cooperation one of its spearhead areas, being "virtually the only arena in which Eastern and Western Europe met to discuss European affairs".[41] The ECE consists of three main parts: the commission, the Secretariat, and the Technical Committees. The Commission holds an annual public plenary session, and oversees the work of the Technical Committees. The ECE was bypassed when the U.S. was choosing an administrator for ERP, because the Americans feared Soviet political obstruction of the ECE. This prophecy came true in part in that Cold War antagonisms did come to play a role in ECE activity. Especially the commission's yearly meeting frequently fell prey to fierce East-West tensions, most often sparked by Soviet provocation.[42]

Yet although it was affected by Cold War, the UNECE actively used its pivotal position between East and West to battle that same divide. To a large extent, this direction was guided by its first Executive Secretary, Swedish economist Gunnar

---

40 For NATO's economic activities see: Ismay, *NATO*, 152.

41 Urwin, *The Community*, 14. The ECE would also facilitate an informal European setting for political affairs. The talks between the Soviets and the Austrians that eventually led to the State Treaty of 1955 were commenced at ECE meetings.

42 David Wightman, "East-West Cooperation and the United Nations Economic Commission for Europe," *International Organization* 11, no. 1 (1957): 1.

Myrdal.[43] According to Myrdal, the UNECE "is a political organization, composed of governments, and operating in a particularly troubled region of the world",[44] which "represents an organized matrix for preserving and strengthening the links between countries on both sides of the divide, which must be preserved and strengthened if we want to build a sounder Europe and a peaceful world".[45] Myrdal deplored the Cold War and lack of East-West cooperation.[46] Myrdal thought that Cold War divisions stood in the way of economic progress for the whole of Europe. He wrote in 1968 that

> In a united Europe we should be able to think, for example, in terms of the construction of oil and gas pipelines from the Middle East serving the great consuming centers as these fuels move from East to West, from South to North, through the continent. [...] We should look upon the coal resources in all parts of Europe as a whole and draw up a program which would take account of geological factors irrespective of political frontiers.[47]

His deputy, Walt W. Rostow, had similar ideas in 1947. He was convinced that "[n]o amount of dollars can, in either the short run or the long run, compensate for adequate supplies of Eastern European grain, Polish coal, Russian and Finnish timber", if Western Europe was to provide itself with these commodities at a minimal cost. According to him "[t]he answer may lie in the ECE".[48]

To be able to accommodate East-West trade, Myrdal thus endeavored to make the ECE an "all-European" organization, including the Soviet Union and its satellite states. He therefore insisted on having a Soviet deputy working with him.[49] In addition, Myrdal kept an open door policy; all governments of the region and interested international organizations could join in deliberations. This included most

---

43 Swede Gunnar Myrdal (1898-1987) studies law and economics. Between 1925 and 1929 he studied abroad in Germany, Great Britain, as well as the United States. In 1930 he was appointed Associate Professor at the Institute of International Studies in Geneva for a year. He also actively engaged in Swedish politics for the Social Democratic Party. Between 1945-1974 Myrdal served as Minister of Commerce. He gave up that post to hold the position of Executive Secretary of the ECE until 1957. He won the Noble Prize of Economic Science in 1974. Well-known economic works by his hand included *An American Dilemma* (1944) and *Asian Drama* (1957).
44 Gunnar Myrdal, "The Research Work of the Secretariat of the Economic Commission for Europe," in *25 Economic Essays in Honour of Erik Lindahl*, ed. Erik Lindahl (Stockholm: Ekonomisk tidskrift, 1956), 267.
45 Gunnar Myrdal, "Twenty Years of the United Nations Economic Commission for Europe," *International Organization* 22, no. 3 (1968): 628.
46 Berthelot and Rayment, "The ECE," 63.
47 Myrdal, "Twenty Years," 625.
48 W.W. Rostow to William Clayton, 22 September 1947, RG 84: Records of the Foreign Service posts of the Department of State, file 2: Records of Diplomatic Posts, Records of Switzerland, box 3, NACP.
49 Kostelecký, *The United*, note 60; and Berthelot and Rayment, "The ECE," 63.

Central and Eastern European countries, who did not join the UN until 1955 (see Table 4.3), and the CMEA, which only gained official observer status in 1974. In the commission and the subsidiary bodies majority voting was avoided, as Myrdal wanted to avoid a split among the countries with different economic and political systems.[50] In practise, divisive proposals were not called to a vote, but withdrawn or postponed instead. Cold War antagonism nevertheless held a *defacto* sway over the process, as East and West initiated a tradition of holding a meeting before the yearly gathering of the Commission and regularly decided to vote *en bloc*.

In contrast to the Commission, the Technical Committees saw far less political rhetoric in their meetings. In case of ECE's work on electricity this was also due to the fact that it was mostly network operators rather than politicians sitting at the negotiating table. They convened privately, without press or public, and verbatim reports were not kept. The rationale behind this was to create an atmosphere where procedural and in particular political discussions could be eliminated. Committees should work on an expert level on concrete cases, to avoid becoming exercises in political confrontation.[51] Topics that might be politically sensitive were often explored first by the Secretariat in consultation with the governments concerned, or were preceded by informal meetings.[52]

The ECE's *Committee on Electric Power* (CoEP) similarly tried to minimize Cold War-antagonisms and to include Central and Eastern European countries as much as possible. It attempted to study electricity-related issues "as though Europe were but a single country, regardless of political frontiers".[53] The ECE only took projects of international scale into consideration. This included international transmission lines, as well as new plants the capacity of which could not be absorbed by the host country alone. As the CoEP, like OEEC, had no funds at its disposal, it acted as a mediator and consultant for such projects. It brought together interested governments, and assessed the economic rationale and technical requirements of specific projects. Once financial requirements were estimated on basis of the technical specifications, finding appropriate financiers was the next stage. These could be the participating countries, private financiers, and the *International Bank for Reconstruction and Development* (IBRD, 1945).

---

50 Melvin M. Fagen, "Gunnar Myrdal and the Shaping of the United Nations' Economic Commission for Europe," *Coexistence* 27 (1988): 427-429.

51 Myrdal once wrote that "[s]cientific activity conceived in terms of *l'art pour l'art* [...] has no place in this type of research organization, whose work must always be *practical* and directly *useful*". Myrdal, "The Research," 268.

52 Fagen, "Gunnar Myrdal," 430.

53 "Examination by the Economic Commission for Europe at its Sixth Session of the Report of the Committee on Electric Power", 20 June 1951, registry fonds GX, file 19/1/6-3306, document EP/26, UNOG.

During the first years, engineers from Hungary, Poland and Czechoslovakia participated in the Committee's work.[54] The Committee figured several familiar faces from OEEC and UNIPEDE meetings, including Hintermayer, De Heem, Ailleret, Bakker, Latour, and Hochreutiner. The first priority for the CoEP planning the coordinated development of the European electricity supply started, which they began by studying the national requirements and interconnections, and appointing sub-committees on thermal power and hydropower.[55] This eventually resulted in the 1952 report *Transfers of Electric Power Across European Frontiers*. The essence of the publication was not to recommend what the future of Europe's electricity network should look like. Arguing against schemes proposed during the interwar period, CoEP-chairman Pierre Smits emphasized in 1951 that "[t]he super-imposition on this system of a European 'super-network', as recommended in some quarters, must at present be considered as a somewhat utopian scheme which is not economically justified".[56] Instead, the report sought to enable governments to "grasp more clearly what opportunities for co-operation exist beyond their frontiers".[57] It was meant to help policy-makers to "think in European terms", like technicians already did.[58] In general terms, the report identified the widely recognized need for an interconnected system, which would enable a better balance between thermal and hydro resources in Europe.[59] The report also pointed out that in general national legislations hampered electricity exchanges between countries, as was also recognized during the interwar years.

On the whole, ECE's work showed similarities with OEEC and ECA activities concerning electricity. Like the TECAID mission, ECE saw potential in electricity transfers between individual countries. The volume of cross-border exchange was expected to be small, yet crucial. These electricity flows helped to prevent potential disruptions of service, to utilize available seasonal surpluses, and increase national system efficiency.[60] ECE also saw the possibilities of developing resources exceeding national needs – a similar rationale to ECA's International Projects. In its 1952 report, ECE mentioned hydroelectricity from Norway, Austria, and Yugoslavia,

---

54 Countries present at the first meetings were Austria, Belgium, Czechoslovakia, Denmark, France, Hungary, Italy, Luxembourg, the Netherlands, Norway, Poland, Sweden, Switzerland, Turkey, United Kingdom, United States, and Yugoslavia.
55 UNECE, *Committee on Electric Power, First Session: Summary of the Second Meeting, October 20, 1947*, UN doc, ser., E/ECE/EP/SR.1/2 (Geneva: UNECE, 1947), 1-3.
56 "Examination by the Economic Commission for Europe at its Sixth Session of the Report of the Committee on Electric Power", 20 June 1951, UNOG.
57 ECE, *Transfers*, 5.
58 Ibid.
59 Ibid., 4.
60 Ibid., 126.

and thermal electricity from Poland and Czechoslovakia. Yet on the level of the committees dealing with electricity, overlap of activities hardly existed. To a very large extent this was guaranteed by engineers staffing these committees, many of whom were active in both organizations, who made sure that the activities remained divided.[61] A major difference was the geographical scope of the ECE. They envisioned an interconnected European system as well, but one that extended beyond the Iron Curtain.

The latter becomes clear when looking to two ECE proposals made during its first decade of existence. The first treats electricity supplies from Poland and Czechoslovakia going to Western Europe, with Austria figuring prominently as transit country. The second concerns Yugoslavia as producer and exporter of hydroelectricity to a number of countries, including Austria and Western Germany. Both options remained on the ECE agenda for several decades.

Bottlenecks and Battle Act

To deal with the immediate shortage of power in Europe, the CoEP examined various European power projects of interest to two or more governments, on a comparative technical basis. At the first session of ECE's CoEP in 1947 the alarm was raised about the situation in Western Germany. The load dispatching office in Bad Homburg reported frequent interruptions in the electricity supply, due to coal shortages, war damaged power plants and a lack of plant maintenance. Reserve capacity was virtually non-existent.[62] The Western part of Germany, and Bavaria in particular, was in need of electricity. Bavaria did enter into an agreement with RWE, but their deliveries would not be able to meet its need until 1952. Aside from the fact that the proper equipment was scarce, several Bavarian industries were geared to run on Bohemian coal from Czechoslovakia.[63] Those deliveries were seen as a problem by U.S. authorities.

---

61 In May 1952 Secretariat members expressed some concern about possible overlap between ECE and OEEC regarding a study. French engineer Crescent, member of the CoEP and chairman of the OEEC Electricity Committee, urged the Secretariat not to worry as the OEEC study was only proposed by the OEEC Secretariat. The OEEC Electricity Committee had the intention to "kill" – to cite Crescent – the proposal. Kostelecky to Myrdal, "Power Study," 5 May 1952, ARR 14, file 1360, box 78, UNOG.

62 "Report on Electric Power System Operation in Western Germany," n.d., registry fonds GX, file 19/1/1-2271, UNOG. Interestingly enough, most day-to-day operational matters were already in 1947 entrusted to German engineers. The export and import of electric power was restricted to Allied Officers. The Soviets did not participate in the dispatch organisation.

63 "Plan for Economic Reconstruction of the German Bizonal Area, 1948/49," n.d., non-registry file 910.33 (43), file G385, LoN. This archival document was presented to me by archivist Ms. Pejovic.

An additional problem was the friction between military and civilian authorities in the FRG and Austria. In 1949, a wartime agreement arranging the export of Austrian electricity to the western part of Germany came to an end. This was a wartime legacy of Austria's electrical integration into the Third Reich, whereby Germany had grown dependent on Austrian supplies (see the transmission lines crossing the Austro-German border in Figure 5.2). The Austrian administration was displeased with the agreement, which furnished German energy needs below cost price. In 1949 Vienna complained with ECA in Washington:

> The Austrian companies producing for Germany were formerly owned almost entirely by German companies and output was almost entirely consumed in Germany. [...] [The] Austrian Government particularly emphasizes to us that they are not prepared to sell power to Germany at less cost than they will have to charge Austrian consumers for power from plants under construction.[64]

During the summer of 1949 the issue gained in significance, as a low water situation occurred due to a dry summer. After delivering several warnings to German authorities, Austria was (allegedly) forced to stop the supply. This only added to the problems in Southern Germany.

In January 1950 a potential solution was presented to the ECE. Representatives of Poland and Czechoslovakia expressed their interest in large-scale deliveries to Bavaria.[65] An acknowledged problem with deliveries from this region was the relative underdevelopment of HV-transmission lines.[66] In the absence of proper transmission lines, electricity from Czechoslovakia seemed the best option. Their proposed power plant would be situated at approximately 30 km from the German border. The length of the needed transmission lines would thus not exceed 50 km. If the price of the Czech supply was to be favorable as well, a CoEP report noted, their offer would certainly be accepted. The only reservation from the ECE secretariat was that these projects were "subject of course to the political and material difficulties which need not be recapitulated".[67] In September 1950 Pierre Sevette (see Figure 4.2), Chief of the Electric Power section of ECE's Secretariat, reported to Myrdal that not only prominent engineers like Ailleret agreed with substance of this project, but also American OEEC officials in Paris. He nevertheless again underlined potential political pitfalls.[68]

---

64 Cablegram from Vienna (unsigned) to ECA Administrator, 6 July 1949, RG 469, file 2.2, box 14, NACP.
65 "Committee on Electric Power," 11 January 1950, registry fonds GX, file 19/6/1/4-3815, document ME/25/50, UNOG.
66 L.H. Black to J. Houston Angus, "Supply of Power to Bavaria," 19 May 1949, ARR 14, file 1360, box 50, UNOG
67 "Committee on Electric Power," 11 January 1950, UNOG.
68 Sevette to Myrdal, 20 September 1950, ARR 14, file 1360, box 50, UNOG.

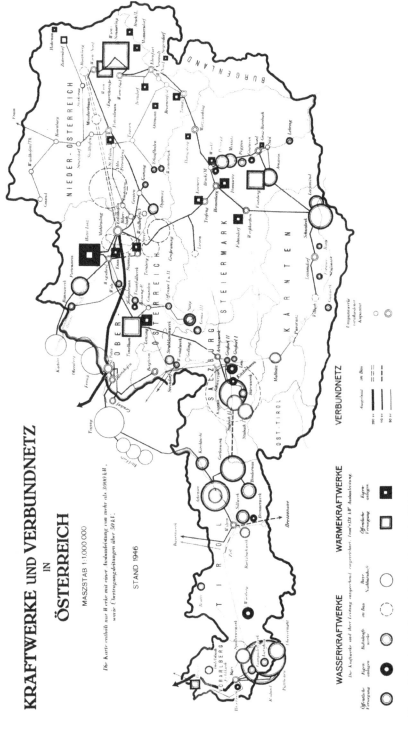

Figure 5.2 – Austria's electricity network in 1946
Source: Map of Austria's grid, 1946, GX, file 19/4/2/2-2716, UNOG.

In November 1950 the Czechoslovaks suddenly stepped out of the project, claiming they needed the electricity for their own economy and society.[69] This meant the ECE needed to turn to Poland again. Their electricity would be generated with Silesian coal as fuel. The site of the new power plant near Oświęcim (German name: Auschwitz) was in the vicinity of rivers and "convenient rail and road connections".[70] This plant with a capacity of 340 MW would utilize excess mining coal from six nearby mines. The costs for the plant were estimated at US$ 57.8 million. This option would need additional transmission lines, however. Accordingly, the electricity would be transmitted from its point of origin in Poland through Czechoslovakia, over a distance of 1,000 to 1,200 km. The choice was either to use partially existing 220 kV lines for load-shifting or to construct new double 220 kV lines. While the latter was estimated at some US$ 45 million, the option of load-shifting was calculated at some US$ 5 million lower. In this scheme the area around Vienna would receive power directly from Poland, whereas Austrian power plants in the Vorarlberg would supply Bavaria.

The latter option made use of existing plans for building an interconnection between Poland, Czechoslovakia, and Austria. Such plans stemmed from the PUP. This concerned a 220 kV line starting at the Polish thermal plant near Oświęcim, traversing Czechoslovakia, and crossing the border at Bisamberg in Austria, near Vienna (see Figure 5.2) Austria would then transmit electricity to Czechoslovakia during summer months. In return, Czechoslovakia would supply electricity generated in thermal plants (and partially from Poland) to its southern neighbor. Part of the work had already commenced during the war, and the Austrian delegate hoped that the Austrian part of the project would be completed by 1948.[71] But Poland, as it turned out, also pulled out of the project in 1950.

There are several reasons why the two plans were withdrawn. Czechoslovakia might have indeed required the electricity to cover its domestic needs. The adoption of the Soviet industrialization model did lead to an emphasis on energy-intensive heavy industry.[72] Another probable issue might have been possible interference of the Soviets, who were at this time not very cooperative within the ECE framework. It hints at strategic reasons that in 1954 Austria declined to build a

---

69 "ECE Committee on Electric Power. Supplement to 'Possibilities for Electric Power Exchanges between Austria, Czechoslovakia, Germany and Poland'," 12 November 1950, registry fonds GX, file 19/6/1/4-3815, document EP/23/add. 1, UNOG.

70 "ECE Committee on Electric Power – Thermal Working Party: Silesian Study Group," 17 March 1949, registry fonds GX, file 19/6/1/4-3815, document EP/WP.2/4, UNOG.

71 UNECE, *Committee on Electric Power, First Session: Summary of the Third Meeting, October 21, 1947*, UN doc, ser., E/ECE/EP/SR.1/3 (Geneva: UNECE, 1947), 1-3.

72 Paul G. Lewis, *Central Europe Since 1945* (London: Longman, 1994), 105.

connection to Hungary fearing that the Soviet Occupation Authority would use the line for exporting power that Austria needed itself.[73]

But other likely explanations exist which are linked to a more general shift in Western attitudes towards the Eastern bloc. In its correspondence with ECE, Poland had already expressed its need for Western electrical equipment.[74] This equipment had grown hard to get as trade between East and West deteriorated. For this specific project, a telegram by U.S. Secretary of State Dean Acheson to the OSR helps to place these events in a broader historical context. In it, he confirmed Poland's trouble with obtaining proper equipment. According to Acheson it appeared "unsound" to encourage the Polish-Czech power export to Bavaria, due to the unreliable Eastern European political situation and problems involved in sending generating equipment from Western to Eastern Europe.[75] In particular, Acheson's telegram pointed to the fact that the equipment in question was on the so-called I-B list. This list related to what would become known as the embargo lists of the *Coordinating Committee for Multilateral Export Controls* (COCOM, 1949).

COCOM was created by Western European allies and the United States in the spring of 1950.[76] It was part of the so-called *Consultative Group*, which had no relation "to any U.S. or European government agency, NATO or the OEEC".[77] COCOM was a way to reinforce the U.S. Export Control Act of 1949 on a wider level. To persuade its allies to participate, the United States passed the *Mutual Defense Assistance Control Act* of 1951, which stipulated in essence that military and economic aid to countries engaged in trade deemed detrimental to U.S. security interests could be terminated.[78] The items, mainly industrial materials and products, which were denied for export to the East were divided over two lists, each with a distinct character. Whereas the first list was definitely designed to slow Soviet development for warfare, the second list aimed at something between *economic warfare*, to weaken the overall

---

73 Sevette to Waring, "Imports of Electric Power by Hungary from Yugoslavia," 21 December 1954, ARR 14, file 1360, box 91, UNOG.

74 W. Micuta to W.W. Rostow, 31 August 1948, ARR 14, file 1360, box 50, UNOG.

75 Telegram Washington (Acheson) to Paris, 6 January 1950, RG 469, file 3.2: Office of the General Counsel, box 36, NACP.

76 The member countries included the United States, Belgium, Canada, Denmark, France, the FRG, Italy, Japan, Luxembourg, the Netherlands, Norway, Portugal and the United Kingdom. In 1996 COCOM was transformed into an organisation of non-proliferation export controls. See Michael Lipson, "The Reincarnation of COCOM: Explaining Post-Cold War Export Controls," *The Nonproliferation Review* Winter (1999): 33 and 36.

77 Quoted in Jacqueline McGlade, "COCOM and the Containment of Western Trade and Relations," in *East-West Trade and the Cold War*, ed. Jari Eloranta and Jari Ojala (Jyväskylä: University of Jyväskylä, 2005), 49, note 6.

78 Gary K. Bertsch, "Introduction," in *Controlling East-West Trade and Technology Transfer: Power, Politics, and Policies*, ed. Gary K. Bertsch (Durham: Duke University Press, 1988), 6.

targeted economy, and a *strategic embargo*, to deny items of indirect military use[79]. List II contained items that could have military relevance, not necessarily linked to warfare as such – so-called *dual-use* items.[80]

Acheson's telegram on COCOM typifies the new phase in Cold War relations after the Korea War started. During the ERP and the subsequent years, electricity systems in Western Europe were to contribute to economic as well as defensive strengthening of the region. COCOM, on the other hand, sought to obstruct such developments within Central and Eastern European countries. Not only did List I contain equipment needed by Poland for the one specific project, List II generally aimed to deny any "significant equipment" for new power plant construction in Eastern Europe.[81] But this line of policy also had serious consequences for collaboration between East and West. This is what probably impelled Poland and Czechoslovakia to opt out of this scheme of international collaboration. Both countries also withdrew from the CoEP, and only returned to ECE meetings in 1953 and 1954 respectively.[82] ECE's scheme had been approved by European and American engineers from a technical point-of-view, and would have provided electricity for a region in need. Politically, however, matters were different. The extension of electrical collaboration across the Iron Curtain ran afoul of security objectives.

This does not imply that the ECE was regarded as unwanted by the Western alliance. In addition to COCOM, NATO countries started to coordinate their attitude towards ECE in 1958, with a view "to making its activities more favorable to Western aims".[83] It was agreed that the Committee of Economic Advisers

---

79 Michael Mastanduno, "Strategies of Economic Containment: U.S. Trade Relations with the Soviet Union," *World Politics* 37, no. 4 (1985): 505-506. Also see Tor Egil Forland, "'Economic Warfare' and 'Strategic Goods': A Conceptual Framework for Analyzing COCOM," *Journal of Peace Research* 28, no. 2 (1991): 191-204.

80 Michael Mastanduno, "The Management of Alliance Export Control Policy: American Leadership and the Politics of COCOM," in *Controlling East-West*, ed. Bertsch, 241.

81 Telegram Paris (Anderson) to Secretary of State, 12 June 1953, RG 469, file 3.2: Records of the Offices of the Director and Deputy Director, box 6, NACP. The precise wording of the telegram is "Cut off intended prevent exports significant equipment for construction of new power plant in bloc". The telegram further deals with the pain-staking slow negotiations that occurred almost immediately once the lists were compiled.

82 David Wightman, *Economic Co-Operation in Europe: A Study of the United Nations Economic Commission for Europe* (London: Stevens, 1956), 157.

83 "Conclusions Agreed by the Committee of Economic Advisers," 12 June 1958, file AC/127: Committee of Economic Advisers, document D/30 (revised), attachment to document C-M(58)94, NATO. This was in line with the recommendations of the report of the Three Wise Men on reform within NATO, in 1956. They did not only advise setting up non-military cooperation – like economic cooperation –, but also to hold NATO consultations before 'meetings of organizations at which the interests of the Atlantic Community may be subject to attempts to weaken or divide the Alliance'. See NATO, Document C-M(56)127 (revised), 'Report of the Committee of Three on Non-Military Co-Operation in NATO', 10 January 1957, 18. Document is available on http://www.nato.int/archives/committee_of_three/index.htm (accessed January 22, 2008).

(ECONAD) regularly discussed ECE's work that concerned the "political interests" of the "Atlantic Alliance".[84] Crucially, NATO did not question the existence of the ECE. It recognized the ECE as the only existing all-European forum, which most Western European countries considered to be "an important bridge" between East and West.[85] For some it was the only place to meet representatives from countries with which they had no diplomatic relations. In addition, it presented a useful source of intelligence for the Atlantic Alliance. ECONAD saw the ECE as a useful instrument, claimed that despite its limited results "it is felt that, if and when political tension decreases, ECE may eventually develop into an important link between the two systems".[86]

Converging interests: Yugoslavia

It was not only the United States that employed economic boycott as a means of achieving foreign policy goals. In 1948, all Soviet economic, financial and technical assistance to Yugoslavia came to a halt. The immediate cause was a row between Stalin and Yugoslav leader Josip Broz Tito (1892-1980). This affected the Yugoslav electricity sector as well, as it meant that an agreement signed in June 1946, providing Soviet technical assistance to the Yugoslav electrical industry, was cancelled.[87] Yugoslavia was subsequently excluded from participating in the CMEA. These political developments, along with a very bad harvest in the same year, had extremely dire consequences for Yugoslavia's current state of economic affairs. It also threatened the ongoing Five Year Plan (see Table 5.1), which was already regarded over-ambitious in various quarters.[88] Tito's Five Year Plan emphasized industrialization: industry was to make a leap from a 40 per cent share in GNP in 1939 to 64 per cent in 1951, whereas agriculture should decrease its

---

84 "Conclusions Agreed by the Committee of Economic Advisers," 12 June 1958, NATO.
85 NATO, AC/127, Document WP/82, "NATO Countries' Policy in the Economic Commission for Europe," 12 March 1962, file AC/127, document WP/82, NATO.
86 Ibid.
87 Leon Gibianskii, "The Soviet Bloc and the Initial Stage of the Cold War: Archival Documents on Stalin's meetings with Communists Leaders of Yugoslavia and Bulgaria, 1946-1948," *Cold War International History Project Bulletin* March, no. 10 (1998): 114-115.
88 Robert Owen Freedman labels the Plan "very ambitious, if not grandiose". See his *Economic Warfare in the Communist Bloc: A Study of Soviet Economic Pressure Against Yugoslavia, Albania, and Communist China* (New York: Praeger, 1970), 20. The IBRD was not very optimistic either. During talks on possible loans IBRD director Eugene Black insisted on a relaxation of 'its entire heavy industrialization program'. See U.S. Department of State, "The Ambassador in Yugoslavia (Allen) to the Secretary of State," in *Foreign Relations of the United States*, vol. 4, *Central and Eastern Europe: The Soviet Union* (Washington, D.C.: U.S. Government Printing Office, 1950), 1448-1449.

Table 5.1 – The Yugoslav Five-Year Plan 1947-1951 (investments in millions of Dinars)

Mining & Metallurgy	31
Electricity	30
Manufacturing industry	55
Communications	72
Agriculture	19
Other	71
Total	278

Calculated on basis of A. A. L. Caesar, "Yugoslavia," 34.

share to 35 per cent by 1951, down from as much as 60 per cent in 1939.[89] Minerals extraction in particular needed to be increased to boost the infant metallurgical industry. In order for this ambitious plan to be successful, energy output would have to grow by a massive 400 per cent, mainly to be generated by hydroelectric plants.[90]

The Tito-Stalin rift initially made Tito receptive to Western aid. Part of this westward orientation was due to the fact that the diplomatic and economic "road" to the East was obstructed by Moscow. The acquisition of knowledge, capital, and materials from the Soviet bloc was out of the question because of the boycott. Replacing the role of the USSR, the ECE and the United States sought to satisfy Yugoslavia's most urgent needs. This time ECE policy was compatible with security interests of the Western block, although different aims were pursued. Although the USSR eventually resumed relations with Yugoslavia at the end of the 1950s, Yugoslavia continued to look West for inspiration and cooperation – while keeping the door to the East open.

Yugoslavia saw the ECE as its main international forum.[91] The ECE Secretariat in turn was quick to recognize Yugoslavia's potential role as an electricity exporting country in the region.[92] Because of the Tito-Stalin row, at least one huge potential resource remained untapped: the Iron Gate, a narrow gorge in the Danube bordering Yugoslavia and Rumania. As relations with Moscow broke down, contact with other Socialists countries also deteriorated. Yugoslavia therefore seriously considered electricity exports to its western neighbors. ECE played an instrumental role

---

89 A huge increase in agricultural productivity was also part of the plan, but industrial growth had to be higher in comparison.
90 A.A.L. Caesar, "Yugoslavia: Geography and Postwar Planning," *Transactions and Papers (Institute of British Geographers)* 30 (1962): 33-43.
91 Kaser, *COMECON*, 75.
92 Sevette to Gunnar Myrdal, "Possibilités d'exportation d'énergie électrique de Yougoslavie," 8 December 1950, ARR 14, file 1360, UNOG.

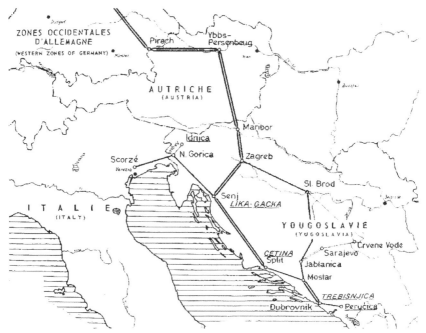

Figure 5.3 – Yougelexport: Yugoslavia, Italy, Austria and Western Germany
Source: Document EP/"Yougelexport" No. 1, 16 March 1954, GX, file 19/6/1/12, UNOG.

in this process. In 1950 Austria, the FRG, Italy and Yugoslavia formed a study group under the aegis of ECE, entitled *Yougelexport*. [93] Within this group, the prospects of exporting electricity from Yugoslavia were studied from a legal, economic, financial and technical point of view. The outline of the project involved the construction of four large power plants in Idnjca, Lika-Gacka, Cetina and Trebisnjica, meant partly for domestic use but mostly for exporting power. Transmission lines over a vast area were also needed because a well-integrated national network was still lacking (see Figure 5.3).

Progress on the project was all but smooth, however. From the institutional point of view, there were different opinions as to what the optimal legal form for the financing structure and trade agreements would be. A partly related problem came in acquiring the necessary finance. The IBRD would not issue a loan to an intergovernmental body, but only to a single government. Some of the participating countries had serious reservations as well as legal difficulties about using such a loan to invest in a foreign country, and Yugoslavia would not be able to contract a loan of that size on its own. An additional problem was that any kind of organi-

---

93 Sevette to Melvin Fagen, "Possibilitiés d'éxportations d'énergie électrique de Yougoslavie," 3 November 1950, ARR 14, file 1360, UNOG.

zation or financing of the project was not permitted to create private property in socialist Yugoslavia.[94] And although the interim technical reports seemed sound, there were diverging opinions about the geological structure of the soil on which the plants were to be constructed. Whereas the Western countries followed the recommendations of the UN expert, the Yugoslavian authorities continued to rely on the conclusions drawn by their own experts. In addition, a diplomatic stir erupted between the FRG and Yugoslavia. The FRG had supplied commercial credits of 400 million Mark which Yugoslavia refused to repay, calling the credits war reparations.[95] The German delegation therefore refused to organize a session to discuss the project scheduled for December 1957, which eventually took place in Vienna.[96] In addition, the Yugoslav authorities also wanted to use electricity generated in the *Yougelexport* framework for the production of aluminum, which would be destined for export.[97] These aluminum factories would be financed by Soviet loans, however, as borrowing money from the Soviet Union was possible again after reconciliation between Tito and Stalin's successor Khrushchev in 1954.[98]. This led to a further increase of tensions between the Yougelexport participants.

Eventually, *Yougelexport* can be considered a mixed success, as most of the plans were executed. In contrast to ECE's initial idea, most plants were built with finance attracted by Yugoslavia itself rather than the study group. By 1959 it was clear that the *Yougelexport*–members would focus on one plant (the one of Lika-Gacka). The plant at Trebisnjica would be financed by U.S. aid, the one at Cetina by the Yugoslav government.[99] This American assistance to Tito was not novel. As early as December 1950 the American Congress passed the Yugoslav Emergency Relief Act, authorizing 50 million US$ to provide immediate relief for the situation resulting from the economic effects of the boycott by Central and Eastern Europe and a severe drought that had hit Yugoslav agriculture. The Truman administration defended its Act stressing that

> It is clearly in our national interest that Yugoslavia be kept free of Soviet domination. Yugoslavia is strategically located, bordering Italy, Austria and Greece, as well as on the edge of Soviet-dominated Europe.[100]

---

94 "Groupe Comité Juridique. Sommaire de la Deuxième Reunion tenu à Venise le 27 Juillet 1953," 11 August 1953, registry fonds GX, file 19/6/1/12, document EP/"YOUGELEXPORT"/No 8, UNOG.

95 Sevette to Tuomioja, 30 April 1958, ARR 14, file 1360, box 109, UNOG.

96 Sevette to Tuomioja, 12 December 1958, ARR 14, file 1360, box 109, UNOG.

97 "Prospects of Exporting Electric Power from Yugoslavia, in Combination with the Production of Aluminium," 12 August 1956, registry fonds GX, file 19/6/1/12-14883, UNOG.

98 Sevette to Tuomioja, 12 December 1958, UNOG. Such a loan could only possible after the reconciliation between Yugoslavia and the Soviet Union, after the death of Stalin in 1953.

99 Sevette to Tuomioja, 17 July 1959, ARR 14, file 1360, box 109, UNOG.

100 ECA, *Eleventh Report to Congress of the Economic Cooperation Administration* (Washington, D.C.: U.S. Government Printing Office, 1950), 40.

At the same time, ECA supplied aid to Yugoslavia through countries participating in the ERP.[101] The stopgap aid and military support supplied by the West in the 1950s gave way to structural development projects in the 1960s and 1970s. This aid materialised also in the electricity sector, which the United States had started to support the in the 1950s. Their particular goal seemed to be to make Yugoslavia more self-sufficient in electric power equipment. By supplying funds for plants in Ljubljana, Zagreb and Maribor, the U.S. believed that "[t]his group of factories is the keystone to Yugoslavia's success in achieving rapid progress in the development of its hydro potential, and it is on this group that Yugoslavia will depend for a continued achievement and independence from imports".[102] The U.S. assumed that the Yugoslav government would try to use current aid flows to achieve a higher degree of self-sufficiency.[103] This could also help to decrease Yugoslavia's balance-of-payments deficit. At the same time arrangements were made to bring four Yugoslav engineers to the United States for technical assistance training.[104] In 1956, another group of Yugoslav engineers were invited to the United States to receive three months of advanced training in the operation and development of the national power system.[105]

But U.S. aid had deeper intentions as well. In 1954, an amount of $20 million ($12,750,000 for electric power) was invested in so-called *Defense Strengthening Projects*. Besides reinforcing the internal economy, these projects added to Yugoslav military strength, and should be capable of supporting the planned factories for gunpowder, arms, tanks and aircrafts.[106] An essential part of these projects involved erecting a HV interconnected grid to improve the balance between thermal and hydroelectric power stations. This was deemed "highly essential if Yugoslavia's military industries, key investments [...] are to be operated at the scales planned".[107] In other words, the electricity supply system had to contribute to the country's defense industry. In the case of Yugoslavia, NATO-countries did not oppose the strengthening of electrical connections between Socialist and capitalist countries. On the contrary, Western countries, and in particular the United States, saw

---

101 Ibid., 40-41.
102 "Survey of the Yugoslav Economy. Prepared by USOM/Yugoslavia with the Assistance of USIS/Yugoslavia, Belgrade," 1 November 1954, RG 59: General records of the Records of the Department of State, file 3.4: Records of offices responsible for European affairs, Records relating to economic affairs, box 4, NACP.
103 "Washington Discussions Concerning Needed Changes in Yugoslav Economic Policy," n.d., RG 469, file 3.2: Office of the Deputy for Defense Affairs, box 2, NACP.
104 Everett Eslick to D.A. Fitzgerald, 4 March 1954, RG 469, file 3.2: Industrial Resources Division, box 1, NACP.
105 "Project Proposal & Approval Summary – Foreign Operations Administration," n.d., registry fonds GX, file 19/6/1/12-14883, UNOG.
106 "Washington Discussions Concerning Needed Changes in Yugoslav Economic Policy," n.d., NACP.
107 Ibid. Citation is on page 21.

Tito's break with Stalin as an opportunity. It was perceived as the first crack in the Soviet firmament that might be followed by others.[108] It also fitted with increased economic support and defense assistance for Southern European countries like Greece, Italy, and Turkey.[109]

Ultimately Yugoslavia chose a middle position in between East and West. After Tito and Stalin's successor Khrushchev re-established contact in 1954, Eastern options became available to them again. Yugoslavia became an associated member of CMEA only a few years later, in 1964. In 1956 Yugoslavia, already a CMEA observer by then, took part in creating a "standing commission for the exchange of electric power among members of the CMEA and for the use of the hydro-resources of the Danube".[110] Subsequently an agreement was signed on the regulation of the flow at the Iron Gate. Yugoslavia and Hungary would profit from land improvement, Rumania would gain irrigation water, and all three would have a new source of hydroelectric power within reach of their respective grids. Again due to deteriorating relations between Belgrade and Moscow, affairs concerning the Iron Gate were arranged bilaterally and outside the CMEA framework.[111] The partners reached a consensus in 1960, and a diplomatic treaty was signed three years later. The 1956 plans had become less ambitious. The 1956 proposal envisioned power plants producing some 35 million MWh per year, in 1963 this was reduced to 10.7 million.[112]

The reestablishment of contacts with the Soviet Union and other CMEA countries did not imply an end to rapprochement to the West. In 1954 it concluded the *Treaty of Alliance, Political Cooperation, and Mutual Assistance* (or Balkan Pact) with Greece and Turkey, obliging each country to assist the others in case of armed aggression. It is important in this respect that both Greece and Turkey had acceded to NATO in 1952. It was therefore hoped that the Pact might be a prelude to further cooperation or perhaps even an associated membership with NATO.[113]

---

108 The U.S. Central Intelligence Agency (CIA) reported: "In the Eastern European Satellites, signs of nationalist sentiment, of mass peasant antagonism to Communist agrarian policies, and of dissension in Communist ranks, have suggested the growth of wavering loyalties and resistance to central direction from USSR. The defection of Tito and the Yugoslav Communist Party is our most striking evidence for the existence of an unstable situation. There is no doubt that this situation caused concern in the Kremlin." See CIA Report, ORE 22-48, September 1948, *(Addendum) Possibility of Direct Soviet Military Action During 1948-49*, recited in Gerald K. Haines and Robert E. Leggett, eds., *CIA's Analysis of the Soviet Union 1947-1991* (Washington, D.C.: Center for the Study of Intelligence - CIA, 2001), 26.
109 Ellwood, *Rebuilding*, 112 ff.
110 Cited by Kaser, *COMECON*, 76.
111 Ibid., 76-77.
112 Ibid., 101.
113 Lorraine M. Lees, *Keeping Tito Afloat: The United States, Yugoslavia, and the Cold War* (University Park: Pennsylvania State University Press, 1997).

In 1961 Yugoslavia gained observer status in the OECD. It was clear that at least the American State Department was very much in favor of Yugoslavia's being integrated in some form into the NATO framework.[114] Illustrative of its in-between position, Yugoslavia took part in the meeting of Western European countries prior to annual meetings of the Economic Commission for Europe, but simultaneously consulted privately with Central and Eastern European countries on their proposals.[115]

Interconnecting regions

In the case of Bavaria, and to a lesser extent Yugoslavia, additional electricity supplies were required to cover postwar needs. Those immediate needs were catered for by the end of 1950s. Western Europe nevertheless witnessed an increasing consumption of energy in general, fuelled by the relative economic prosperity of the 1950s and 1960s. With the prospects of coal production on the decline, Western Europe could not match further growth by indigenous supply alone. Increasingly, fuels – both coal and oil – were imported from overseas and the overall use of coal declined. Policy-makers and planners thus felt some sense of urgency about energy policy.

This urgency showed in the sheer quantity of high-level and authoritatively studies into the European energy economy in those years, in particular by the OEEC. 1955 saw the OEEC report *Some Aspects of the European Energy Problem*, authored by French engineer and director of the French state railways, Louis Armand.[116] A year later, just before the Suez crisis, a second major OEEC study was published, entitled *Europe's Growing Need of Energy*.[117] The report, commissioned by the OEEC under the aegis of professor Austin Hartley, wrote that the future of hard coal production in Western Europe depended "primarily on the possibility of producing coal at a price that will make its use fully competitive with that of alternative fuels".[118] Electricity, recognized by the Hartley report as a source of heat, light and power, needed to keep up with demand. On average, the annual

---

114 "United States policy towards Yugoslavia," n.d., RG 59, file 3.4, box 3, NACP.
115 "Evaluation of the seventeenth plenary session of the Economic Commission for Europe," file AC/127, document WP/90/1, NATO.
116 Louis Armand, *Some Aspects of the European Energy Problem: Suggestions for Collective Action* (Paris: OEEC, 1955).
117 OEEC, *Europe's Growing Need of Energy: How Can They Be Met? A Report Prepared by a Group of Experts* (Paris: OEEC, 1956). Members included Walker Cisler, Swiss Pierre Uri, and for a while the Frenchman Louis Armand.
118 Ibid., 40.

rise of electricity demand in Western Europe was estimated at 7 per cent. This implied a doubling of demand every 10 years.[119] The electricity industry began to seek ways to be able to meet that future demand.

One solution considered was to expand the geographical scope of cooperation. Despite objections of NATO countries, the idea of increased East-West collaboration gained strength within the industry in the following years. This is clear from UNIPEDE gatherings and to some extent from discussions within UCPTE. In 1964 the UNIPEDE Study Committee on Interconnections reckoned that interconnection in Western Europe had "reached a very advanced stage of development and at the present time all the countries of Europe are connected to their immediate neighbors".[120] In addition, their Central and Eastern European counterparts expressed similar intentions at ECE meetings. The countries within Central and Eastern Europe had instituted a power pool too: CDO/IPS. The process of creating this power pool was accompanied by substantial network expansion. By the early 1960s a 380 kV system had emerged (see Figure 5.4). The core of the CDO system was formed by the interconnection between the GDR, Poland, Czechoslovakia, Hungary, and the Ukrainian SSR. Romania and Bulgaria joined in 1963 and 1964 respectively. It has not yet been possible to reconstruct the atmosphere in which these talks took place, so it is not possible to speculate on what the driving forces of this collaboration were.

Expansion of interconnected operation thus had to come either from strengthening internal links, or by involving new countries outside of UCPTE. UNIPEDE concluded in 1964 that "[a]ny new progress in interconnection will arise either from a reinforcement of the existing links or from the setting up of new submarine links, or the establishment of links with countries of eastern Europe".[121] According to UNIPEDE's 1964 general report on interconnections, technical difficulties prevented a parallel interconnection between East and West.[122] Synchronous interconnections were not possible without risking instability. This did not render any form of interconnection impossible, however. In existing forms of East-West cooperation this problem was solved by isolating specific links from the rest of

---

119 Ibid., 33-34.
120 François Cahen and Bernard Favez, "Control of Frequency and Power Exchanges within the Framework of International Interconnections (report IV.2)," in *UNIPEDE Congress of Scandinavia* (Paris: Imprimerie Chaix, 1964), 23.
121 Ibid.
122 Giorgio Riccio, "Rapport général du président du Comité (report no. IV)," in *UNIPEDE Congress of Scandinavia* (Paris: Imprimerie Chaix, 1964), 4.

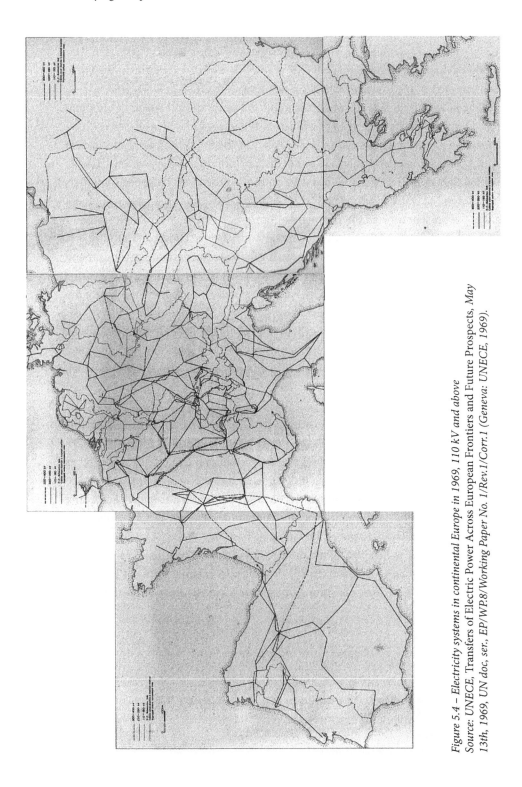

Figure 5.4 – Electricity systems in continental Europe in 1969, 110 kV and above
Source: UNECE, Transfers of Electric Power Across European Frontiers and Future Prospects, May 13th, 1969, UN doc, ser., EP/WP8/Working Paper No. 1/Rev.1/Corr.1 (Geneva: UNECE, 1969).

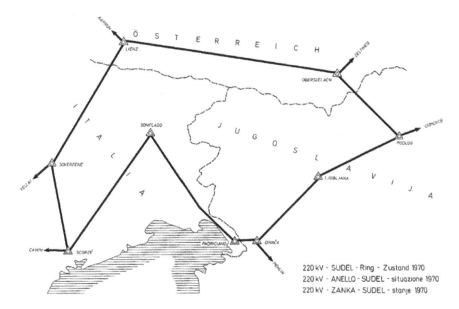

Figure 5.5 – SUDEL grid in 1970
Source: UCPTE, SUDEL (1970).

the network, in so-called *radial* or *isolated operation*.[123] This implies that a power plant or part of the system was separated from the system, and connected across the border to the other system while operating at the other system's frequency.[124] In case of SUDEL a ring was gradually constructed (see Figure 5.5). This ring was operated separately from the UCPTE network in Italy and Austria, and from the CDO network in Yugoslavia. For example, in 1963 an isolated transmission line between Austria and Czechoslovakia was brought into use, allowing the exchange of electricity on a seasonal basis.

Yet whereas stress was laid upon technical hindrances, political geography was important as well. Two countries that did have East-West connections by the early 1960s both held special almost non-aligned positions. While working in the SUDEL framework with Austria and Italy, we already saw how Yugoslavia re-established contact with CMEA countries. As we have seen, Tito was able to occupy a position between the two antagonizing blocks. Austria also came to hold

123 UNECE, *The Interconnexion of the Electric Power Transmission Systems of Countries in Eastern and Western Europe, September 30, 1971, pp.1-2.,* UN doc, ser., EP/WP.8/Working paper No.16/Corr.2 (Geneva: UNECE, 1971), 1-2.
124 Helmuth Allmer, "Extension Planning of the Austrian Interconnected Network with Regard to HVDC Back-to-Back Links," in *UNECE Seminar on High Voltage Direct Current Techniques, Stockholm, May, 1985,* UN doc, ser., EP/SEM.10/Report no. 2 (Geneva: UNECE, 1985), 2.

a position as "bridge" between East and West, which was not only due to its geography but to its political position as well. Austria emerged from Four Power custody in 1955 with the signing of the State Treaty, an important stipulation of which was its continuing political neutrality.[125] As a consequence, Austria could neither join NATO nor its Eastern counterpart, the Warsaw Pact. In practice, this gave Austrian policy-makers and network operators more leeway in establishing contacts with their Eastern neighbors.

Austria and Yugoslavia were thus in a good position to engage in East-West cooperation. Other Western European countries were not, however, despite the growing support for such connections from various bodies in the electricity industry. Again, political and strategic interests prevailed. This is apparent from the sequence of events following a new initiative by ECE. At the 18th Session of the ECE in 1963, several countries – Poland, Czechoslovakia, Austria and Yugoslavia – requested the Secretariat to examine the possibilities of reinforcing the interconnection between the networks of Eastern and Western European countries.[126] Therefore ECE Secretariat member Pierre Sevette made three consecutive trips to Budapest, Warsaw, and Berlin in 1963, to prepare a proposal. He did not consult Western European capitals. Ideas and opinions were entrusted to paper in a draft plan, which was sent around to European capitals for review.

The draft plan made reference to Europe's energy supply. It remarked that "untapped hydro-power resources in Europe are dwindling markedly".[127] The availability of interconnections between national networks in Europe made it possible to reduce reserve capacity and to affect seasonal exchanges between hydro and thermal electricity plants. Yet it underlined the satisfactory level of interconnection in Western Europe and substantially improved level in Central and Eastern Europe. Yet, according to the plan, "[t]here are comparatively few important interconnection lines between countries situated in the west and countries situated in the east of Europe, except the 220-kV line between Austria and Czechoslovakia".[128] This assessment was reflected in the actual proposals made in this ECE draft, which was akin to earlier ECE plans (see Figure 5.6). The draft plan included the return of Poland and Czechoslovakia as exporters to the FRG. The FRG should be responsible for financing new plants. This required transmission via the GDR, where

---

125 Warren W. Williams, "The Road to the Austrian State Treaty," *Journal of Cold War Studies* 2, no. 2 (2000): 97-107.
126 Sevette to Zachmann, and Meller-Conrad and Batros, 3 July 1963, registry fonds GX, file 19/6/1/15-32212, UNOG.
127 "Project de plan d'une étude relative aux possibilités de renforcement de l'interconnexion des réseaux de transmission d'énergie électrique en Europe," 1963, ARR 14, file 1360, box 109, UNOG.
128 Ibid.

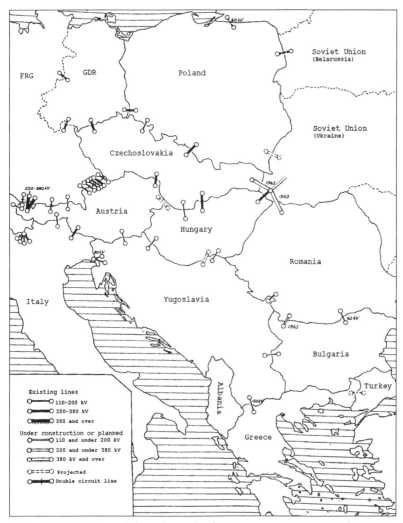

Figure 5.6 – Existing and planned cross-border interconnections in Central Europe in 1963
Source: UNECE, Outline of a Study on the Possibilities of Increasing Interconnexion Between
Electric Power Transmission Networks in Europe, *UN doc, ser., ME/31/64/C.2(a) (Geneva:
UNECE, 1964).*

"there were already certain transmission lines in existence in this region that could
easily be interconnected again with the network of the FRG".[129] Austria was a candidate to import Polish power, too. Another familiar project was the export of
Yugoslavian electricity to Austria and the FRG, centered again on Yugoslavia's un-
derutilized hydroelectric potential.[130] Though very brief, the draft also drew atten-

---

129 Ibid. Translation from French by the author.
130 Ibid.

tion to a possible connection between Scandinavia and the European mainland.[131] ECE argued for these schemes by pointing to the intensive collaboration within regions and arguing that even more benefits could be reaped by building interconnections between them.[132]

Several Central and Eastern European governments responded to the report in a positive manner, including the Soviet Union.[133] However, most Western European countries abstained from the plan. The FRG was by far the most outspoken, and saw the involvement of the GDR as the principal obstacle. Its opposition to electricity supplies from Yugoslavia was motivated by "political reasons", namely Yugoslavia's official recognition of the GDR.[134] Similarly, the FRG minister of economic affairs opposed electricity trade with Poland. According to the ECE proposal this required bringing back into operation electricity lines with the GDR, which were shut off in the early 1950s. Two other economically motivations for opposing the plan were cited as well. First, the electricity supply industry was not willing to finance foreign large-scale power supplies; second, acquiring Polish thermal power was not in line with the FRG's efforts to support its own mining industry.[135] Crucially, the bottom line of the FRG was that "a basis of mutual confidence is absolutely necessary if long-term contracts are envisaged on large-scale power supplies from one country to another". It was convinced that starting negotiations at that moment were "bound to be unsuccessful and must necessarily lead to a discussion, or at least mention, of delicate political problems which the ECE in Geneva has so far avoided to touch upon".[136] Interestingly enough, the United Kingdom, Belgium and the United States responded in a remarkably similar way. All four governments rejected ECE's draft proposal by pointing to the lack of "mutual confidence" between East and West.[137]

This was due to the fact that the Western European response was a coordinated one. In April 1964 NATO's ECONAD reviewed the ECE proposal regards East-West interconnections. The German representative on ECONAD strongly

---

131 Ibid.
132 Ibid.
133 Lebedev (General Secretary USSR Committee for the USSR participation in international power conferences) to Sevette, 1 December 1964, registry fonds GX, file 19/6/1/15-32212, UNOG.
134 Sevette to Van Rhyn, 5 October 1964, registry fonds GX, file 19/6/1/15-32212, UNOG.
135 Heesemann (Der Bundesminister für Wirtschaft) to Velebit, 17 July 1964, registry fonds GX, file 19/6/1/15-32212, UNOG.
136 Ibid.
137 George Tesoro to Velebit, 8 October 1964; J.F, de Liedekerke to Velebit, 13 October 1964; and T. Solesby to Velebit, 29 July 1964. All in registry fonds GX, file 19/6/1/15-32212, UNOG. All three countries – obviously – were not involved in the project from a geographical standpoint.

argued that the initiative was premature.[138] He reminded those assembled that collaboration in Western Europe was based upon mutual confidence between reliable partners – by which he was most likely aiming at the fruitful cooperation between UCPTE-partners. Adding to that, he stressed how this Western European cooperation happened without the intervention of the respective governments – with the exception of the liberalization of electricity exchanges.[139] Within Western Europe confidence was maintained through close personal contacts, which guaranteed help from neighbors in case of emergencies. "The core of the problem" in the case of Central and Eastern European countries, was that such a relation of trust had yet to be established. Therefore the proposal could not be taken into consideration "unless a basis of real mutual confidence has been established, even if such supplies are offered at very favorable prices".[140] In the meeting of the ECE's Western members, prior to the 19th meeting of the ECE, they agreed to reject the East-West electricity proposal. France, the Netherlands, the United Kingdom, and the United States all agreed with the position presented by the FRG in the meeting of ECONAD.[141]

Yet this dismissive position towards East-West collaboration was on the verge of changing. By late 1966 the FRG's policy towards the GDR no longer received full backing of the NATO Alliance. Many urged the FRG to intensify and explore the opportunities of East-West collaboration.[142] While NATO issued an investigation into future possibility, a more open policy towards Central and Eastern Europe was supported by Willy Brandt, who had just taken office in the FRG as foreign minister.[143] During his subsequent term as Bundeskanzler he followed a policy of appeasement towards the FRG's Eastern neighbors, the so-called *Ostpolitik*.[144] Coincidently, a similar change in U.S. policy could be observed as well. Indicative for the overall American position was a 1966 speech by president Lyndon B. Johnson, referring to "the winds of change which are blowing in Eastern Europe":

---

138 "Text of the Statement on Exchanges of Electric Power between East and West, Made by the German Representative at the Meeting of 2nd April, 1964," 8 April 1964, file AC/127, document R/132, annex, NATO. The document does not mention name nor gender of the representative in question. I choose to use the pronoun 'he' for matters of convenience.
139 Ibid.
140 Ibid.
141 Outgoing telegram Department of State to U.S. Mission Geneva (George Tesoro), 4 August 1964, RG 59, file 2: Central files of the Department of State, box 939, NACP.
142 Helga Haftendorn, "The Adaptation of the NATO Alliance to a Period of Détente: The 1967 Harmel Report," in *Crises and Compromises: The European Project 1963-1969*, ed. Wilfried Loth (Baden-Baden: Nomos Verlag, 2001), 285-286.
143 Ibid., 287. The outcome of the result was the so-called Harmel Report, after Belgian foreign minister Pierre Harmel.
144 Garton Ash, *In Europe's*.

> Our policy must reflect the reality of today – not yesterday. [...] Our
> purpose is not to overturn other governments, but to help the people of
> Europe to achieve together: a continent in which the peoples of Eastern
> and Western Europe work shoulder to shoulder together for the common
> good; a continent in which alliances do not confront each other in bitter
> hostility, but instead provide a framework in which West and East can act
> together in order to assure the security of all.[145]

In November 1965 the ECE Secretariat reported that several countries had "renewed interest" in studying the electricity transfers across borders. Most notably, Poland had offered to build power stations with Western money, and to use
new generation capacity to transmit electric power to Western neighbors. Poland
could thus exploit her coal resources while obtaining valuable foreign currency
by selling electricity. It would already have 300 MW of capacity available for export purposes outside of peak periods.[146] U.S. opposition to East-West electricity
cooperation had also become less restrictive. While still labeling these electricity
transfers "obnoxious" in 1966, the U.S. supported the program on the condition
that any such ECE study keep clear of the "inter-German problem".[147] In other
words, as long as the re-unification of the two Germanies was not placed back on
the agenda, no substantial opposition would be voiced. This was in analogy with
the opinion of the government in Bonn. The FRG did support increased East-West
cooperation, but did not change its position regarding the German question until
a final peace settlement was reached.[148]

Although the NATO Alliance loosened its position, this did not mean strategic
intentions were not part of the considerations. In fact, they can be seen as part
of a broader change of policy towards Central and Eastern European countries
that can be discerned within NATO. ECONAD studied economic measures that
might "loosen the ties between the USSR and the various satellites".[149] Replacing
the dominant role of the Soviet Union as main supplier to that region was seen as a
viable option. Goods and services for which Central and Eastern European countries depended upon the Soviet Union included energy, part of which was electricity. The ECE was seen as one of the main bodies to encourage trade between East

---

145 Lyndon B. Johnson, "Remarks in New York City before the National Conference of Editorial Writers"
(New York, October 7, 1966), http://www.presidency.ucsb.edu/ws/print.php?pid=27908.
146 Airgram from U.S. Mission Geneva to Dept of State, 17 November 1965, RG 59, file 2, box 939, NACP.
147 Telegram Department of State to U.S. Mission Geneva, 17 November 1965, RG 59, file 2, box 939,
NACP.
148 Haftendorn, "The Adaptation," 295.
149 "NATO Countries' Trade Policies Towards the European Satellite Countries," 31 March 1964, file
AC/127, document D/150 (revised), NATO.

and West.[150] ECONAD recognized the possible central role Yugoslavia could play in establishing closer economic relations with the Eastern bloc.[151] Earlier experiences with Yugoslavia had "demonstrated that the West was able, by a flexible and generous policy, to assist effectively a Communist country in parrying the worst effects of an abrupt severance of economic links with the entire Soviet bloc".[152] This is further illustrated by a message from the U.S. State Department to its Geneva Mission. It reminded them that Yugoslavia and Rumania had recently connected their networks and that the U.S. Embassy in Bucharest had reported on possible UNIPEDE membership for Rumania. The latter move "could be a practical step towards linking it with western economic organization as well as strengthening Rumanian-Yugoslav economic ties, as counterbalance to CMEA electric power integration".[153]

Besides the intra-German problem, the U.S. also suggested that ECE should only undertake this type of studies "if found useful by countries immediately concerned".[154] The wide support from Central and Eastern Europe its proposal to continue to study East-West interconnections received seems to confirm that plenty of countries did find it useful. This might be linked with the significant improvement of relations between ECE and CMEA. Before 1965, ECE officials only occasionally participated in CMEA meetings of a specialized nature. That year the ECE Secretariat was invited for the first time to take part in some CMEA committees – those on coal, electric power, statistics, and automation.[155] Contact and collaboration between the two bodies would grow closer in the next couple of years. In 1969 the Executive Committee of the CMEA labeled its cooperation with the ECE Secretariat "particularly useful and intensive".[156]

While ECE remained a place for East-West negotiations, it inspired other developments outside of ECE's scope. By 1965 an informal group had formed, comprising Austria, Czechoslovakia, and Poland. Although not an official group, they convened in the Palais des Nations (ECE's headquarters in Geneva) to discuss proposals whereby electricity would be transmitted to Austria. Austria in turn then

---

150 Ibid.
151 Ibid.
152 "Yugoslavia's Economic Relations with the West since 1948 and the Relevance of this Experience to the Present Situation of the Eastern European Countries," 24 May 1965, file AC/127, document WP/156, NATO.
153 Harriman to Tesoro, 3 December 1964, RG 59, file 2, box 939, NACP.
154 Telegram U.S. Mission Geneva to Department of State, 3 December 1965, RG 59, file 2, box 939, NACP. The term "obnoxious" was used in an Airgram from U.S. Mission Geneva to Dept of State, 17 November 1965, RG 59, file 2, box 939, NACP.
155 "Cooperation with Council for Mutual Economic Assistance (CMEA)," 8 February 1966, ARR 14, file 1856, UNOG.
156 Cited in Kostelecký to Stanovnik, 29 April 1968, ARR 14, file 1856, UNOG.

increased its capabilities of exporting electricity to the neighboring FRG, Italy and Switzerland.[157] This bilateral approach had already born fruit and would eventually do so again.

The path of least resistance: Austria and Yugoslavia

In the course of the 1970s, the prospects of meeting future electricity demands came under future pressure. To one extent, the price of oil skyrocketed after a boycott of Arab petroleum suppliers. In addition, societal opposition to construction of transmissions lines and power plants grew. This was related to environmental concerns in general as well as resistance to nuclear energy more specifically. In 1973 the Organization of Arab Petroleum Exporting Countries (OAPEC) targeted its "oil weapon" mainly against Denmark, the Netherlands, Portugal, Rhodesia, South Africa, and the United States, as a repercussion for the Western support for Israel during the Yom Kippur War. The crisis, starting in October 1973, had two distinctive phases; first, a drop in oil production, and second, a steep price increase. The crisis did not result in an acute supply crisis. As a general rule, Western European countries kept 90 days of oil reserve and had about 30 additional days in shipment. Nor was the embargo well organized.[158] The high oil prices nevertheless presented a challenge to Western Europe, including the electricity sector. This challenge was all the greater because the future of atomic energy had become dim. It was no longer perceived as a viable alternative to classic thermal plants in most European countries. During the 1960s, growth had been already lower than anticipated.[159]

Another issue for the sector was the increased awareness of environmental pollution and societal opposition to new projects in general, resulting in "painfully slow approval procedures, sharpened environmental regulations, and drastic price hikes [making] the construction of new generation units and expansion of the transmission network increasingly more difficult".[160] Increasingly, the electricity supply industry had difficulties obtaining approval for expanding generation ca-

---

157 Telegram U.S. Mission Geneva to Department of State, 3 December 1965, RG 59, file 2, box 939, NACP.
158 Romano Prodi and Alberto Clô, "Europe," *Daedalus* 104, no. 4 (1975): 97-98.
159 For example, the report *A Target for Euratom* spoke of a contribution of 15 million kW by nuclear energy to the total electricity generation capacity by 1967. In practice, by early 1965 only 3,5 million kW was installed in the Community. Calculated on the basis of ECE, *The Electric Power Situation in Europe in 1964-1965 and its Future Prospects* (United Nations: New York, 1966): 54-56, table 24. Figure is gross production capacity.
160 UCPTE, *Rapport Annuel 1981-1982* (Rhode-St.Genese: UCPTE, 1983), 305.

pacity and the network, not only from governments but also from the general public. An example was given in the 1975-1976 Annual Report of UCPTE. In April 1976 a 220-kV line a 220 kV line between Kelsterbach and Uberach (both FRG) short-circuited following a brushfire. Local electricity supply failed immediately, and other adjacent lines were shut off as well, because they were overloaded. This situation overburdened yet more lines, with the result that large parts of Bavaria and Austria experienced a blackout that lasted between eight minutes to two hours.[161] According to UCPTE, this interruption should not have taken place, if the construction of the 380 kV line Grosskrotzenburg – Uberach – Burgstadt had been completed. This transmission line, originally scheduled to enter operation in 1972, was stymied by opposition of municipalities, landowners, and action committees.[162]

These factors not only put pressure on the current practices of network-building and operation, but also the security of supply of electricity. The electrical industry – again – looked to the East. The two countries that had previously seen the least political resistance to East-West linkages, Austria and Yugoslavia, led the way. In both countries HVDC interconnections with the CDO network were built. The adoption of HVDC helped to overcome differences in system operation. In April 1974 the UCPTE held a discussion on electricity trade. Austrian Wilhelm Erbacher, then UCPTE president, noted that in the future larger trade flows of electricity between UCPTE-members would become more complicated for two reasons. First, he pointed to social opposition against to the construction of plants and lines. Second, he stressed that in the current difficult situation, domestic utilization of electricity and other energy sources had priority. The latter issue had already showed during the oil crisis, when exchange was less then normal, and only mutual assistance in emergency situations increased (see Figure 5.7). In the light of these difficulties, Erbacher proposed several options, including more flexible exchange and export agreements as well as Western financing the construction of plants in countries with domestic reserves of primary energy sources, such as Poland.[163]

Central and Eastern European countries were both *attractive* and *attracted* to satisfying Western European energy needs. Within CMEA, petroleum was priced according to a formula based on five-year averages. Even though prices did increase, they did so only gradually and so the Eastern European did not felt the immediate impact of the oil crisis since they were not fully exposed to world market prices.[164] In addition, due to decreasing economic growth rates in the 1960s

---

161 UCPTE, *Rapport Annuel 1975-1976* (Arnhem: UCPTE, 1977), 91.
162 Ibid.
163 Meeting Comité Restreint, 9 March 1974, UCTE Archives, Brussels (hereafter: UCTE).
164 Kazimierz Grzybowski, "The Council for Mutual Economic Assistance and the European Community," *The American Journal of International Law* 84, no. 1 (1990): 491.

Central and Eastern European countries were not able to finance their Western imports by the export of raw material and industrial products alone. The extension of credit in East-West trade added to their indebtedness. As a consequence, the CMEA program of development and integration became sidetracked.[165] From this vantage point, trade with the Western world was a way to obtain hard foreign currency, especially as Poland and Hungary had serious debt problems. This provided an incentive to raise energy exports to the West – including electric energy.

Erbacher, the chairman of the *Österreichische Elektrizitätswirtschaft AG* (Verbund), clearly intended to obtain Central and Eastern European energy sources. In 1954 he had already been part of the negotiations for an interconnection between Austria and Czechoslovakia. In October of the same year, Erbacher informed the UCPTE of a deal between Verbund and Polish authorities. The contract, with a term of 25 years, comprised an Austrian loan of 3 billion Schillings to enable Poland to buy Austrian electrical equipment. The price of the electricity transmitted to Austria was partially fixed, and for 70 per cent determined by world market prices of solid and liquid fuels – radically different from the Polish price structure of fuels.[166] This deal in principle sealed deliberations going on since 1948, and the bilateral talks outside of the ECE-framework started in 1964. In 1974, Erbacher made explicit reference to the latter planning group consisting of Austria, Poland and Czechoslovakia, and that Austria started to look into the possibilities of building Direct Current connections.[167] The result of that strategy can be read from Figure 5.7, as Austria's electricity imports from CDO increased after 1968, and saw even further expansion during the two fuel crises.

It must be stressed that Austria's solution to utilize electricity from Eastern neighbors was to a certain extent obvious because of its history of collaboration and its geography. Most other Western European countries did not pursue East-West connections as an option, simply because their eastern border did not coincide with the Iron Curtain. Yet more western situated countries were able to make use of electricity generated in Central and Eastern Europe as Austria established itself as a transit country between East and West. This role was especially sought after by Erbacher's successor, Walter Fremuth (born 1931). He wanted Austria to become a *Drehscheibe* ("turntable") in Europe, between the UCPTE and CDO systems. From the outset, he not only intended to strengthen Austria's domestic network, but also wanted to "build strong connections with all neighbors, with the

---

165 Lewis, *Central*, 217.
166 Meeting Comité Restreint, 9 October 1974, UCTE.
167 Ibid.

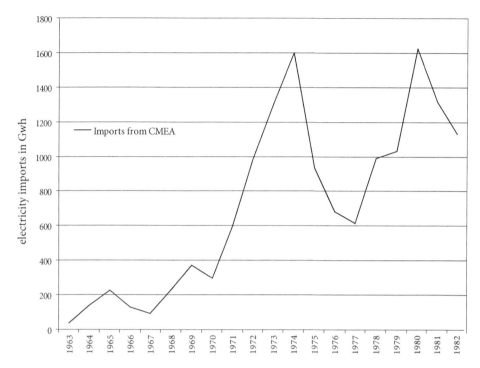

Figure 5.7 – Austrian electricity imports from CMEA, 1968-1982 (in GWh)
Source: UNECE, Annual Bulletin of Electric Energy Statistics for Europe, *several years.*

exception of Liechtenstein".[168]

As chairman of Verbund, Fremuth also had good reasons to strengthen relations with Central and Eastern Europe. He also had to deal with Austria's electricity
supply which was under threat, due to a growing number of out-of-date thermal
power plants and problems surrounding the nuclear power plant Zwentendorf.[169]
The latter had cost 9 billion Schillings, but could not be taken into operation because of societal opposition to atomic energy as a whole.[170] As Zwentendorf remained inoperative, other sources of energy should be found to cover Austria's
needs. Fremuth saw Czechoslovakia, Poland and the Soviet Union as possible energy suppliers to meet domestic demands. Yet it also fitted with his overall ideas
about European collaboration. In terms of energy, Europe – encompassing both

---

168 Walter Fremuth, interviewed by the author, 8-9 March 2007. The remark about Liechtenstein was
meant ironic and should be taken with a grain of salt.
169 "Verbundgeneral Fremuth: "Mister 100.000 Volt"," *A3 Volt. Das österreichische Magazin für Elektronik
und Elektrotechnik* November/December (1980): 14.
170 See Helmut Hirsch and Helga Nowotny, "Information and Opposition in Austrian Nuclear Energy
Policy," *Minerva* 15, no. 3-4 (1977): 316-334.

East and West in Fremuth's mind – only had limited resources. That alone provided an important incentive for European collaboration. Several years after WWII, Fremuth had joined the Pan European movement.[171] He was, and still is, convinced of the necessity for economic and political cooperation in Europe. In addition, Fremuth also had considerable experience in doing business with Socialist countries. Through his previous job as General Director of the *Girozentrale und Bank der Österreichischen Sparkassen AG*, Fremuth was well-connected in economic and political circles of the GDR and the Soviet Union. As chairman of Verbund he was backed by Austrian Bundeskanzler Bruno Kreisky, who not only supported Fremuth's efforts to secure electricity suppliers from Czechoslovakia and Poland, but also was a known proponent of East-West détente.[172]

One of Fremuth's first measures was to construct two new thermal power plants. Initially this plan was opposed by the Green party, who objected to the pollution from coal-fired plants. Eventually Verbund decided to use the best possible technologies to minimize the polluting effects.[173] Interestingly enough, the coal fired in these newly-built plants largely came from Poland. Through an arrangement made in 1980, Austria imported large quantities of hard coal from Poland at an indexed price. In addition, the earlier proposed option of Direct Current connection was also – successfully – pursued. On September 1, 1983 an interconnection station in Dürnrohr, Austria became operational (see Figure 5.8, north-west of Vienna). According to an Austrian engineer, it was "a milestone on the way to a new era in electricity transport with Austria playing a central role in electricity transit between East and West".[174] The link with a capacity of 550 MW was of the High Voltage direct current back-to-back type (HVDC), connected 380 kV Austrian power lines with 400 kV Czechoslovak ones at the Slavětice substation. Before the implementation of HVDC, island operation was the only possible option for exchanging power between the two large continental systems. Now both countries did not have to isolate parts of their system in order to exchange electricity. The basis of the new link was the contract between Austria and Poland, by which the

---

171 He eventually stepped out of the Movement as he opposed the course taken by Otto von Bismarck. Fremuth, interview by the author, 8-9 March 2007.

172 Ibid. At several occasions, Kreisky spoke out for more East-West collaboration, also in the field of energy. In a talk given at Chatham House, London, in July 1978, he underlined that "[t]here can be no doubt that an all-European cooperation in the energy sector, which is not only imaginable but also feasible, may well be realised and would constitute a strong link between East and West European economies". See Bruno Kreisky, "On Promoting Detente," *International Affairs* 54, no. 4 (1978): 621-622.

173 Fremuth, interview by the author, 8-9 March 2007.

174 Allmer, "Extension."

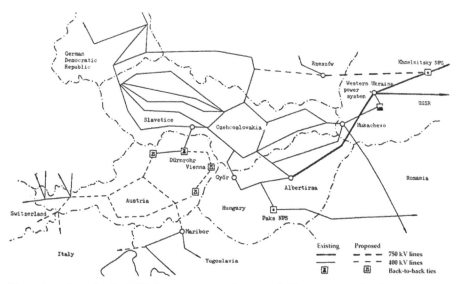

Figure 5.8 – Cross-border HVDC connections and 400-750 kV lines in Central and Eastern Europe, existing and proposed in 1985
Source: UNECE, Group of Experts on Problems of Planning and Operating Large Power Systems, 17th Session, 1985, *UN doc, ser., EP/GE.2/R.73 (Geneva: UNECE, 1985).*

latter supplied power through Czechoslovakia.[175] Over a period of 13 years some 1,600 GWh was transmitted to Austria annually, on a capacity of 400 MW. Already during the planning phase, the Swiss *Elektrizitätsgesellschaft Laufenberg* contacted the Verbund for a 150 MW participation. This HVDC allowed for the first time large exchanges of electricity between the systems of the UCPTE and the CDO. The capacity of the HVDC link thus was rated at 550 MW.[176]

The Austrian HVDC interconnection inspired others. A 1985 ECE Seminar in Stockholm focused upon HVDC and its possible applications in Europe as subject. Many papers featured Dürnrohr, or mentioned its success. This increased contact – and interconnection with the East – was obviously not only due to an improved transmission technology. It thrived in an environment of better overall relations between East and West, and with Western Europe interested in tapping into new

175 V. Novotny, "The First Experience of the Back-to-Back HVDC Link of the Czechoslovak and Austrian Power Systems," in *UNECE Seminar on High Voltage Direct Current Techniques, Stockholm, 6-9 May, 1985,* UN doc, ser., EP/SEM.10/Report no. 21 (Geneva: UNECE, 1985).
176 G Moraw and K.W. Kanngiesser, "The HVDC Back-to-Back Tie Duernrohr as Synchronous Link between the Eastern and Western European Super Grids: Technical Data and Required System Performance," in *UNECE Seminar on High Voltage Direct Current Techniques, Stockholm, 6-9 May, 1985,* UN doc, ser., EP/ SEM.10/report no. 23 (Geneva: UNECE, 1985).

sources of energy.[177] Although Cold War tensions did mount on several occasions, the forms of cooperation established in the 1960s and 1970s proved to be lasting and stable. In 1968 ECE had set up a Group of Experts on Problems of Planning and Operating of Large Power Systems. Although not directly clear from its name, the group studied – amongst other subjects – methods and possibilities to strengthen interconnections between East and West. Interestingly enough, the ECE now coordinated this work with the power pools. UCPTE, UFIPTE, NORDEL, and SUDEL were all given an opportunity to review the draft document, and send revisions, recommendations and corrections.[178] This suggests widespread interest in East-West relations.

Within ECE, efforts were also made to integrate the Balkan region, where no regional pool existed. These included plans for HVDC interconnection between Yugoslavia and the CDO network. The first steps towards integrating the Balkan area were made in the mid-1970s by the ECE, in collaboration with the United Nations Development Program (UNDP). Together they set up a new program wherein Yugoslavia was central, the so-called *Electric Power Transmission Systems of the Balkan countries* project (Balkan project).[179] The main objectives of interconnecting the region were to reduce national reserve capacities, coordinate possible seasonal exchanges, and eventually to import and export electricity. Around the same time, UNDP started so-called European Co-operative Programs, based on the results of the Helsinki Conference on Co-operation and Security in Europe (CSCE).[180]

The CSCE institutionalized the process of détente, as countries from all parts of Europe participated in an effort to promote better mutual confidence, secure political relations, and to expand collaboration in the field of economy, science, technology, and environment.[181] ECE was recognized by the CSCE as an important forum for strengthening overall economic bonds in Europe, a role ECE had longed to play for quite some time. Yet whereas the Final Act spoke out for more

---

177 This also included natural gas and oil, which will not be dealt with here. See for example Bruce W. Jentleson, *Pipeline Politics: The Complex Political Economy of East-West Energy Trade* (Ithaca: Cornell University Press, 1986).
178 UNECE, *Ad Hoc Group of Experts on Problems of Planning and Operating Large Power Systems, 2nd Session, 'Transfers of Electric Power Across European Frontiers and Future Prospects', March 31, 1969*, UN doc, ser., EP/WP.8/Working paper No.1/Rev.1 (Geneva: UNECE, 1969).
179 The others were Romania, Turkey, Greece, Albania, and Bulgaria.
180 "Coordination Committee for the Studies Relating to the Development of the Interconnection of the Electric Power Transmission Systems of the Balkan Countries, Fifth Session," 6-9 December 1977, registry fonds GX, file 19/6/1/15-32212, UNOG.
181 CSCE, *Conference on Security and Co-operation in Europe: Final Act* (Helsinki: CSCE, 1975). Though "mutual confidence" is not explicitly mentioned in the Final Act, a lot of stress is placed upon building a relation of confidence between European countries.

"exchanges of electrical energy within Europe with a view to utilizing the capacity of the electrical power stations as rational as possible",[182] earlier drafts had proposed ECE as the leading organization, and called for the "unification of electrical power systems".[183] Yet for ECE not to achieve these broader aims did not seem much of an issue, as it still regarded itself as a pivotal player in the process. An ECE official explained in 1985 that "whenever interconnection concerns countries of Eastern and Western Europe, it falls inevitably within the mandate of the *Economic Commission for Europe*".[184]

In practice, however, ECE did stimulate electricity exchanges and network unification. A significant part of the Group of Experts focused on possibilities to reinforce East-West interconnections. This was mostly true for Balkan project as well. Already in 1968 a British consultant mentioned to the director of the CoEP that by expanding HV transmission lines between the Balkan countries "[...] Greece would thereby come into the orbit of a general European interchange".[185] An important technical obstacle existed, however. Some of the participating countries were synchronized with the CDO system, whereas the Yugoslav system operated at the same frequency as the Western European countries. This necessitated additional study.[186]

Yugoslavian authorities strongly spoke out for close relations with both UCPTE and CDO. At a UNIPEDE conference in 1976, a representative claimed that "[i]t is unacceptable for the Yugoslav system to operate permanently in parallel operation only with one of the European interconnections, whereas the periodical operation with either one or the other interconnection, depending on current energy and economic interests, could not naturally be accepted as a way of operation by those interconnections".[187] By applying HVDC, the Balkan countries could choose whether they would remain synchronous with the large regional networks; it was a way of forging East-West interconnections without large-scale adaptation of the

---

182 Ibid., 21.

183 In particular, both Austria and the Soviet Union stressed such a role for ECE inserted in the Final Act. The United States clearly thought otherwise. Handwritten notes on these drafts by U.S. policy-makers strongly suggest their objections. On a Soviet proposal for long-term collaboration in the field of energy under the aegis of ECE it was written "unacceptable". Various notes in a folder labeled "Conference on Security and Cooperation in Europe (CSCE) 1976-1979",RG 59, file 3.4: Office of Soviet Union Affairs, box 1, NACP.

184 UNIPEDE, *Twentieth Congress, Athens 1985, Proceedings of the Working Sessions and Other Functions* (Paris: Imprimerie Chaix, 1985), 305. The quote is from the ECE Director of the Energy Division, Mario Trigo Trinidade.

185 K. Goldsmith to Gustaaf van Rhijn, 4 June 1968, registry fonds GX, file 19/6/1/16-38412, UNOG.

186 Ibid.

187 Representative of the Yugoslav power company in UNIPEDE, *Seventeenth Congress, Vienna 1976, Proceedings of the Working Sessions and Other Functions* (Paris: Imprimerie Chaix, 1976), 308.

Table 5.2 – The Yugoslav grid between East and West, 1955-1980

	Number of interconnections*		Imports (GWh)		Exports (GWh)	
	with CDO	with UCPTE	From CDO	From UCPTE	to CDO	to UCPTE
1955	0	3	0	0	0	44
1960	1	4	0	30	94	30
1970	6	7	162	199	78	74
1980	10	10	1,132	175	464	1,249

* interconnection lines above 50 kV only.
Calculated on basis of: UNECE, *Annual Bulletin*; and UNECE, *The Electric Power Situation in Europe*, various years.

regional systems – and avoiding a though technical yet political decision. Yugoslavia could thus remain "unaligned", or at least aligned with both.

Eventually Yugoslavia chose to be synchronously connected to the UCPTE system. Being synchronized with Western Europe necessitated closer collaboration as well – more than with Eastern Europe. But it also profited from its linkages with its eastern neighbors. Yugoslavia would also finally start to commonly exploit the hydroelectric potential of the Iron Gate, at her eastern borders. From 1975 Yugoslavia was in parallel operation with Italy. It became a full UCPTE-member in October 1987, making Yugoslavia "officially" a full and interconnected partner of the Western European system, although it had been in close touch with the UCPTE for decades.[188] With that, Greece also became connected the Western European system. If we look at Table 5.2, we see how Yugoslavia's connections to both East and West grew substantially in the 1960s and 1970s. In addition, one can also observe how Yugoslavia's "bridge" function between the two parts of Europe developed. During the 1970s, Yugoslavia became net-importer of electricity from Central and Eastern Europe, while it became a net-exporter to its Western neighbors (see Table 5.2).

Uniting Europe

The development of interconnections between the systems of CDO and UCPTE was accelerated after the mid-1980s. At a UNIPEDE meeting in 1988, more connections between East and West were announced. Austria planned several HVDC

---

188 UCPTE, *Rapport Annuel 1986-1987* (Heidelberg: UCPTE, 1988).

links with the Soviet Union and Hungary, and the FRG also agreed on connecting with the Soviets and the GDR.[189] Several of these are depicted in Figure 5.9. Note how a ticker dark borderline separates the Eastern and Western parts of Europe, and how Yugoslavia is placed on the Western side of the Iron Curtain.

The most symbolic indicator of détente and of East-West network development was renewed interest for interconnections between the FRG and the GDR in the course of the 1980s. This was a vexed issue in the early 1960s, as it aroused strong criticism from both the FRG and the United States. The idea of inter-German collaboration was never dead and buried, however. After rejecting the ECE suggestion in 1965, the FRG itself started to consider building a transmission line to West Berlin in 1974.[190] Although this would not have entailed direct cooperation with the GDR, the proposed line was to cross the latter country's territory. At the same time, both "Germanies" were part of the CSCE by which they pledged to increase and improve relations between European countries – included between each other.

At a 1988 meeting a FRG engineer presented plans to connect West and East Germany, as well as the West Berlin to the FRG. It foresaw in the construction of a HVDC transmission line, which should be operational by 1991.[191] The link was applauded by ECE. According to Mario Trinidade, ECE Energy Division director, this was "a step towards developing the potential to increase the level of optimization of the European electrical supply system, by removing some interconnection constraints".[192] Yet to Trinidade its value exceeded economic significance alone. Trinidade expressed his enthusiasm in a fashion that reminds us of Interwar arguments. Besides helping to optimize European electricity systems, the interconnection between the FRG and GDR showed "that electric power lines can carry not only electric power but a refreshing message of peace and this should be very rewarding for us all".[193]

The 1988 UNIPEDE meeting saw two papers about the future structure of Europe's electricity supply. One report by a group of experts dealt with the prospects of system operations and control. It suspected that problems related to these latter issues would substantially grow, but at the same time the "structure of the

---

189 See the table in Ibid., 368.

190 One such instance was a Meeting Comité Restreint in 1974. A representative of the RWE explained there that the possibility of building an AC 400-kV line between the FRG to West Berlin, and on to Poland was under scrutiny. Meeting of the Comité Restrein, 11 January 1974, UCTE.

191 This plan was presented in a general discussion on interconnections. See UNIPEDE, *Twenty-First Songress, Sorrento 1988*, vol. 2, *Proceedings of the Working Sessions and Other Functions* (Paris: Imprimerie Chaix, 1988), 377.

192 Ibid., 365-366.

193 Ibid., 377-378.

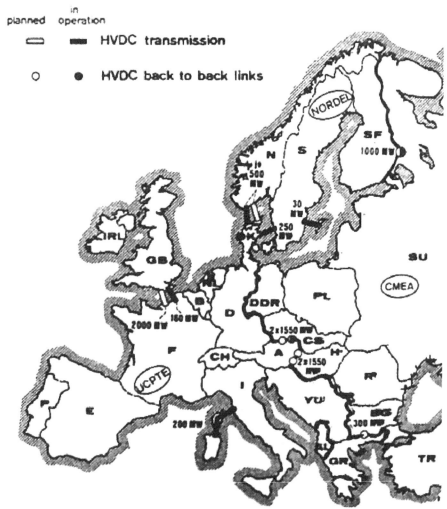

Figure 5.9 – European power pools and HVDC links in 1985
Source: G. Moraw and K.W. Kanngiesser, "The HVDC back-to-back tie Duernrohr as asyn-
chronous link between the Eastern and Western European super grids; Technical data and re-
quired system performance," in UNECE Seminar on High Voltage Direct Current techniques,
Stockholm, May, 1985, *UN doc, ser., EP/SEM.10/report no. 23 (Geneva: UNECE, 1985).*

European power system will not undergo much change over the next decade".[194]
The next year's social-political turmoil heralded further developments that proved
these expectations wrong. Another UNIPEDE report on interconnections was

---

194 M. Pavard, "Long-Term Prospects for the Development of Operation and Control of European Interconnected Systems (report 40.2)," in UNIPEDE, *Twenty-First Congress, Sorrento 1988,* vol. 2, 1.

more accurate, predicting more "uncertainty" for the next 10 years.[195] On the evening of November 11, 1989, an enthusiastic crowd started to tear down the wall dividing Berlin. The unification of the two Germanies was only a matter of time, taking place in 1990. The interconnection of the networks of the former FRG and GDR proved more time-consuming. Three separate systems existed: the FRG network, which was synchronous with the UCPTE network, the GDR network in parallel with the CDO system, and the electricity system of West Berlin which functioned as an island. Towards the end of 1992 West Berlin was even in synchronous operation with the CDO network for a while. Only in September 1995 would the grids of East and West Germany be linked. Commenting on the consolidation of the GDR into the new FRG in 1990, a representative of the UCPTE observed that "[f]or the first time politicians were ahead of electricians".[196]

Political change was not limited to Germany alone. In several Central and Eastern European countries, the power of the Communist Party had seriously eroded. Nationalistic aspirations proliferated and were nourished, as national historical figures and concepts were revitalized. The idea of distinct Central Europe, or *Mitteleuropa*, became en vogue in the 1980s. According to the East German dissident Rudolf Bahro the preconditions for an undivided Europe was to create circumstances that would enable the Soviet Union to "let Eastern Europe go".[197] Constructing transnational infrastructures that connected Western to Eastern Europe was such a condition. The opportunity arose in 1991 with the break-up of the Soviet Union, whereby Central and Eastern European countries lost their Soviet tutelage.

Already in 1990, Hungary had announced that it wanted to operate its own network synchronized with the UCPTE system.[198] Although officials of the Austrian Verbund expressed their support for synchronous operation of CMEA countries, other UCPTE member were more hesitant.[199] This is confirmed by Walter Fremuth, at that time an influential figure within UCPTE. He remembered that several more western located countries initially were hesitant to enter synchronous intercon-

---

195 C. Barbesino, "Problems and Methods of Planning National and International Connections (Report 88E.40.1)," in *Twenty-first congress, Sorrento 1988*, vol. 2, 2.

196 "Pour la première fois les politiciens sont en avance sur les electriciens." Meeting Comité Restreint, 16-17 October 1990, UCTE.

197 Cited in Hans-Georg Betz, "Mitteleuropa and Post-Modern European Identity," *New German Critique* 50 (1990): 176-177.

198 Meeting Comité Restreint, 17-18 April 1990, UCTE; and Meeting of Comité Restreint, 24 January 1990, UCTE.

199 Ibid. Judging from the meeting's report, it was a Dutch UCPTE member that wanted to postpone a discussion on synchronous interconnection with Central and Eastern European countries.

nection with Central and Eastern Europe.[200] In any event, also Austrian members – including Fremuth – were of the opinion that such a structural change would require several years to be completed. The region would need considerable investments in order to be able to meet the technical standards in force in Western Europe. For the moment, Fremuth advised that new interconnections should be of the HVDC type.[201]

Despite some hesitant voices, a first meeting between representatives of CDO and UCPTE was held in Amsterdam in 1990. Gradually, more within UCPTE grew to consider seriously synchronous interconnection of Central and Eastern European countries. CDO members' wish for joining the UCPTE also was economically motivated. Since January 1991 Central and Eastern European countries had to pay for Russian energy sources with convertible currency, resulting in a relative price increase.[202] The now renewed discussion on the future of the electricity network in Europe was under scrutiny by three different sources; a mixed UNIPEDE-UCPTE group, a Nordel-UCPTE group, and an internal UCPTE group on East-West connections.[203] The role of the ECE, the most constant promoter of such interconnection, was rather negligible this time. Neither Fremuth in Austria nor the UCPTE had any sort of extended contact with ECE regarding the rapprochement towards Central and Eastern Europe.[204] Reflecting upon the process of change, ECE itself underlined its facilitating role in the preceding decades:

> For 40 years, the ECE has been the only forum where those responsible in the East and West could set their projects face to face and make their policies known. [...] The men which it had brought together formed, at the moment when political evolution allowed it, an immediately available core to start up the integration projects [...].[205]

The study conducted by the UNIPEDE-UCPTE working group indicated that synchronous interconnection would be possible, but only after technical issues were solved.[206] It estimated that it would take between five and ten years before

---

200 Fremuth, interview by the author, 8-9 March 2007.
201 Meeting Comité Restreint, 17-18 April 1990, UCTE.
202 Meeting Comité Restreint, 16-17 October 1990, UCTE.
203 Meeting Comité Restreint, 7 July 1992, UCTE.
204 Fremuth, interview by the author, 8-9 March 2007. My own extensive research in the ECE archives confirm Fremuth's statement. I only retrieved a very limited correspondence between Geneva and Vienna, or with UCPTE on the subject.
205 J. Thiry, "Interconnection of European Electric Power Systems: Present Situation and Prospects up to the Year 2000," in *IEA/OECD Seminar on East-West Energy Trade* (Vienna: IEA/OECD, 1991), 159-178.
206 Henri Persoz and Jean Remondeulaz, "Consolidating European Power," *IEEE Spectrum* 29, no. 10 (1992): 65.

the interconnection was a fact. The study also estimated the economic benefits of interconnection at a decrease of operation costs of some 100 million US$ per year.[207] Synchronous interconnection should initially focus on Czechoslovakia, Poland and Hungary and only later would Rumania, Bulgaria and Turkey be considered.[208] The Central and Eastern European countries – Czechoslovakia, Hungary, and Poland – in turn responded by establishing a new regional organization, CENTREL, in October 1992.[209] Within CENTREL they undertook a series of organizational and technical measures to reach the same reliability as the UCPTE system. Thereafter further steps towards synchronized interconnection were undertaken.[210] In the meantime the UCPTE working group on CENTREL, headed by Fremuth, prepared for synchronization.[211] At that time the interconnection was scheduled for 1997 at the earliest.[212] CENTREL countries, however, were very dedicated to pressing ahead faster. According to Michel Albert, then UCPTE vice-chairman, they desired to complete the interconnection at "the earliest possible stage". Such sentiments were shared in Western Europe. Two engineers involved in the UNIPEDE-UCPTE working group underlined the need for a speedy process. This was not only because East-West interconnections were intertwined with the long-term perspectives of Europe's electricity system, but also because "Europe is making history very quickly today, and those involved in electric power cannot afford to be left behind".[213] They continued to stress that "the interest of electric interconnections and the solidarity it represents is too great for experts in electricity not to achieve their goal [...]".[214]

CENTREL countries met UCPTE operational standards sooner than anticipated, in September 1993. CENTREL proved to be able to operate according to UCPTE standards without the actual interconnection.[215] The actual interconnection of the CENTREL and UCPTE network took place on October 18, 1995, at 12.30 pm.[216] The electrical divide between East and West had been bridged. Only one month after the merger of the German systems was successfully completed, four Central and Eastern European countries were connected to the Western

---

207 Meeting Comité Restreint, 16-17 October 1990, UCTE.
208 Meeting Comité Restreint, 8 March 1992, UCTE; and Persoz & Remondeulaz, "Consolidating," 65.
209 Czechoslovakia would split into the Czech Republic and Slovakia in 1993.
210 Michel Albert, "Enlarged Interconnection Between the East and the UCPTE," *Perspectives in Energy* 4 (1997): 16.
211 Interview Fremuth, March 8-9, 2007.
212 Meeting Comité Restreint, 21 March 1993, UCTE.
213 Persoz and Remondeulaz, "Consolidating," 65.
214 Ibid.
215 T.J. Hammons et al., "European Policy on Electricity Infrastructure, Interconnections, and Electricity Exchanges," *IEEE Power Engineering Review* 18, no. 1 (1998): 14.
216 Albert, "Enlarged," 17.

European system. After a year of operation without problems, HVDC connections between the two regional networks were shut down as unnecessary.[217] In 2001 all four countries became full UCPTE members. The developments provoked references to earlier proposals for a Europe-wide network. Two German engineers brought into remembrance how Oskar Oliven envisioned an "all-European" interconnected electricity system in 1930. "In those days the ideas of Oliven were considered a vision', they explained, 'but today such ideas have become realistic".[218]

Creating a European Market

The synchronous interconnection of the UCPTE with former CDO-countries took place within the framework of cooperation between network operators, started in the 1950s. The European Community – the European Union (EU) since 1992 – contributed to this process only indirectly. The majority of feasibility studies in Poland, the Czech Republic, Slovakia, and Hungary were financial supported through the EU's PHARE program.[219] PHARE was called into being to prepare former CMEA countries to accede to the EU, which eventually took place in 2004. A more direct influence was felt by the electricity sector when the EC pressed on with its plan for a Common Market – later renamed the Internal Market – for electricity.[220]

A European electricity system was clearly constructed outside the process of European integration, which started with the *European Coal and Steel Community* (ECSC) in 1951. Although it observed the work of UNIPEDE, and the electricity committees of both OEEC and ECE, the ECSC did not deal with electricity transmission itself.[221] Energy policy was discussed in the negotiation process that led to the signing of the Treaty of Rome in 1957, which established the *European*

---

217 Hammons et al, "European Policy," 14.
218 Harald Brumshagen and Jürgen Schwarz, "The European Power Systems on the Threshold of a New East-West Co-Operation," *IEEE Transactions on Energy Conversion* 11, no. 2 (1996): 474.
219 Albert, "Enlarged," p.16. PHARE originally was the abbreviation of *Pologne Hongrie Aide à la Reconstruction Economique*, but gradually its aid was distributed to other Central and Eastern European, and Balkan countries.
220 More elaborate publications have been published on the politics of the European Community and the internal energy market. See for example Padgett, "The Single"; and Schmidt, *Liberalisierung*. Here the main focus will be on how this effect the electricity industry.
221 This is a general observation in consulting the archives of the European Commission and High Authority. For the 1950s and 1960s, the ECSC archives hold a wide range of publications by the OEEC and OECD, ECE, and UNIPEDE.

Economic Community (EEC).[222] Amongst other aspects, the EEC aimed for a gradual progress towards a general common market. Although the energy sector was identified as one where urgent action was needed, the intention to start up the integration of the "classic" energy sector was not part of the Treaty.[223] Only the "modern" nuclear energy sector became a spearhead for integration in the newly set up *Atomic Energy Community*, or Euratom (1957).[224] Thus in 1957, energy policy became divided over three different bodies: coal was dealt with by the ECSC, nuclear energy was part of Euratom's tasks, and electricity and gas fell under the EEC. To formulate an energy policy, the three Communities formed an *Interexecutive Working Group* starting in 1959.[225] It drafted several policy documents including major ones in 1961[226] and 1964[227] in order to initiate an energy policy.

With the signing of the Merger Treaty in 1965 (in force since 1967), the three Communities transformed into the *European Community* (EC). The Working Group was thereby dissolved and replaced by the Directorate-General for Energy (DG XVII). Although countries of the European Community were struck by the 1973 Arab oil embargo, this did not immediately lead to an extension of Community energy policy.[228] Just several months before the oil crisis, several meetings on potential problems with Middle East oil supply were held, but little agreement was reached.[229] While the EC failed to organize a common, the major

---

222 "Commission de l'énergie classique: Projet de rapport," 10 October 1955, fonds 3: Negotiations for the Treaties institutionalising the EEC and EURATOM, File Nego 65: Comité Intergouvernemental créé par la Conférence de Messine, document Mae 441 f/55 mvo, Central Archives of the Council of the European Union, Brussels (hereafter CACEU). On the EEC see Gerbet, *La construction*, 194.

223 Comité Intergouvernemental créé par la Conférence de Messine, *Rapport des Chefs de Délégation aux Ministres des Affaires Etrangères*, document Mae 120 f/56 (corrigé) (Brussels: Secrétariat, 1956), 126-129. According to this report, this was due to technical conditions, which prevented the setting up of a common market for electricity and gas, like existed for coal. A similar argument was made earlier by in a French memorandum to the Heesemann Committee. See "Memorandum de la delegation Francaise sur l'action européenne dans le domaine de l'énergie classique," fonds 3, file Nego 65, document Mae 407 d/55 doc.304, CACEU.

224 On the history of Euratom, see Pascal Girerd, *Trente ans d'expérience Euratom. La naissance d'une Europe nucléaire*, ed. Olivier Pirotte, Pierre Marsal, and Sylvaine Morson (Bruylant, 1988).

225 "Procedure pour l'élaboration d'une politique de l'énergie", Annex to Meeting of Interexcutive Working Group, 27 July 1959, collection High Authority of European Coal and Steel Community (hereafter CEAB), file 9: Division Economie et Energie, no. 624, Historical Archives of the European Commission, Brussels (hereafter: HEAC). This point is also made by Cailleau, "Energy," 472-474.

226 "Conseil special de ministres, 74ᵉ session, 16 mai 1961. Note introductive du Secretariat. Objet: Poursuite de l'échange de vues sur les problèmes posés par la coordination des politiques énergétiques," 5 May 1961, CEAB, file 2, no. 2074, document 279 f/61, HAEC.

227 This was the so-called *Protocol of Agreement on Energy Policy*, signed by the Council of Ministers. John A. Hassan and Alan Duncan, "Integrating Energy: The Problems of Developing an Energy Policy in the European Communities, 1945-1980," *Journal of European Economic History* 22, no. 1 (1994): 164.

228 Prodi and Clô have claimed that the recent expansion from six to nine countries did not help building consensus Prodi and Clô, "Europe," 91.

229 Lucas, *Energy*, 56-58.

attempt to stand up to the increasing oil prices came from across the Atlantic. The U.S. initiative to establish the International Energy Agency (IEA) and to develop contingency plans for oil within the OECD framework was willingly received by most Western countries.

Only after 1985 with the signing of the *Single European Act* (SEA) did the EC become an actor in the electricity sector. By means of the SEA the EC began to pursue a policy of completing the Common Market by 1992, also for energy. The aim of the internal market was to ensure the free movement of goods, persons, services and capital.[230] In 1985 the European Commission concluded that "Europe" was at a crossroads and should move forward to complete the Internal Market, so as not to "drop back into mediocrity".[231] According to the European Commission, it was "self-evident that a large market without internal frontiers could not be completed or operate properly unless the Community had instruments enabling it to avoid imbalances interfering with competitiveness and inhibiting the growth of Community as a whole".[232] This required the removal of physical barriers, such as frontier posts, fiscal barriers such as tariffs and duties, and finally the technical barriers to the free movement of goods and the freedom to provide services.[233]

There were a number of technical barriers for network-bound services such as gas and electricity. Though it was again not explicitly included in the Act, the Commission showed a clear interest in conducting energy policy. In 1986 the Commission clearly spoke out in favor of an internal energy market, whereby the electricity sector – among others – had to be liberalized.[234] With regard to electricity, the Commission's document *The Internal Market* praised the existence of a highly interconnected system in the Community, wherein only Ireland and Greece did not participate.[235] Furthermore, it recognized that international exchanges were managed without interference of executive powers, but by groups of electricity utilities such as UCPTE and Nordel.[236] These (voluntary) exchanges, power plants and transmission networks were controlled and "owned by monopolies".[237] The interconnections did therefore not constitute a common carrier system, meaning that no-one other than the owning parties had access to the network.

---

230 'Single European Act', in: *Official Journal of the European Communities*, L169, (1987), pp.1-29, there p.7.
231 European Commission, *Completing the Internal Market: White Paper from the Commission to the European Council*, COM (85) 310 final (Brussels, 1985), 57.
232 European Commission, "The Single Act: A New Frontier for Europe. Communication from the Commission to the Council," *Bulletin of the European Communities* 1/87 (1987): 7.
233 European Commission, *Completing*, 8.
234 A similar point is made by Schmidt, *Liberalisierung*, 191.
235 European Commission, *The Internal Energy Market*, COM (88) 238 final (Brussels, 1988), 68-69.
236 Ibid.
237 Ibid., 69.

The Commission argued that this system should transform into an open internal market, whereby electricity is produced on a competitive basis while being subject to the Community policy regarding environmental protection and Community energy policy.[238] Differences in fiscal and financial preferences granted to utilities, as well as state support, had to be harmonized within the Community. The same applied to ownership structures of network ownership and national electricity pricing systems. The latter in particular should be made more transparent.[239] The main benefits from the changes were argued to be an increase in energy trade between member states, a further rationalization of the sectors, an enhanced security of supply, and reduced energy costs.[240]

Interesting enough, the Commission's document seemed to downplay the process towards an integrated European system, which went as far back as the 1920s. Whereas it recognized the existing interconnectedness, it did not see this as "European". "The 'cost of non-Europe' in the energy sector", it wrote, "is affecting our economic performance [...]".[241] This was hardly a bone of contention for the electricity industry. The proposed changes were met with considerable opposition for other reasons. For one, the EC and UCPTE had different outlooks on the term "liberalization". The latter had already used the term for the removal of barriers to short and long-term exchange in the 1950s and 1960s. In 1987 UCPTE claimed that the industry itself had taken the initiative to liberalize cross-border electricity flows from early on, which put the sector ahead of other sectors.[242] In addition, it regularly stated that cross-border trade was hardly absent in the sector, and had been going for nearly 50 years.[243] For the EC, liberalization was about increasing the number of players.

Another point of friction was that the Commission's policy line required alterations in the structure of electricity production and transmission. This would potentially have significant consequences for the way UCPTE coordinated international flows of electricity. As utilities represented within UCPTE indeed held national or regional monopolies, complying with new regulations implied a separation – or *unbundling* – of their production and transmission activities. In addition, the respective networks had to be opened to so-called *Third Party Access*, that is, to new electricity producers. Taken together, these changes would fundamentally alter the membership structure of UCPTE. The Internal Market would lead to increased competition

---

238 Ibid., 70.
239 Ibid., 71 and 74.
240 Padgett, "The Single," 57.
241 European Commission, *The Internal*, 6.
242 UCPTE, *R.A. '86-'87*, 95.
243 UCPTE, *Rapport Annuel 1997* (Madrid: UCPTE, 1998), 13.

across borders between utilities that now closely coordinated and collaborated to arrange international exchanges. The common carrier principle was also expected to introduce new players to the market, further complicating international coordination. In addition, unbundling transmission and production gave rise to concerns about meeting future needs. In particular, UCPTE expected that competitive pressures would jeopardize the system's security. This in turn increased the possibilities of black-outs.[244] It stated that there was "a price to be paid for foreseeable changes resulting from the increase in the multiplicity of relations".[245] In 1992 then-president Walter Fremuth emphasized that the protection of consumers and the security of supplies could not be solely achieved by "the introduction of an organizational structure based exclusively upon competition".[246] In 1992 the EC, then renamed to the *European Union* (EU), also made its first strides in network-building. The 1992 Treaty on European Union had a special passage on Trans-European Networks, concerning transport, communication, and energy networks.[247] Through the TEN-program the EU sought to promote the interconnection of European countries, thereby strengthening the prerequisites for the internal market.

Although the sector expressed its objections the implementation of the internal electricity market it quite frankly had to comply with new regulations. The decisions were taken outside their sphere of influence, by their respective member states and the Commission. Organizational changes of UCPTE as well as UNIPEDE seem to reflect an understanding of the new reality. Both reoriented towards Brussels. In 1996 UCPTE president Michel Albert proclaimed that the 1996 Directive was "not entirely satisfactory" but an "acceptable position". Although UNIPEDE – the organization representing electricity producers – closely followed Community action, its global and open membership did not lend itself to responding efficiently to developments in Brussels.[248] The UCPTE agreed that it was important to have "clear and transparent" contacts with the Commissioner, Directorate-General for Energy and Transport, and their colleagues.[249] After some discussion, it was decided in 1990 to set up a new organization, to be able to represent the industry as a whole; the *European Grouping of the Electricity Supply Industry* (EURELECTRIC).[250] EURELECTRIC, which has established itself in the

244 Ibid., 15.
245 Ibid., 7.
246 UCPTE, *Rapport Annuel 1992* (Madrid: UCPTE, 1993), 9.
247 "Treaty on European Union," *Official Journal of the European Communities* C 191 (1992): article 129b.
248 Lyons, *75 Years*, 45.
249 UCPTE, *Rapport Annuel 1989* (Arnhem: UCPTE, 1990), 11.
250 UNIPEDE, *Annual Report 1992* (Paris: UNIPEDE, 1993), 60-61.

Belgian capital, was made up from representatives of the 12 member states, plus one each from UNIPEDE, Nordel, and the UCPTE. In 1991 it gained the status of European Economic Interest Grouping. UNIPEDE and EURELECTRIC merged in 1997.[251] UCPTE too settled permanently in Brussels in 2001, and since 1998 dropped the "P" of production from its name, signifying the advanced state of unbundling among its members.

In the process, a change of the basic functions of UCTE took place. In 1999 a new organization, the *European Transmission System Operators* (ETSO), was established by UCTE, Nordel, as well as the TSOs of Ireland and Great Britain. ETSO's prime tasks were to harmonize network access and conditions for usage, in particular for international electricity trade.[252] UCTE, on the other hand, took upon itself two primary tasks. First, UCTE focused upon system security, laying down the technical rules for system operation related to interconnected synchronous operation in the UCTE area. Second, it held a close watch on system adequacy, supplying information to members, market players, and authorities.[253]

The time-table set in 2003 for further liberalization implied that the electricity market should be open to all non-household consumers by July 1, 2004, and to all customers by July 1, 2007. Yet the EU did not only look to the future, but also to the East. Already in 2001 it suggested that the internal market could include non-EU members and candidate members.[254] The Commission explicitly mentioned the UCTE and CENTREL members, and also referred to the strengthening or new construction of interconnections between EU and non-EU members. It seems as if it wanted to have the internal market and the UCTE system coincide.

The EU substantially grew three years later. In May 2004 the European Union was expanded with 10 new members, most of which from Central and Eastern Europe.[255] UCTE viewed this step as a political move which was technically anticipated by UCTE.[256] Five out of ten new EU-members already participated within UCTE. It led the UCTE to conclude that it had been "a visionary pioneer of the European integration process".[257] Its "approach to system development proved to

---

251 Lyons, *75 Years*, 45.
252 See ETSO's website, http://www.etso-net.org/association/aboutus/etso/e_default.asp (Accessed October 21, 2007).
253 UCTE, *Rapport Annuel 2001* (Brussels: UCTE, 2002), 27.
254 European Commission, *Proposal for a Decision of the European Parliament and of the Council Amending Decision No 1254/96*, COM(2001) 775 final (Brussels, 2001), 11.
255 Being Poland, the Czech Republic, Bulgaria, Romania, Slovakia, Slovenia, Hungary, as well as the three Baltic States Latvia, Estonia, and Lithuania.
256 UCTE, "Press Release: UCTE Welcomes Tomorrow's Enlargement of EU - 5 of the 10 New Member Countries are Already Firmly Interconnected and their TSOs are Full Members of UCTE" (Brussels, 2004).
257 Ibid.

be right" as nearly 90 per cent of the people joining the EU were already supplied through the European interconnection system of UCTE.

Conclusions

It is not without reason that this chapter's title includes the term *securing*. In several ways, the notion of security was important to the way European networks were formed, or being formed after the war. According to the NATO alliance the political and military security of Western Europe was at stake in electricity development. Electricity networks not only added to economic growth and prosperity, as was shown in Chapter 4, but also enhanced the military potential of the region. With that being the case, a similar development ideally had to be prevented in Central and Eastern Europe, which supposedly posed the main threat along with the Soviet Union. Therefore the COCOM boycott was installed, by which strategic goods had to be denied to that region. As the Bavarian electricity project in the 1950s showed, these embargo lists contained equipment relevant to electricity network-building. Until well into the 1960s, and possibly longer, Western European security interests exerted a strong influence on the building of a European system. They thwarted network expansion to Czechoslovakia and Poland, but stimulated collaboration with Yugoslavia. In general, however, while cooperation and interconnection on the Western side of the Iron Curtain was stimulated, linkages with countries *across* that divide were not. On the contrary, East-West connections were not compatible with American containment policy. Since 1947 nearly all proposals for East-West interconnections were thwarted by political interference. Not just geopolitical interests complicated cooperation between Central and Eastern Europe, and Western Europe. Technical issues also prevented interconnections between regional power pools.

An apparent lack of "mutual confidence" – an oft-heard additional precondition for close cooperation – between Central and Eastern European engineers and those from other regions was an equally important consideration in this regard. Partially to maintain security of supply, the Western European electricity sector wished build upon secure and close mutual relationships with its Eastern neighbors. Only a few forums existed where engineers from both East and West could exchange views and get acquainted, the most important being the Committee on Electric Power of the ECE. The phase of building up trust was seemingly long, but nevertheless necessary. The ECE's method of work avoided political interference as much as possible by emphasizing questions of technical and economic feasibility. Although in practice ECE's work was highly political, it nevertheless was very compatible with the convictions of network operators, who, like the ECE, focused upon technical matters, and refrained from politicizing issues of collaboration.

In 1965 the American-led opposition against East-West interconnections started to fade. This policy shift should be placed within the international atmosphere of détente at that time. While this change of heart opened up perspectives for closer collaboration, other aspects of the Western Europe energy situation provided further incentives for collaboration with Central and Eastern European countries. Western Europe's energy needs continued to rise; yet fulfilling these needs became more complicated by high fuel prices, unexpected troubles surrounding the introduction of nuclear power plants, and popular and political environmental concerns. Behind the Iron Curtain, these problems hardly were an issue. Western currency and advanced electrical equipment made collaboration with the West advantageous for Central and Eastern European countries.

From the 1970s an important shift in actors took place. Whereas initially the ECE had taken the lead in promoting East-West linkages, the centre of gravity gradually moved towards bilateral initiatives, and later on to rather informal organizations made up by network-operators and electrical engineers, such as UCPTE and UNIPEDE. An incremental bilateral approach was taken wherein Austria – not part of the NATO Alliance – led the way. Projects initially proposed by ECE thereby remained under consideration. Though network extensions were shaped by socio-political factors, it was network operators themselves who took the initiative. The newly established European Community in 1957 did not really attempt to steer and influence the organization of the European system until the 1980s. This began to change around 1985, with the introduction of the Single European Act. On the planned path towards a European internal market, the existing formations of restricted network access, monopoly ownership structures and opaque price formation had to be replaced by open access, unbundling of transmission and distribution, and price systems based on competition.

The unpredicted fall of the Berlin Wall in 1989 led to a redefinition of the future architecture of Europe's electricity network, which resulted in a Europe-wide synchronous system by 1995. Though the electricity sector in Central and Eastern, as well as Western, Europe had for a long time longed to collaborate more closely, it was only after this political turmoil that a strong and intense form of cooperation could grow. The willingness was shown by the speed with which CENTREL-countries adopted the UCPTE standards that would allow European-wide synchronous operation.

Chapter 6 Conclusion
From cooperation to competition

The first two chapters of this book both opened by examining exceptional circumstances in Italy. In each case, Italy's electricity supply was under threat. International solutions were sought to overcome "local" problems in 1921 as well as in 2003. In the first case, collaboration with French and Swiss electricity producers ensured that Italy's North remained provided with sufficient electricity. Engineers seized upon the event to argue for more international cooperation, by building more international interconnections and liberalizing legislation in order to allow more cross-border electricity flows. Their rationale was that it would enable mutual assistance in cases like in 1921, which in turn would increase system reliability. It also opened perspectives for improving economic mix by interconnecting different types of plants.

An extensive interconnected network existed in 2003. In addition to national systems, a well-integrated European system had been developed. But the "goodwill" between countries, which was used to describe the spirit in 1921, seemed to have vanished. As transmission lines were damaged, neighboring countries decided to isolate Italy from the interconnected operation in order to prevent problems in their respective countries – rather than coming to Italy's aid. The result was the largest blackout in Italian history.

That loss of solidarity can be related to reforms initiated by the EU, whereby "goodwill" was replaced by competition. The European Commission sees a "truly competitive single European electricity network as the way to bring down prices, improve security of supply and boost competitiveness".[1] According to the *International Energy Agency* (IEA), energy market liberalization has on the one hand led to reduced overcapacity, improved overall system efficiency, and often led to falling prices.[2] On the other, however, IEA reckons that market reform "has fundamentally altered the underlying drivers for sound governance and weakened

---

1 European Commission, *A European Strategy for Sustainable, Competitive and Secure Energy. Green Paper*, COM (2006) 105 final (Brussels, 2006), 5.
2 IEA, *Lessons from Liberalised Electricity Markets* (Paris: IEA/OECD, 2005), 12.

previous arrangements for maintaining effective transmission system security".[3] To strengthen these arrangements, ironically, the European Commission has proposed to develop a mechanism "to prepare for and ensure rapid *solidarity* and possible assistance to a country facing difficulties following damage to its essential infrastructure".[4]

Looking back at transnational network-building, the development of a European system arguably was the most profound change in the 82-year time span I have charted here. One might expect that the European character of the system was the result of EU involvement. But, as I have shown, the creation of a European electricity system remained for a long time separate from the processes of political and economic integration that led to the EU. In fact, the notion of such a system was already conceived of during the interwar period and the process that led to its realization was initiated after 1921. It resulted in a vast increase of interconnections, institutionalized international collaboration, and less restrictive regulations concerning the in- and outflow of electricity. Tracing this longer history of interconnection and negotiation has revealed important answers to the questions I raised in my introduction, namely: 1) How, when and why did the notion of a European electricity system take root? 2) How did it develop throughout the decades up to the end of the twentieth century, and how did it affect actual network construction? 3) Which actors played an influential role? In this concluding chapter, I will address these questions explicitly, starting by examining the roots of the idea of a European electricity system. Subsequently, I will review the characteristics of the various phases in the system's development and identify the most important actors. Finally, in a short epilogue, I will reflect on how the processes I have highlighted here shed light on the present state of European system development.

The roots of the European system

If we are to agree with Henri Persoz, whom I paraphrased in the first chapter, then the development of a European system is just a phase in the process which will eventually lead to the interconnection of the whole globe.[5] He argues that the importance of load management, economic mix, and the increase of system

---

3   IEA, *Learning from the Blackouts: Transmission System Security in Competitive Electricity Markets* (Paris: IEA/OECD, 2005), 109.
4   European Commission, *A European*, 8. My emphasis.
5   Persoz, "Les grands," 783-784.

reliability are the main drivers of this increasing growth. These principles correspond with Thomas Hughes' findings for the development of regional systems, as described in his *Networks of Power*.

Similar ideas lay at the root of concepts for a European system. Between 1929 and around 1937, the idea of such a system gained acceptance in many circles, and was regarded as a "natural" extension of processes of interconnection taking place on (micro-)regional, and to some extent, national, levels. Many engineers in particular saw the ever-increasing scale of networks as self-evident and logical. Although there was hardly consensus as to where "Europe" was as a geographical unit, the notion nevertheless provided for a more bounded framework wherein electricity systems could be organized. In addition, many engineers believed that such a system would help to overcome national legislation, which supposedly hampered the ongoing process of internationalization of the electricity industry. The financial sector also had a vested interest in "Europe". Before electricity became nationally regulated, financial flows and technical knowledge moved across borders through the *Unternehmersgeschäfte*, which operated internationally. Their possibilities were limited by the new regulations, and they, too, came to see "Europe" as an opportunity to revive internationalization.

Yet technical and economic factors only partially explain the genesis of a European system. They do not explain why *Europe* became a guiding concept in system-building. In addition to technical-economic drivers, an ideological mix of arguments was used to legitimate the development of a European system. This ideological mix consisted of political convictions, economic policy, and ideas of socio-economic advancement. Plans for a European electricity system were always intertwined with visions of Europe as a socio-political and economic unit. If we place the ideas on European system-building within this broader historical context, plans like those of Schönholzer and Viel appear to be more than "mere" utopian or unrealistic sketches. These plans, as well as later initiatives, were products of their time, and often related to specific issues of the epoch.

The shift to thinking in terms of a European system was linked to the growing popularity of ideas of European unification. Such ideas gained prominence after WWI, which left European countries economically and politically weak. Oliven's and Viel's plans for a European network coincided with the apogee of the European movement during the interwar period, and were certainly influenced by it. This was underlined by the fact that several engineers involved (Heineman, Loucheur, and Ulrich) were members of the European movement. They explicitly linked their projects to ongoing processes of economic and political European integration.

Technical and economic as well as ideological arguments were used to legitimize a European system. There were, of course, differences between engineers and Europeanists – although these categories were not mutually exclusive. Many engineers saw a European network as a way to increase system reliability and economy, and to conserve the international character of the industry. For Europeanists, a European grid also had ideological connotations. To them, it should lead to the electrification, and thereby modernization of relatively backward region of Central and Eastern Europe. Such economic growth would enable that region to sell agricultural goods to Western Europe, and acquire industrial products. Planning such a vast undertaking was supposed to revive international investment and create employment. Lastly, according to the likes of Albert Thomas it created a physical bond that would foster a "European spirit", which would help to sustain peace in Europe.

As a consequence, engineers and Europeanists also had different opinions on the route towards a European system. Europeanists wished to plan the short-term construction of a network, to reap the presupposed benefits immediately. This corresponded with the initial set up of the studies conducted by the LoN and the ILO. Their idea of a European system contained strong elements of planned economic development, aiming at tackling "European" problems. Engineers, on the other hand, stressed that a European system was a program for the coming decades. They had little faith in planning a vast network, and opted instead for a more gradual approach whereby networks of neighboring nations would become interconnected. According to several engineers, this gradual growth was more in line with the ongoing national network-building. This is confirmed by statistical evidence. In the subsequent decades, the tensions between the concepts of a planned system and gradual system development occasionally re-emerged.

By a planned system I mean a predesigned scheme, such as Oliven's, whereby transmission lines in the first place connected centers of production and consumption, regardless of existing network or national frontiers. In most cases the construction of such a system was to be financed, built and operated as a multilateral and centralized effort. The gradual development of a system, or as what Hughes has called an *evolving system*[6], assumes a process whereby existing systems gradually become interconnected. No superseding control or institution is in charge of the intermeshing process, but it is coordinated and negotiated among participating actors.

---

6 See Hughes, *Networks,* 363ff.

Building the European system

Interwar plans saw no immediate results due to the nationalistic and strategic network-building that became dominant around 1937. Network extensions or enhancements aiming to protect the system or to minimize damage in case of warfare had highest priority. The triumphal march of German armies after 1939 did not end nationalistic network-building but led to a situation whereby network planning in Europe became dominated by German interests. A European Nazi network was planned to help secure German dominance in Europe. In practice, however, network-building remained in the hands of engineers – not only German, but also local ones. Despite ambitious German plans for a European network, new connections between Germany and its occupied areas only gradually became operational.

After WWII, electricity supply became tied into discussions of the overall economic reconstruction of Europe. The notion of a European system had survived the war intact and apparently untainted. The aims behind post-WWII network-building within a European framework were twofold; to stimulate economic recovery and growth, and to prepare for a potential new conflict. While the first was the prime concern of the engineers involved, the second was primarily shaped by political decision-making enforced through the NATO Alliance. Both relied largely upon the same principles, namely close cooperation between utilities through interconnected operation.

Starting in 1945, discussions about electricity network-building took place within several intergovernmental organizations (IGO), but were conducted, largely, by the same group of engineers. Here again the issue of planning versus gradual development surfaced. In addition their support for national electricity systems, American policy-makers longed to stimulate Western European cooperation through the ERP. They hoped to set up internationally owned power plants and have the produced electricity be pooled. The American position did not go unchallenged. European engineers discussed international network operation, while bearing interwar plans in mind. Some of them thought, like the Americans, in terms of a planned European system, but proponents of a gradual development prevailed. As an alternative to a planned system, engineers wanted to use existing installations as efficiently as possible. International coordination of electricity production and exchange, they believed, should be left to engineers themselves. The outcome was the UCPTE, a power pool wherein Western European engineers worked in what they called a "spirit of mutual trust".

Within the UCPTE, national systems became increasingly interconnected. Production and exchange of electricity were closely coordinated, despite the absence of central control. The UCPTE successfully lobbied to remove gradually restrictions on electricity exchanges, which further stimulated the growth of cross-border flows. The UCPTE, as well as other regional power pools later on, were without governmental representation, and explicitly set up outside of IGOs like the OEEC. These power pools represent an example of hidden integration as described by Schot.[7]

While engineers saw their role as vital for economic growth, more ideological arguments were heard as well. Cooperation in the first years after WWII was also seen as an act of solidarity, which could contribute to more peaceful relations in Europe. This was made clear by Italian engineer Silva, who stated in 1949 that the work of electrical engineers would be "always directed, as silently as indefatigably, towards the realization of a future of happiness and peace".[8]

Other ideological incentives influenced network-building as well. The regional division in power pools partially represented the geopolitical and "techno-geographical" reality, and showed how Cold War sentiments affected network-building. Policy-makers in Western Europe also saw the integration of electricity systems in Europe as a means to increase their defensive capabilities in case of a new armed conflict. This strategy was "sold" under the banner of the ERP along with its more peaceful aims. "Europe" in this sense was "Western Europe", consisting of Western European countries and NATO allies like Greece, and represented a defensive bulwark against possible Soviet aggression.

This Cold War divide in Europe was contested by UNECE. Inspired by its first Executive Secretary Gunnar Myrdal, UNECE tried to be an "all-European" organization and to strengthen ties between both sides of the divide. Its CoEP looked at projects as if "Europe were a single country", but at the same time rejected the notion of a planned European super-network. Their attempts to forge East-West interconnections encountered strong political opposition from the NATO Alliance. NATO only supported such projects in the case of Yugoslavia, and then only because they coincided with strategic political aims.

By 1964, many engineers thought the limits of interconnected operation in Western Europe had been reached. Any further progress, they argued, would come from either submarine links, or connections with Central and Eastern European countries. In addition, political developments made East-West linkages more likely. First, since 1965 Central and Eastern European countries strongly

---

7 See Introduction, note 21.
8 Quoted in Chapter 4, note 162.

expressed their interest in cooperating with Western Europe. Second, around 1966 the NATO Alliance became less strict in its position on East-West connection, although interconnections between the FRG and GDR remained nonnegotiable. These changes did not mean that the process of East-West interconnections shifted significantly. It followed, as ever, the path of least resistance, with pioneering countries being Yugoslavia and Austria. Further stimuli to East-West interconnections occurred in the 1970s. Energy imports from Central and Eastern Europe became even more attractive as fuel prices rose in the Western world, and as the expansion of networks and construction of new power plants in the West met increasing opposition. Debt crises in several Central and Eastern European countries made Western Europe an equally interesting partner.

From the 1970s, a number of HVDC linkages were constructed between East and West. HVDC interconnection was a way to interconnect networks operating at different technical standards. Around 1988 several additional HVDC interconnections between East and West were announced, including ones between the two Germanies. Yet the Berlin wall fell and changed the political geography in Europe. Several Socialist countries were quick to apply for synchronous interconnection with UCPTE countries. By 1995 four former Central and Eastern European countries had successfully joined the UCPTE. A large European synchronized network had come into existence.

Another major change took place in following years. Since the early 1990s, the EU had strongly influenced the electricity sector by changing substantially the rules of the game. Whereas the first steps towards political and economic integration were taken in the 1950s in Western Europe, European cooperation in the electricity sector had taken place outside this process. Now, as a means of forging a European electricity market, the EU sought to separate production and transmission activities so that more parties could enter the electricity market. Previously, electricity was regarded to be a homogenous good or service. Now, according to a UCTE president, "electricity has [...] assumed the characteristics of a branded commodity, to which it is now possible to assign a name, or even a color".[9] "Europe" in this new phase still represented a political and economic unit, but also a market, where electricity can be bought and sold.

---

9 UCTE, *Rapport Annuel 1999* (Brussels: UCTE, 2000), 5. Part of presidential address by Jürgen Stotz.

Epilogue

Throughout this book I have examined the various types of "Europe" visible throughout eight decades of system-building. I have placed network development and system-builders in a more general historical context. It is only then that we see that the plans for a European electricity system are more than utopian or un-realistic sketches; they a product of their time and related to specific issues of the epoch. The notion of such a system was conceived during the interwar period. The suggestion remained in the minds of engineers and policy-makers until after WWII and beyond. In general, it were the latter that thought in terms of a planned network. Engineers proposed, and were eventually responsible for, a gradual con-struction of the system. The European aspect in transnational system-building re-mained present throughout time.

The idea of a European system proved not only durable, but also flexible. Various actors at various times perceived the system as performing different ideo-logically-inspired functions; stimulating economic growth and development, add-ing to military strength, helping to maintain peace. In the process, "Europe" was equally flexible, and its form varied along with these various functions the system was called upon to perform. Such visions of a European system with ideological connotations continue to emerge. For example, a recent article in *The Economist* spotlighted an idea by Jürgen Schmidt to build a HVDC European network that would be able to cover Europe's base load by wind power, accounting for some 30 per cent.[10] Utilizing wind energy prevents relying upon fossil fuels and nuclear energy – both contemporary socio-political issues. If the wind fails, hydroelec-tric plants from Norway can "spring into action and fill in the gap for up to four weeks", explained Schmidt.

The vision of the so-called *Global Electricity Network Initiative* (GENI) is even of a scale beyond Europe.[11] It propagates a globe-spanning electricity network which in particular aims to utilize renewable energy sources. According to GENI such a vast system helps to decrease pollution, reduce hunger and poverty, increase trade and cooperation and thus peace, and stabilize population growth.[12] A closer look at these initiatives, when placed into historical perspective, show great similarities with earlier plans for a European system. Here too, part of the legitimization is a wish for a more rational use of resources and efficient organization of the electric-ity supply. At the same time they also address broader political and social issues

---

10 "Where the Wind Blows," *The Economist*, 2007. I thank Geert Verbong for pointing my attention to this article.
11 See www.geni.org (accessed October 26, 2007).
12 Ibid.

of their own time. During the interwar stress was placed upon preventing a new war and rejuvenating the economy. Current projects refer to current issues such as global warming and global poverty.

The GENI initiative raises a question already posed in the Introduction; to what extent is the drive for a European interconnected system part of a wider, possibly global movement of interconnection? In other words, is the process of interconnecting continuing into other continents, like Persoz predicted? Others have hinted at the possibilities of doing so. Former UCTE-president Michel Albert wrote that "synchronous interconnection has no technical limits" – though he also stressed that problems of organization and coordination would be involved with further growth, as well as the increase of losses on long distance transmission.[13]

At least at the surface, there seems to be some basis for these expectations. A further result of the synchronized interconnection between East and West, in addition to strengthening of linkages within the region, has been that more countries have been added to the synchronized zone. Morocco has been connected to Spain since 1997, and gradual progress is being made toward constructing a ring around the Mediterranean, including Northern African countries. In the north east, the so-called Baltic Ring Study examined possibilities for stronger interconnections between the eleven countries around the Baltic Sea between 1996 and 1998. At this moment, UCTE-countries are in negotiation with Russia about synchronous interconnection. If this comes about, the synchronous zone would extend well into Asia, because Russia is connected with its eastern neighbors as well. A question for the future is whether such expansions into Africa and Asia still can and will be accommodated under the banner of Europe.

In the meantime, for the European system it is not now so much a question of the system's growth, but of strengthening it internally. Due to the electricity market, one of the primary tasks of the interconnected European system is to facilitate trade. This involves a more intensive use of cross-border capacity, and has led to congestion in some areas, like around Italy. As the UCTE stated in its report on the 2003 blackout, the system is not designed for this task.[14] These changes provoke new questions, like who is responsible for the security of supply and the performance of the system as such, and how are risks distributed among network users? The IEA stated in a 2005 report that "commercial interests, arising as a result of electricity reform, raise questions about transparency, objectivity and legal liability associated with system operation".[15] Although one might still expect that Europe's

---

13 Albert, "Enlarged Interconnection," 7.
14 UCTE, *Final Report*, 3.
15 IEA, *Learning*, 109.

future will be brightly lit, the question yet remains as to who is responsible for keeping the lights on.

In response to this, and other challenges to the energy supply, the European Commission stressed in 2006 that Europe needs a common response, and not one "based solely on 25 individual energy policies".[16] Furthermore, as the first of six priority areas, the Commission emphasized that "[c]onsumers need a single European grid for a real European electricity [...] market to develop". Again, also in 2006, a European network is seen as a viable response to contemporary problems.

---

16 European Commission, *A European*, 4.

Sources and bibliography

Archival sources

Austrian State Archives, Vienna (OS)
    File: "Allgemein (Handel/Gewerbe/Industrie) (1918-1940)"
    File: "Bundesministerium für Handel und Wiederaufbau (1945-1991)"

Belgian State Archives, Brussels (BSA)
    Collection *Société Financière de Transports et d'Entreprises Industrielles* (SOFINA)

Central Archives of the Council of the European Union, Brussels (CACEU)
    Collection Council of Ministers of the European Union, fonds 3: Negotiations for the
    Treaties institutionalising the EEC and EURATOM

Centre d'archives et de recherches européennes: Institut européen de l'Université de Genève
    File AP 2: Richard N, von Coudenhove-Kalergi

Diplomatic Archive, Brussels (Diplobel)
    File 4643: "Commission consultative des Communication et transit"
    File 11440: "Pan-Europa"

Historical Archives of the European Commission, Brussels (HAEC)
    High Authority of European Coal and Steel Community collection.
    EEC and ECSC Collections (BAC)

Historical Archives of the European Union, Florence (HAEU)
    Fonds Organisation for European Economic Cooperation
    File OEEC.EL: Electricity Committee
    File OEEC.EN: Energy Committee
    Fonds Organization for Economic Cooperation and Development
    File OECD.EL: Electricity Committee
    File OECD.EN: Energy Committee

International Labor Organisation Archives, Geneva (ILO)
    Fonds Cabinet Albert Thomas
    File series D 600
    File series L 1/14
    File series L 4/15

League of Nations Archives, Geneva (LoN)
    Registry file 9A: Transit
    Registry file 9E: Communications and Transit Section, Electric Power

Registry file 10: Economic and Financial Section
Registry file 14A: International Transit Conference
Registry file 14: Transit
Princeton files: Office of Alexander Loveday

National Archives at College Park, Maryland, United States (NACP)
Record group 59: General Records of the Department of State
Record group 84: Records of the Foreign Service Posts of the Department of State
Record group 260: Records of U.S. Occupation Headquarters, World War II
Record group 331: Records of Allied Operational and Occupation Headquarters, World War II
Record group 469: Record of U.S. Foreign Assistance Agencies

North Atlantic Treaty Organisation Archives, Brussels (NATO)
File AC/89: Working Group on Comparison of Economic Trends in the NATO and Soviet Countries
File AC/119: Committee of Political Affairs
File AC/127: Committee of Economic Advisers
File AC/143: Industrial Planning Committee

Swiss Federal Archives, Bern
File E 8190 (A): "Amt für Energiewirtschaft 1930-1969"

Truman Library, Independence, Missouri
Paul. G. Hoffman Papers

UC(P)TE Archives, Brussels (UCTE)
Reports of the Comité Restreint

United Nations Organisation at Geneva Archives (UNOG)
File G.X.1: General and Miscellaneous
File G.X 10: Economic Commission for Europe
File G.X. 19: Electric Power
File G.X 12: Emergency Economic Commission for Europe
File G/ECE 632: Electric Power
File G/ECE 633: Electric Power.
File G/ECE 643: General Energy.
File Accession of Retired Records (ARR) 14, number 1360: Files of Office of Executive Secretary Gunnar Myrdal (1947-1957)
File ARR 14, number 1822
File ARR 14, number 1856
File ARR 14, number 1961

Interview

Interview with Walter Fremuth, conducted in Vienna on March 8-9, 2007.

Newspaper and magazine articles

"Black out, Marzano apre inchiesta 'Troveremo presto i responsabili." *La Repubblica*, September 28, 2003, http://www.repubblica.it/2003/i/sezioni/cronaca/blackitalia/marzano/marzano.html.

"Blackout, per Parigi e Berna la responsabilità è italiana." *La Repubblica*, September 28, 2003, http://www.repubblica.it/2003/i/sezioni/cronaca/blackitalia/cause/cause.html.

"Blackout, tre morti in Puglia, Sicilia ancora al buio." *La Repubblica*, September 28, 2003, http://www.repubblica.it/2003/i/sezioni/cronaca/blackitalia/citta/citta.html.

"Confindustria: 'L'elettricità è emergenza nazionale." *La Repubblica*, September 28, 2003, http://www.repubblica.it/2003/i/sezioni/cronaca/blackitalia/confind/confind.html.

"Verbundgeneral Fremuth: 'Mister 100.000 Volt." *A3 Volt. Das österreichische Magazin für Elektronik und Elektrotechnik* November/December (1980): 14-16.

"Where the wind blows." *The Economist*, July 26, 2007.

Blattmann, H. "Hochspannung zwischen Schweiz und Italien. Bericht zur Ursache des Blackouts." *Neue Zürcher Zeitung*, September 28, 2003.

Blattmann, H. "Zu früh für Schuldzuweisungen." *Neue Zürcher Zeitung*, September 28, 2003.

Galinier, Pascal. "Les risques et faiblesses d'un réseau sature. La panne en Italie souligne la fragilité de l'Europe de l'électricité." *Le Monde*, September 30, 2003.

Heineman, D.N. "Internationale Elektrizitätswirtschaft." *Wirtschaftshefte der Frankfurter Zeitung*, 1927.

Heineman, Dannie. "Esquisse d'une nouvelle Europe." *L'Européen 7* (1931): 1-7.

Ulrich, Marcel. "Un projet de réseau européen. Le transport de l'énergie electrique." *l'Européen* 25 (1932).

Published documentation

League of Nations documents

International Economic Conference, Geneva, May 1927. Documentation: Electrical Industry. Vol. 16. Geneva: League of Nations, 1927.

World Economic Conference: Discussion and Declarations on the Report of the Conference at the Council of the League of Nations on June 16th, 1927. Geneva: League of Nations, 1927.

Advisory and Technical Committee for Communications and Transit, Procès-Verbal of the Second Session, Held at Geneva, March 29th- 31st, 1922. LoN doc, ser., C.212.M.116.1922.VIII. Geneva: LoN, 1922.

Advisory and Technical Committee for Communications and Transit: Minutes of the 4th Session: Report of the Sub-Committee for Hydro-Electric Questions. LoN doc, ser., C.486.M.202.1923.VIII. Geneva: LoN, 1923.

Advisory and Technical Committee for Communications and Transit: Minutes of the 6th Session Held at Geneva, March 12th – 14th, 1924. LoN doc, ser., C.196.M.61.1924.VIII. Geneva: LoN, 1924.

Commission of Enquiry for European Union. LoN doc, ser., C.724.M.324.1932.VII. Geneva: LoN, 1932.

II. Public Works. LoN doc, ser., C.395.M.158.1931.VII. Geneva: LoN.

Mémoire du Bureau International du Travail. Genève, le 29 juin 1931. LoN doc, ser., C.E.U.E./C/1. Geneva: LoN, 1931.

Memorandum from the Director of the International Labour Office on Certain Questions Dealt with by that Office, of Special Interest to European States. LoN doc, ser., C.39.M.19.1931. VII. Geneva: LoN, 1931.

Memorandum of the Secretary-General of the Committee on Transport and Transit of Electric Power and the Regime of International Exchange of Electric Power in Europe. LoN doc, ser., C.C.T.566. Geneva: LoN.

Minutes of the Seventh Session of the Commission. LoN doc, ser., C.532.M370.1937.VII. Geneva: LoN, 1937.

Monetary and Economic Conference: International Questions Relating to Public Works. LoN doc, ser., C.377.M.186.1933.VIII. Geneva: LoN, 1931.

Monetary and Economic Conference: International Questions Relating to Public Works. LoN doc, ser., C.377.M.186.1933.VIII. Geneva: LoN, 1933.

Proposals Put Forward by the Belgian Government for the Agenda of the Commission of Enquiry for European Union, on December 11th, 1930. LoN doc, ser., C.706.M.298.1930.VII / C.E.U.E.3. Geneva: LoN, 1930.

Report on the Fourth Session of the Committee. LoN doc, ser., C.379.M.188.1933.VIII. Geneva: LoN, 1933.

Resolution Adopted by the Commission of Enquiry for European Union Relating to Transport and Transit of Electric Power. LoN doc, ser., C.417.M.173.1931.VIII. Geneva: LoN, 1931.

Second General Conference on Communications and Transit. Electric Questions: Report Concerning the Draft Conventions and Statutes Relating to the Transmission in Transit of Electric Power and the Development of Hydraulic Power on Watercourses Forming Part of a Basin Situated in the Territory of Several States. Vol. 3. LoN doc, ser., C.378.M.171.1923. VIII. Geneva: LoN, 1923.

Transport and Transit of Electric Power and Regime of the International Exchange of Electric Power in Europe. LoN doc, ser., C.98.M.33.1934.VIII. Geneva: LoN.

Transport and Transit of Electric Power, and Regime of the International Exchange of Electric Power in Europe. LoN doc, ser., C.380.M.256.1937.VIII. Geneva: LoN.

Transport and Transit of Electric Power, and Regime of the International Exchange of Electric Power in Europe. LoN doc, ser., C.266.M.159.1938.VIII. Geneva: LoN, 1938.

Unemployment: Proposals of the International Labour Organisation. LoN doc, ser., C.275.M.127.1931.VII, Annex 14. Geneva: LoN, 1931.

Various Communications by the Secretariat: 3. Transmission in Transit of Electric Power. LoN doc, ser., C.531.M.265.1932.VIII. Geneva: LoN, 1932.

Verbatim Record of the 10th Ordinary Session of the Assembly of the League of Nations, 6th Plenary Meeting. LoN doc, ser., A.10.1929. Geneva: LoN, 1929.

Work of the Second Conference with a View to Concerted Economic Action: Statement by M. Colijn. LoN doc, ser., C.144.M.45.1931.VII. Geneva: LoN, 1931.

OEEC Documents

Armand, Louis. *Some Aspects of the European Energy Problem: Suggestions for Collective Action.* Paris: OEEC, 1955.

OEEC. *Europe's Growing Need of Energy: How Can They Be Met? A Report Prepared by a Group of Experts.* Paris: OEEC, 1956.

———. *Interconnected Power Systems in the USA and Western Europe: The Report of the Tecaid Mission, the Report of the Electricity Committee.* Paris, 1950.

———. *The Organisation for European Economic Co-operation: Two Years of Economic Co-Operation.* Paris: OEEC, 1950.

United Nations Documents

Allmer, Helmuth. "Extension Planning of the Austrian Interconnected Network with Regard to HVDC Back-to-Back Links." In *UNECE Seminar on High Voltage Direct Current Techniques, Stockholm, May, 1985.* UN doc, ser., EP/SEM.10/report no. 2. Geneva: UNECE, 1985.

Moraw, G, and K.W. Kanngiesser. "The HVDC Back-to-Back Tie Duernrohr as Asynchronous Link Between the Eastern and Western European Super Grids; Technical Data and Required System Performance." In *UNECE Seminar on High Voltage Direct Current Techniques, Stockholm, May, 1985*. UN doc, ser., EP/SEM.10/report no. 23. Geneva: UNECE, 1985.

Novotny, V. "The First Experience of the Back-to-Back HVDC Link of the Czechoslovak and Austrian Power Systems." In *UNECE Seminar on High Voltage Direct Current Techniques, Stockholm, 6-9 May, 1985*. UN doc, ser., EP/SEM.10/Report no. 21. Geneva: UNECE, 1985

UNECE. *Ad Hoc Group of Experts on Problems of Planning and Operating Large Power Systems, 2nd Session, 'Transfers of Electric Power Across European Frontiers and Future Prospects',* March 31, 1969. UN doc, ser., EP/WP.8/Working paper No.1/Rev.1. Geneva: UNECE, 1969.

———. *Annual Bulletin of Electric Energy Statistics for Europe*. United Nations: Geneva, years 1955-1993.

———. *Annual Bulletin of Electric Energy Statistics for Europe and North America*. United Nations: Geneva, years 1994-1995.

———. *Committee on Electric Power, First Session, Fifth meeting, October 14, 1947*. UN doc, ser., E/ECE/EP/SR.1/5. Geneva: UNECE, 1947.

———. *Committee on Electric Power, First Session: Summary of the Second Meeting, October 20, 1947*. UN doc, ser., E/ECE/EP/SR.1/2. Geneva: UNECE, 1947.

———. *Committee on Electric Power, First Session: Summary of the Third Meeting, October 21, 1947*. UN doc, ser., E/ECE/EP/SR.1/3. Geneva: UNECE, 1947.

———. Group of Experts on Problems of Planning and Operating Large Power Systems, 17th Session, 1985. UN doc, ser., EP/GE.2/R.73. Geneva: UNECE, 1985.

———. *Outline of a Study on the Possibilities of Increasing Interconnexion Between Electric Power Transmission Networks in Europe*. UN doc, ser., ME/31/64/C.2(a). Geneva: UNECE, 1964.

———. *Report of the Committee on Electric Power to the Economic Commission for Europe*. UN doc, ser., E/ECE/127-C 24. Geneva: UNECE, 1951.

———. *The Interconnexion of the Electric Power Transmission Systems of Countries in Eastern and Western Europe, September 30, 1971*. UN doc, ser., EP/WP.8/Working paper No.16/Corr.2. Geneva: UNECE, 1971.

———. *Transfers of Electric Power Across European Frontiers and Future Prospects, May 13th, 1969*. UN doc, ser., EP/WP.8/Working Paper No. 1/Rev.1/Corr.1. Geneva: UNECE, 1969.

———. *Transfers of Electric Power Across European Frontiers. Study by the Electric Power Section*. UN doc, ser., E/ECE/151. Geneva: United Nations, 1952.

EU(-related) documents

Comité Intergouvernemental créé par la Conférence de Messine. *Rapport des Chefs de Délégation aux Ministres des Affaires Etrangères*, document Mae 120 f/56 (corrigé). Brussels: Secrétariat, 1956.

European Commission. *A European Strategy for Sustainable, Competitive and Secure Energy: Green Paper*. COM (2006) 105 final. Brussels, 2006.

———. *Completing the Internal Market: White Paper From the Commission to the European Council*. COM (85) 310 final. Brussels, 1985.

———. *Proposal for a Decision of the European Parliament and of the Council Amending Decision No 1254/96/EC Laying Down a Series of Guidelines for Trans-European Energy Networks*. COM(2001) 775 final. Brussels, 2001.

———. *The Internal Energy Market*. COM (88) 238 final. Brussels, 1988.

———. "The Single Act: A New Frontier for Europe. Communication from the Commission to the Council." *Bulletin of the European Communities* 1/87 (1987).

"Treaty on European Union." *Official Journal of the European Communities* C 191 (1992).

UC(P)TE Documents

UCPTE. *1951-1976: 25 Jaar UCPTE*. Arnhem: UCPTE, 1976.

———. *Rapport Annuel 1951-1952*. Paris: UCPTE, 1952.

———. *Rapport Annuel 1975-1976*. Arnhem: UCPTE, 1977.

———. *Rapport Annuel 1976-1977*. Arnhem: UCPTE, 1978.

———. *Rapport Annuel 1981-1982*. Rhode-St.Genese: UCPTE, 1983.

———. *Rapport Annuel 1986-1987*. Heidelberg: UCPTE, 1988.

———. *Rapport Annuel 1989*. Arnhem: UCPTE, 1990.

———. *Rapport Annuel 1992*. Madrid: UCPTE, 1993.

———. *Rapport Annuel 1997*. Madrid: UCPTE, 1998.

———. *SUDEL*, n.p.: UCPTE, 1970.

———. *U.C.P.T.E. 1951-1971: 20 ans d'activitè*. Rome: UCPTE, 1971.

UCTE. *Final report of the Investigation Committee on the 28 September 2003 Blackout in Italy*. Brussels: UCTE, 2004, http://www.ucte.org/_library/otherreports/20040427_UCTE_IC_Final_report.pdf.

———. "Press Release: UCTE Welcomes Tomorrow's Enlargement of EU - 5 of the 10 New Member Countries are Already Firmly Interconnected and Their TSOs are Full Members of UCTE," Brussels, 2004.

———. *Rapport Annuel 1999*. Brussels: UCTE, 2000.

———. *Rapport Annuel 2001*. Brussels: UCTE, 2002.

UNIPEDE Documents, Proceedings

"Minutes of the 'Comité d'Études des Interconnexions Internationales.'" In *Compte rendu des travaux du huitième congrès international tenu à Bruxelles en septembre 1949, Rapports des Comités d'Études IV à IX*, 2:108-127. Paris: Imprimerie Chaix, 1949.

"Minutes of the 'International Interconnections Study Committee.'" In *Tenth Congress of UNIPEDE, London, 1955*, 1:126-149. Paris: Imprimerie Chaix, 1955.

Barbesino, C. "Problems and Methods of Planning National and International Connections (report 88E.40.1)." In *Twenty-First Congress, Sorrento 1988, Proceedings of the Working Sessions and Other Functions*, edited by UNIPEDE, 2: Paris: Imprimerie Chaix, 1988.

Berni, Amicare. "La construction d'un réseau d'interconnexion européen au point de vue technique et économique (report no. 2.)." In *Compte rendu des travaux du huitième congrès international tenu à Bruxelles en septembre 1949. Rapports des Comités d'Études IV à IX*, 2: Paris: Imprimerie Chaix, 1949.

Cahen, François, and Bernard Favez. "Control of Frequency and Power Exchanges within the Framework of International Interconnections (report IV.2)." In *UNIPEDE Congress of Scandinavia*. Paris: Imprimerie Chaix, 1964.

Cahen, François, and Réne Pélisser. "La compensation des pointes de puissance par l'interconnexion internationale (report no.3)." In *Compte rendu des travaux du huitième congrès international tenu à Bruxelles en septembre 1949. Rapports des Comités d'Études IV à IX*, 2: Paris: Imprimerie Chaix, 1949.

Civita, D. "Sur la situation électrique dans les différents pays. Législation et statistique." In *Comptre rendu des travaux du premier congrès international tenu à Rome en septembre 1926*, edited by UNIPEDE, 489-600. Rome: L'Universale Tipografia Poliglotta, 1926.

De Heem, Louis. "Expérience acquise dans le fonctionnement interconnecté du réseau belge avec les réseaux des pays voisins." In *Report to UNIPEDE Congres: Comité d'études des interconnexions internationales*. IV.1. Rome: UNIPEDE, 1952.

Fehr, E. "Conditions jurisdiques et économiques de l'exportation hors de Suisse de l'énergie électrique (report no. 12)." In *Compte rendu des travaux du huitième congrès interna-*

tional tenu à Bruxelles en septembre 1949. Rapports des Comités d'Études IV à IX, 2: Paris: Imprimerie Chaix, 1949.

Hochreutiner, René. "L'Interconnexion au service des échanges d'énergie en Europe occidentale (report no. 9)." In *Compte rendu des travaux du huitième congrès international tenu à Bruxelles en septembre 1949, Rapports des Comités d'Études IV à IX*, 2: Paris: Imprimerie Chaix, 1949.

Maggi, Leonardo. "Considérations générales sur les interconnexions (report no. 13)." In *Compte rendu des travaux du huitième congrès international tenu à Bruxelles en septembre 1949, Rapports des Comités d'Études IV à IX*, 2: Paris: Imprimerie Chaix, 1949.

Niesz, H. "L'échange d'énergie électrique entre pays, au point de vue économique et technique." In *Transactions of the World Power Conference, Basle, Sectional meeting*, 1:1025-1063. Basel: Birkhäuser & Cie, 1926.

Pavard, M. "Long-term Prospects for the Development of Operation and Control of European Interconnected Systems (report 40.2)." In *Twenty-First Congress, Sorrento 1988, Proceedings of the Working Sessions and Other Functions*, 2: Paris: Imprimerie Chaix, 1988.

Riccio, Giorgio. "Rapport général du président du Comité (report no. IV)." In *UNIPEDE Congress of Scandinavia*. Paris: Imprimerie Chaix, 1964.

Selmo, Luigi. "Les interconnexions européennes (report no. 4)." In *Compte rendu des travaux du huitième congrès international tenu à Bruxelles en septembre 1949. Rapports des Comités d'Études IV à IX*, 2: Paris: Imprimerie Chaix, 1949.

UNIPEDE. *Annual Report 1992*. Paris: UNIPEDE, 1993.

———. *Production et de la Distribution d'Énergie Électrique*. Paris:UNIPEDE, years 1932-1946.

———. *Seventeenth Congress, Vienna 1976, Proceedings of the Working Sessions and Other Functions*. Paris: Imprimerie Chaix, 1976.

———. *Twentieth Congress, Athens 1985, Proceedings of the Working Sessions and Other Functions*. Paris: Imprimerie Chaix, 1985.

———. *Twenty-First Congress, Sorrento 1988, Proceedings of the Working Sessions and Other Functions*. Vol. 2. Paris: Imprimerie Chaix, 1988.

———. *L'Économie électrique: bulletin périodique de l'Unipede*. UNIPEDE: Paris, years 1928-1952.

United States Government Documents

United States. *The United States Strategic Bombing Survey: Over-All Report (European War)*. Washington, D.C.: Government Printing Office, 1945.

CEEC. *Committee of European Economic Co-Operation. General Report*. Vol. 1. Washington, D.C.: U.S Government Printing Office, 1947.

CEEC. *Committee of European Economic Co-Operation, Technical Reports*. Vol. 2. Washington, D.C.: U.S. Government Printing Office, 1947.

ECA. *Eleventh Report to Congress of the Economic Cooperation Administration*. Washington, D.C.: U.S. Government Printing Office, 1950.

———. *First Report to Congress of the Economic Cooperation Administration*. Washington, D.C.: U.S. Government Printing Office, 1948.

———. *Second Report to Congress of the Economic Cooperation Administration*. Washington, D.C.: U.S. Government Printing Office, 1948.

———. *Tenth Report to Congress of the Economic Cooperation Administration*. Washington, D.C.: U.S. Government Printing Office, 1955.

———. *Thirteenth Report to Congress of the Economic Cooperation Agency*. Washington, D.C.: U.S. Government Printing Office, 1951.

———. *Twelfth Report to Congress of the Economic Cooperation Agency*. Washington, D.C.: U.S. Government Printing Office, 1950.

U.S. Agency for International Development. *U.S. Overseas Loans and Grants: Obligations and*

Loan Authorizations, July 1, 1945-September 30, 2006. Washington, D.C.: USAID, 2006,
    http://qesdb.usaid.gov/gbk/gbk2006.pdf.

U.S. Department of State. "The Ambassador in Yugoslavia (Allen) to the Secretary of State."
    In *Foreign Relations of the United States*, 4. *Central and Eastern Europe: The Soviet Union*,
    Washington, D.C.: U.S. Government Printing Office, 1950.

Office of Military Government U.S. Sector Berlin. A Four Year Report: July 1, 1945 - September 1,
    1949. Berlin: Office of Military Government U.S. Sector Berlin, 1949.

World Power Conference Documents, Proceedings

Bundesministerium für Handel und Verkehr. "The Development of and Utilisation of
    Water Power in Austria." In *The Transactions of the First World Power Conference: Power*
    Resources of the World, Available and Utilised, 1:684-705. London: Percy Lund Humphries
    & Co. Ltd., 1924.

Génissieu, E. "Échanges d'énergie entre pays." In *Transactions of the World Power Conference,*
    Basle Sectional meeting, 1:1001-1024. Basle: E. Birkhäuser & Cie., 1926.

Haas, Robert. "Austausch Elektrischer Energie zwischen verschiedenen Ländern." In
    Transactions of the World Power Conference, Basle Sectional Meeting, 1:987-999. Basle: E.
    Birkhäuser & Cie., 1926.

Landry, Professor. "Exchange of electrical energy between countries. General report on Section
    B." In *Transactions of the World Power Conference, Basle Sectional meeting*, 1:1112-1124.
    Basle: E. Birkhäuser & Cie., 1926.

Masarykova Akademie Práce. "Review of the Natural Sources of Energy and Their Use in
    Czechoslovakia." In *Transactions of the World Power Conference, Basle Sectional Meeting*,
    1:760. Basle: E. Birkhäuser & Cie., 1926.

Oliven, Oskar. "European Super Power Lines: Proposal for a European Super Power System."
    General Address Presented at the World Power Conference, Berlin, 1930.

Polish National Committee. "Polish Power Resources and their Development." In *The*
    Transactions of the First World Power Conference: Power Resources of the World, Available
    and Utilised, 1:1099-1158. London: Percy Lund Humphries & Co. Ltd., 1924.

de Verebélÿ, L. "General Survey of Hungary's Power Resources and their Future Development,
    with Special Reference to Electrification." In *Transactions of the World Power Conference,*
    Basle Sectional meeting 1926, 1:924. Basle: E. Birkhäuser & Cie., 1926.

Other

CSCE. *Conference on Security and Co-operation in Europe: Final Act.* Helsinki: CSCE, 1975.

Thiry, J. "Interconnection of European Electric Power Systems: Present Situation and Prospects
    up to the Year 2000." In *IEA/OECD Seminar on East-West Energy Trade*, 159-178. Vienna:
    IEA/OECD, 1991.

Tribot Laspière, Jean, ed. *Construction et exploitation des Grands réseaux de transport d'énergie*
    électrique à très haute tension. Compte-rendu des travaux de la Conférence Internationale
    tenue à Paris du 21 au 26 novembre 1921. Paris: l'Union des Syndicats de l'Électricité, 1922.

Union of the Electricity Industry–EURELECTRIC. *Power Outages in 2003. Task Force Power*
    Outages. Brussels: EURELECTRIC, June 2004.

Scholarly books, articles and dissertations

Adas, Michael. *Machines as the Measure of Men: Science, Technology, and Ideologies of Western*
    Dominance. Ithaca: Cornell University Press, 1989.

Albert, Michel. "Enlarged Interconnection between the East and the UCPTE." *Perspectives in*
    Energy 4 (1997): 13-17.

Badenoch, Alexander, and Andreas Fickers. "Introduction: Untangling Infrastructures and
    Europe: Mediations, Events, Scales." In *Europe Materializing? Transnational Infrastructures*

and the Project of Europe, edited by Alexander Badenoch and Andreas Fickers. London: Palgrave, forthcoming.

Baer, Josette. "Imagining Membership: The Conception of Europe in the Political Thought of T.G. Masaryk and Václav Havel." *Studies in East European Thought* 52 (2000): 203-226.

Barjot, Dominique, and Ginette Kurgan. "Les réseaux humains dans l'industrie électrique." *Annales historiques de l'électricité* 2, (2004): 69-88.

Barrère, Julien. "La genèse de l'Europe électrique: Les logiques de l'interconnexion transnationale (début des années 1920-fin des années 1950)." PhD diss., Université de Bordeaux-III, 2002.

Beltran, Alain, Ginette Kurgan, and Henri Morsel. "Présentation." *Bulletin d'histoire de l'électricité* 22 (1993): 7-22.

Berend, Iván T. *Decades of Crisis: Central and Eastern Europe before World War II.* Berkeley: University of California Press, 1998.

Berger, Helge, and Albrecht Ritschl. "Germany and the Political Economy of the Marshall Plan, 1947-1952: A Re-Revisionist View." In *Europe's Postwar Recovery,* edited by Barry Eichengreen, 199-245. Cambridge: Cambridge University Press, 1995.

Berthelot, Yves, and Paul Rayment. "The ECE: A Bridge between East and West." In *Unity and Diversity in Development Ideas: Perspectives from the UN Regional Commissions,* edited by Yves Berthelot, 51-131. Bloomington & Indianapolis: Indiana University Press, 2004.

Berthonnet, Arnaud. *Guide du chercheur en histoire de l'électricité.* Éditions La Mandragore. Paris, 2001.

Bertsch, Gary K. "Introduction." In *Controlling East-West Trade and Technology Transfer: Power, Politics, and Policies,* edited by Gary K. Bertsch, 1-27. Durham: Duke University Press, 1988.

Betz, Hans-Georg. "Mitteleuropa and Post-Modern European Identity." *New German Critique* 50 (1990): 173-192.

Bijker, Wiebe E., Thomas Parke Hughes, and T.J. Pinch, eds. *The Social Construction of Technological Systems: New Directions in the Sociology and History of Technology.* Cambridge: MIT Press, 1987.

Binder, Beate. *Elektrifizierung als Vision: Zur Symbolgeschichte einer Technik im Alltag.* Tübingen: Vereinigung für Volkskunde, 1999.

den Boer, Pim. "Europe to 1914: The Making of an Idea." In *The History of the Idea of Europe,* edited by Kevin Wilson and Jan van der Dussen, 13-82. London: Routledge, 1993.

Boll, Georg. *Entstehung und Entwicklung des Verbundbetriebs in der deutschen Elektrizitätswirtschaft bis zum europäischen Verbund. Ein rückblick zum 20-jährgen Besiehen der Deutschen Verbundsgesellschaft e.V., Heidelberg.* Frankfurt: Verlags- u. Wirtschaftges, d. Elektrizitätswerke m.b.H., 1969.

Bongrain, Hervé. "L'Électricité au service de la Défense nationale." In *Histoire générale de l'électricité en France,* edited by Henri Morsel, vol. 3. *Une oeuvre nationale: L'Équipement, la croissance de la demande, le nucléaire (1946-1987),* 556-576. Paris: Fayard, 1996.

Bonhage, Barbara. "Unternehmerische Entscheidungen im Spannungsfeld gesamtwirtschaftlicher Veränderungen: Eine Fallstudie zum organisatorischen Wandel der Bank für elektrische Unternehmungen in der Zwischenkriegszeit und im Zweiten Weltkrieg." Lizentiatsarbeit, Philosophischen Fakultät I der Universität Zürich, 1998.

Borneman, John, and Nick Fowler. "Europeanization." *Annual Review of Anthropology* 26 (1997): 487-514.

Bossaut, Gérard. *L'Europe occidentale à l'heure américaine: Le Plan Marshall et l'unité européenne (1945-1952).* Brussels: Editions Complexe, 1992.

Bouneau, Christophe, Michel Derdevet, and Jacques Percebois. *Les réseaux électriques au coeur de la civilisation industrielle.* Boulogne: Timée-Editions, 2007.

Bouneau, Christophe. "L'Économie électrique sous l'Occupation: Des contraintes de la production aux enjeux de l'interconnexion." In *Les entreprises du secteur de l'énergie sous l'Occupation*, edited by Denis Varaschin, 119-132. Arras: Artois Presses Université, 2006.

———. "La genèse de l'interconnexion électrique internationale de la France du début du siècle à 1946." In *Les réseaux Europééns transnationaux XIXe - XXe siècles: quels enjeux?*, edited by Michèle Merger, Albert Carreras, and Andrea Giuntini, 77-98. Nantes: Ouest Éditons, 1994.

———. "Les réseaux de transport d'électricité en Europe occidentale depuis a fin du XIXe siècle: De la diversité des modèles nationaux à la recherche de la convergence européenne." *Annales historiques de l'électricité* 2 (2004): 23-37.

———. "Transporter." In *Histoire générale de l'électricité en France*, edited by Maurice Lévy-Leboyer and Henri Morsel, vol. 2, *l'Interconnexion et le marché, 1919-1946* 2:777-902. Paris: Fayard, 1994.

Braun, Hans-Joachim. "Die Weltenergiekonferenzen als Beispiel internationaler Kooperation." In *Energie in der Geschichte: Zur Aktualität der Technikgeschichte. 11th Symposium of ICOHTEC*, edited by Hans-Joachim Braun, 10-16. Düsseldorf: Verein Deutscher Ingenieure.

Brion, René, and Jean-Louis Moreau. *Inventaire des archives du groupe SOFINA (Société Financière de Transports et d'Entreprises Industrielles) 1881-1988*. Brussels: Archives Générales du Royaume, 2001.

Brion, René. "Le rôle de la Sofina." In *Le financement de l'industrie électrique, 1880-1980*, edited by Monique Trédé-Boulmer, 215-232. Paris: Association pour l'histoire de l'électricité en France, 1994.

Broder, Albert. "L'Expansion internationale de l'industrie allemande dans le dernier tiers du XIXe siècle: Le cas de l'industrie électrique, 1880-1913." *Relations internationales* 29 (1982): 65-87.

Brumshagen, Harald, and Jürgen Schwarz. "The European Power Systems on the Threshold of a New East-West Co-Operation." *IEEE Transactions on Energy Conversion* 11, no. 2 (1996): 462-474.

Bugge, Peter. "The Nation Supreme: The Idea of Europe 1914-1945." In *The History of the Idea of Europe*, edited by Kevin Wilson and Jan van der Dussen, 83-150. London: Routledge, 1993.

Bussière, Eric. "L'Organisation économique de la SDN et la naissance du régionalisme économique." *Relations internationales* 75 (1993): 301-313.

———. *La France, la Belgique et l'organisation économique de L'Europe, 1918-1935*. Paris: Comité pour l'histoire économique et financière de la France, 1992.

Caesar, A.A.L. "Yugoslavia: Geography and Postwar Planning." *Transactions and Papers (Institute of British Geographers)* 30 (1962): 33-43.

Cailleau, Julie. "Energy: From Synergies to Merger." In *The European Commission, 1958-1972. History and Memories*, edited by Michel Dumoulin, 471-490. Brussels: Office for Official Publications of the European Communities, 2007.

CAPAS. "Évolution du système électrique européen. Nouveaux défis pour la recherche." Académie royale des Sciences, 2006.

Cardot, Fabienne, ed. *1880-1980. Un siècle d'électricité dans le monde: Actes du Premier colloque international d'histoire de l'électricité*. Paris: Presses Universitaires de France, 1987.

Carls, Stephen D. *Louis Loucheur and the Shaping of Modern France, 1916-1931*. Baton Rouge: Louisiana State University Press, 1993.

Chandler, Alfred D. *The Visible Hand: The Managerial Revolution in American Business*. Cambridge: Belknap Press, 1977.

Cisler, Walker L. *Partners in Electric Power: Development under the Marshall Plan*. New York: The Newcomen Society in North America, 1955.

Clavin, Patricia, and Jens-Wilhelm Wessels. "Transnationalism and the League of Nations: Understanding the Work of its Economic and Financial Organisation." *Contemporary European History* 14, no. 4 (2005): 465-492.

Clavin, Patricia. "Introduction: Defining Transnationalism." *Contemporary European History* 14, no. 4 (2005): 421-440.

———. *The Great Depression in Europe, 1929-1939*. Basingstoke: Macmillan, 2000.

Cohrs, Patrick O. "The First 'Real' Peace Settlements after the First World War: Britain, the United States and the Accords of London and Locarno, 1923-1925." *Contemporary European History* 12, no. 1 (2003): 1-31.

Conze, Vanessa. *Richard Coudenhove-Kalergi. Umstrittener Visionär Europas*. Zurich: Muster-Schmidt, 2004.

Coopersmith, Jonathan. *The Electrification of Russia, 1880-1926*. Ithaca: Cornell University Press, 1992.

Coudenhove-Kalergi, R.N. *Paneuropa*. Vienna: Editions Paneuropéennes, 1928.

———. *Paneuropa ABC*. Vienna: Paneuropa-Verlag, 1931.

Coutard, Olivier, ed. *The governance of large technical systems*. London: Routledge, 1999.

———. "Imaginaire et developpement des reseaux techniques. Les apport de l'histoire de l'électrification rurale en France et aux Etats-Unis." *Réseaux* 5, no. 109 (2001): 76-94.

de Grazia, Victoria. *Irresistible Empire: America's Advance through 20th-Century Europe*. Cambridge: Belknap Harvard, 2005.

Delaisi, Francis. *Les deux Europes*. Paris: Payot, 1929.

———. *Political Myths and Economic Realities*. London: N. Douglas, 1927.

Delanty, Gerard. *Inventing Europe: Idea, Identity, Reality*. New York: St. Martin's Press, 1995.

Deschamps, Etienne. "L'Européen (1929-1940): A Cultural Review at the Heart of the Debate on European Identity." *European Review of History - Revue européenne d'histoire* 9, no. 1 (2002): 85-95.

Devinat, Paul. *L'Organisation scientifique du travail en Europe*. Geneva: Bureau International du Travail, 1927.

du Réau, Elisabeth. *L'Idée d'Europe au XXe siècle: Des mythes aux réalités*. Brussels: Editions Complexe, 1996.

Dubin, Martin David. "Transgovernmental Process in the League of Nations." *International Organization* 37, no. 3 (1983): 469-493.

Dumoulin, Michel, and Yves Stelandre. *L'Idée européenne dans l'entre-deux-guerres*. Louvain-la-Neuve: Academia Bruylant, 1992.

Dumoulin, Michel. "La reflexion sur les espaces regionaux en Europe à la aube des annees trente." In *Organisations internationales et architectures européennes 1929-1939. Actes du colloque de Metz 31 mai - 1er juin 2001. En hommage à Raymond Poidevin*, edited by Sylvian Schirman, 17-33. Metz: Centre de Recherche Histoire et Civilisation de l'Université de Metz, 2003.

Ebasco Services Incorporated. *Electric Power Program, Kingdom of Greece*. New York: Economic Cooperation Administration, 1950.

Eichengreen, Barry. *Golden Fetters: The Golden Standard and the Great Depression, 1919-1939*. London: Oxford University Press, 1992.

Ellwood, David W. *Rebuilding Europe: Western Europe, America and Postwar Reconstruction*. London: Longman, 1992.

Esposito, Chiarella. *America's Feeble Weapon: Funding the Marshall Plan in France and Italy, 1948-1950*. Westport: Greenwood Press, 1994.

Evangelista, Matthew. *Unarmed Forces: The Transnational Movement to End the Cold War*. Ithaca: Cornell University Press, 1999.

Faddeev, N.W. *Der Rat für Gegenseitige Wirtschaftshilfe*. Berlin: Staatsverlag der Deutschen Demokratischen Republik, 1965.

Fagen, Melvin M. "Gunnar Myrdal and the Shaping of the United Nations' Economic Commission for Europe." *Coexistence* 27 (1988): 427-435.

Fells, Ian. *World Energy 1923-1998 and Beyond: A Commemoration of the World Energy Council on its 75th Anniversary*. London: Atalink Projects / World Energy Council , 1998.

Fine, Martin. "Albert Thomas: A Reformer's Vision of Modernization, 1914-'32." *Journal of Contemporary History* 12, no. 3 (1977): 545-564.

Fleury, Antoine. "Avant-propos." In *Le Plan Briand d'Union fédérale européenne: Perspectives nationales et transnationales, avec documents*, edited by Antoine Fleury and Lubor Jílek, IX-XVI. Bern: Peter Lang, 1998.

———. "La Suisse et Radio Nations." In *The League of Nations in Retrospect: Proceedings of the Symposium*, 196-220. Berlin: Walter de Gruyter, 1983.

———. "Une évaluation des travaux de la Commission d'Étude pour l'Union Européenne 1930-1937." In *Organisations internationales et architectures européennes 1929-1939. Actes du colloque de Metz 31 mai - 1er juin 2001. En hommage à Raymond Poidevin*, edited by Sylvian Schirmann, 35-53. Metz: Centre de Recherche Histoire et Civilisation de l'Université de Metz, 2003.

Forland, Tor Egil. "'Economic Warfare' and 'Strategic Goods': A Conceptual Framework for Analyzing COCOM." *Journal of Peace Research* 28, no. 2 (1991): 191-204.

Freedman, Robert Owen. *Economic Warfare in the Communist Bloc: A Study of Soviet Economic Pressure against Yugoslavia, Albania, and Communist China*. New York: Praeger, 1970.

Fridlund, Mats, and Helmut Maier. "The Second Battle of the Currents." Working paper, Department of History of Science and Technology, Royal Institute of Technology, 1996.

Gaddis, John Lewis. *We Now Know: Rethinking Cold War History*. Oxford: Clarendon Press, 1997.

Gall, Alexander. "Atlantropa: A Technological Vision of a United Europe." In *Networking Europe. Transnational Infrastructures and the Shaping of Europe, 1850-2000*, edited by Erik van der Vleuten and Arne Kaijser, 99-128. Sagamore Beach: Science History Publications, 2006.

———. *Das Atlantropa-Projekt: Die Geschichte einer gescheiterten Vision. Herman Sörgel und die Absenkung des Mittelmeers*. Frankfurt: Campus Verlag, 1998.

Garton Ash, Timothy. *In Europe's Name: Germany and the Divided Continent*. New York: Random House, 1993.

Gehler, Michael, and Wolfram Kaiser. "Transnationalism and Early European Integration: The Nouvelles Equipes Internationales and the Geneva Circles, 1947-1957." *The Historical Journal* 44, no. 3 (2001): 773-798.

Gellner, Ernest. *Nations and Nationalism*. Ithaca: Cornell University Press, 1983.

Gerbet, Pierre, Marie-Renée Mouton, and Victor-Yves Ghébali. *Le rêve d'un ordre mondiale de la SDN à l'ONU*. Paris: Imprimerie Nationale, 1986.

Gerbet, Pierre. *La construction de L'Europe*. Paris: Imprimerie nationale, 1983.

Giannetti, Renato. "Resources, Firms and Public Policy in the Growth of Italian Electrical Industry from Beginnings to the 30's." In *1880-1980. Un siècle d'électricité dans le monde: Actes du Premier colloque international d'histoire de l'électricité*, edited by Fabienne Cardot, 41-50. Paris: Presses Universitaires de France, 1987.

Gibianskii, Leon. "The Soviet Bloc and the Initial Stage of the Cold War: Archival Documents on Stalin's Meetings with Communists Leaders of Yugoslavia and Bulgaria, 1946-1948." *Cold War International History Project Bulletin* March, no. 10 (1998): 114-115.

Girerd, Pascal. *Trente ans d'expérience Euratom. La naissance d'une Europe nucléaire.* Edited by Olivier Pirotte, Pierre Marsal, and Sylvaine Morson. Bruylant, 1988.

Greaves, H.R.G. *The League Committees and World Order: A Study of the Permanent Expert Committees of the League of Nations as an Instrument of International Government.* London: Oxford University Press, 1931.

Grzybowski, Kazimierz. "The Council for Mutual Economic Assistance and the European Community." *The American Journal of International Law* 84, no. 1 (1990): 284-292.

Guérin, Denis. *Albert Thomas au BIT, 1920-1932: De l'internationalisme à L'Europe.* Geneva: Institut européen de l'Université de Genève, 1996.

Gugerli, David. *Redeströme: Zur Elektrifizierung der Schweiz, 1880-1914.* Zurich: Chronos Verlag, 1996.

Guieu, Jean-Michel. "Le Comité fédérale de Coopération européenne: L'Action méconnue d'une organisation internationale privée en faveur de l'union de l'Europe dans les années trente (1928-1940)." In *Organisations internationales et architectures européennes 1929-1939. Actes du colloque de Metz 31 mai - 1er juin 2001. En hommage à Raymond Poidevin*, edited by Sylvian Schirmann, 73-91. Metz: Centre de Recherche Histoire et Civilisation de l'Université de Metz, 2003.

Haas, Peter M. "Introduction: Epistemic Communities and International Policy Coordination." *International Organization* 46, no. 1 (1992): 1-35.

Haftendorn, Helga. "The Adaptation of the NATO Alliance to a Period of Détente: The 1967 Harmel Report." In *Crises and Compromises: The European Project 1963-1969*, edited by Wilfried Loth, 285-322. Baden-Baden: Nomos Verlag, 2001.

Haines, Gerald K., and Robert E. Leggett, eds. *CIA's Analysis of the Soviet Union 1947-1991.* Washington, D.C.: Center for the Study of Intelligence - CIA, 2001.

Hallon, Ľudovít. "Systematic Electrification in Germany and in Four Central Europe States in the Interwar period." *ICON* 7 (2001): 135-147.

Hammons, T.J., Y. Kucherov, L. Kapolyi, Z. Bicki, M. Klawe, S. Goethe, et al. "European Policy on Electricity Infrastructure, Interconnections, and Electricity Exchanges." *IEEE Power Engineering Review* 18, no. 1 (1998): 8-21.

Hassan, John A., and Alan Duncan. "Integrating Energy: The Problems of Developing an Energy Policy in the European Communities, 1945-1980." *Journal of European Economic History* 22, no. 1 (1994): 159-176.

Hausman, William J., Mira Wilkins, and John L. Neufeld. "Multinational Enterprise and International Finance in the History of Light and Power, 1880s-1914." *Revue économique* 58, no. 1 (2007): 175-190.

Hausman, William, Mira Wilkins, and Peter Hertner. *Global Electrification: Multinational Enterprise and International Finance in the History of Light and Power.* Cambridge: Cambridge University Press, 2008.

Hay, Denys. *Europe: The Emergence of an Idea.* New York: Harper & Row, 1966.

Hecht, Gabrielle. "Technology, Politics and National Identity in France." In *Technologies of Power: Essays in Honor of Thomas Parke Hughes and Agatha Chipley Hughes*, edited by Gabrielle Hecht and Michael Thad Allen, 253-294. Cambridge/London: MIT Press, 2001.

——. *The Radiance of France: Nuclear Power and National Identity after World War II.* Cambridge: MIT Press, 1998.

Heineman, Dannie. "Das Wirtschaftliche Gleichgewicht Europas." *Paneuropa* 6, no. 2 (1930): 48-56.

——. "Préface." In *Les deux Europe*, edited by Francis Delaisi, 7-20. Paris: Payot, 1929.

——. *Outline of a New Europe.* Brussels: Vromant, 1930.

Heller, Agnes. "Europe: An Epilogue?." In *The idea of Europe. Problems of National and Transnational Identity*, edited by Brian Nelson, David Roberts, and Walter Veit, 12-25. Providence: Berg, 1992.

Henderson, W.O. "Walther Rathenau: A Pioneer of the Planned Economy." *Economic History Review* 4, no. 1 (1951): 98-108.

Hertner, Peter. "Financial Strategies and Adaptation to Foreign Markets: the German Electro-Technical Industry and its Multinational Activities: 1890s to 1939." In *Multinational Enterprise in Historical Perspective*, edited by Alice Teichova, Maurice Lévy-Leboyer, and Helga Nussbaum. Cambridge: Cambridge University Press, 1986.

Hertner, Peter. "Les sociétés financières suisses et le développement de l'industrie électrique jusqu'à la première guerre mondiale." In *1880-1980. Un siècle d'électricité dans le monde: Actes du Premier colloque international d'histoire de l'électricité*, edited by Fabienne Cardot, 341-356. Paris: Presses Universitaires de France, 1987.

Hirsch, Helmut, and Helga Nowotny. "Information and Opposition in Austrian Nuclear Energy Policy." *Minerva* 15, no. 3-4 (1977): 316-334.

Hoffman, George W. "The Survival of an Independent Austria." *Geographical Review* 41, no. 4 (1951): 606-621.

Hogan, Michael J. "American Marshall Planners and the Search for a European Neocapitalism." *The American Historical Review* 90, no. 1 (1985): 44-72.

——. *The Marshall Plan: America, Britain, and the Reconstruction of Western Europe, 1947-1952.* Cambridge: Cambridge University Press, 1987.

Hughes, Thomas P. "The Evolution of Large Technical Systems." In *The Social Construction of Technological Systems*, edited by Wiebe E. Bijker, Thomas P. Hughes, and T.J. Pinch. Cambridge: MIT Press, 1987.

——. "Visions of Electrification and Social Change." In *1880-1980. Un siècle d'électricité dans le monde: Actes du Premier colloque international d'histoire de l'électricité*, edited by Fabienne Cardot, 327-340. Histoire de l'électricité. Paris: Presses Universitaires de France, 1987.

——. *American Genesis: A Century of Invention and Technological Enthusiasm, 1870-1970.* London: Viking, 1989.

——. *Networks of Power: Electrification in Western Society, 1880-1930.* Johns Hopkins University Press, 1983.

——. *Rescuing Prometheus: Four Monumental Projects that Changed the Modern World.* New York: Pantheon Books, 1998.

Hutter, Clemens M. "Kriege, Krisen und kein Groschen Startkapital." In *Energie für unser Leben, 1947 bis 1997. 50 Jahre Verbund*, 61-84. Vienna: Österreichische Elektrizitätswirtschafts-Aktiengesellschaft, 1997.

IEA. *Learning from the Blackouts: Transmission System Security in Competitive Electricity Markets.* Paris: IEA/OECD, 2005.

——. *Lessons from Liberalised Electricity Markets.* Paris: IEA/OECD, 2005.

International Labor Office. *The Social Aspects of Rationalisation: Introductory Studies.* Geneva: P.S. King, 1931.

Iriye, Akira. *Global Community: The Role of International Organizations in the Making of the Contemporary World.* Berkeley: University of California Press, 2002.

Ismay, Lord. *NATO. The First Five years, 1949-1954.* Paris: NATO, 1954.

Jentleson, Bruce W. *Pipeline Politics: The Complex Political Economy of East-West Energy Trade.* Ithaca: Cornell University Press, 1986.

Johnson, Edward. "Early Indications of a Freeze: Greece, Spain and the United Nations, 1946-47." *Cold War History* 6, no. 1 (2006): 43-61.

Johnson, Robert H. "International Politics and the Structure of International Organization:

The Case of UNRRA." *World Politics* 3, no. 4 (2006): 520-538.

Kaijser, Arne. "Controlling the Grids: The Development of High-Tension Power Lines in the Nordic Countries." In *Nordic Energy Systems: Historical Perspectives and Current Issues*, edited by Arne Kaijser and Marika Hedin, 31-54. Chicago: Science History Publications, 1995.

———. "Nature's Periphery: Rural Transformation by the Advent of Infrasystems." In *Taking Place: The Spatial Contexts of Science, Technology and Business*, 151-186. Sagamore Beach: Science History Publications, 2006.

———. "Trans-Border Integration of Electricity and Gas in the Nordic Countries, 1915-1992." *Polhem* 15 (1997): 4-43.

Kaser, Michael. *COMECON: Integrated Problems of the Planned Economies*. London: Oxford University Press, 1965.

Kindleberger, Charles P. *The World in Depression, 1929-1939*. London: Allen Lane, 1973.

Kline, Ronald R. *Consumers in the Country. Technology and Social Change in Rural America*. Baltimore: The Johns Hopkins University Press, 2000.

Kostelecký, Václav. *The United Nations Economic Commission for Europe: The Beginning of a History*. Stockholm: Arbetarrörelsens arkiv och bibliotek, 1989.

Kreisky, Bruno. "On Promoting Detente." *International Affairs* 54, no. 4 (1978): 618-625.

Krüger, Peter. "European ideology and European Reality: European Unity and German Foreign Policy in the 1920s." In *European Unity in Context: The Interwar Period*, edited by Peter M.R. Stirk, 84-98. London: Pinter, 1989.

Kupper, Patrick, and Tobias Wildi. *Motor-Columbus: From 1895 to 2006. 111 Years of Motor-Columbus*. Baden: Motor-Columbus, 2006.

Kurgan van Hentenryk, Ginette. "La patronat de l'électricité en Belgique, 1895-1945." In *Stratégies,gestion,management: les compagnies électriques et leurs patrons,1895-1945: Actes du 12e colloque de l'Association pour l'histoire de l'électricié en France les 3,4 et 5 février 1999*, 55-69. Paris: Fondation Electricité de France, 2001.

———. "Le régime économique de l'industrie électrique belge depuis la fin du XIXe siècle." In *1880-1980. Un siècle d'électricité dans le monde: Actes du Premier colloque international d'histoire de l'électricité*, edited by Fabienne Cardot, 119-134. Paris: Presses Universitaires de France, 1987.

Lanthier, Pierre. "Logique électrique et logique électrotechnique: la cohabitation des électriciens et des électrotechniciens dans la direction des constructions électriques français: une comparaison internationale." In *Stratégies, gestion, management: les compagnies électriques et leurs patrons, 1895-1945: Actes du 12e colloque de l'Association pour l'histoire de l'électricité en France les 3, 4 et 5 février 1999*, edited by Dominique Barjot, Henri Morsel, Sophie Coeuré, and Coraline Clément, 35-53. Paris: Fondation Electricité de France, 2001.

Laughland, John. *The Tainted Source: The Undemocratic Origins of the European Idea*. London: Little, Brown and Company, 1997.

Le Marec, Pierre. "L'Organisation des Communications et du Transit." PhD diss., Université de Rennes, 1938.

Lees, Lorraine M. *Keeping Tito Afloat: The United States, Yugoslavia, and the Cold War*. University Park: Pennsylvania State University Press, 1997.

Legge, Joseph. *Grundsätzliches und Tatsächliches zu den Elektrizitätswirtschaften in Europa*. Dortmund: Gebrüder Lensing, 1931.

Lewis, Paul G. *Central Europe since 1945*. London: Longman, 1994.

Lipgens, Walter. *Documents in the History of European Integration*. Vol. 1. *Continental Plans for European Union, 1939-1945*. Berlin: Walter de Gruyter, 1985.

Lipson, Michael. "The Reincarnation of COCOM: Explaining Post-Cold War Export Controls." *The Nonproliferation Review* Winter (1999): 33-51.

Loucheur, Louis, and Jacques de Launay. *Carnets secrets, 1908-1932*. Brussels: Éditions Brepols, 1962.

Lucas, N.J.D. *Energy and the European Communities*. London: Europa Publications, 1977.

Lundestad, Geir. "Empire by Invitation? The United States and Western Europe, 1945-1952." *Journal of peace research* 23, no. 3 (1986): 263-277.

Lundgreen, Peter. "Engineering Education in Europe and the USA, 1750-1930: The Rise to Dominance of School Culture and the Engineering Professions." *Annals of Science* 47, no. 1 (1990): 33-75.

Lyons, Paul K. *75 Years of Cooperation in the Electricity Industry*. Brussels: Union of the Electricity Industry/EURELECTRIC, 2000.

Maier, Charles S. "Alliance and Autonomy: European Identity and U.S. Foreign Policy Objectives in the Truman Years." In *The Truman Presidency*, edited by Michael J. Lacey, 273-298. Cambridge: Cambridge University Press, 1989.

———. "The Two Postwar Eras and the Conditions for Stability in Twentieth-Century Western Europe." *The American Historical Review* 86, no. 2 (1981): 327-352.

———. *In Search of Stability: Explorations in Historical Political Economy*. Cambridge: Cambridge University Press, 1987.

———. *Recasting Bourgeois Europe: Stabilization in France, Germany, and Italy in the Decade after World War I*. Princeton: Princeton University Press, 1988.

Maier, Helmut. "'Lauchhammer', 'Döbern' und 'Ragow': Imaginäre und reale Verknotungen der Niederlausitzer Landschaft in die Elektrizitätswirtschaft des 20. Jahrhunderts." In *Die Niederlausitz vom 18. Jahrhundert bis heute: Eine gestörte Kulturlandschaft?, Band 19 der Cottbuser studien zur Geschichte von Technik, Arbeit und Umwelt*, edited by Günter Bayerl and Dirk Maier, 149-195. Münster: Waxmann, 2002.

———. "'Nationalwirtschaftlicher Musterknabe' ohne Fortune. Entwicklungen der Elektrizitätspolitik un des RWE im 'Dritten Reich'." In *Elektrizitswirtschaft zwischen Umwelt, Technik und Politik. Aspekte aus 100 Jahren RWE-Geschichte, 1898-1998*, edited by Helmut Maier, 129-194. Freiberg: TUB, 1998.

———. "Systems Connected: IG Auschwitz, Kaprun, and the Building of European Power Grids up to 1945." In *Networking Europe: Transnational Infrastructures and the Shaping of Europe, 1850-2000*, 129-158. Sagamore Beach: Science History Publications, 2006.

———. *Erwin Marx (1893-1980), Ingenieurwissenschaftler in Braunschweig, und die Forschung und Entwicklung auf dem Gebiet der elektrischen Energieübertragung auf weite Entfernungen zwischen 1918 und 1950*. Verlag für Geschichte der Naturwissenschaften und der Technik, 1993.

af Malmborg, Mikael. "Swedish Neutrality, the Finland Argument and the Enlargement of "Little Europe"." *Journal of European Integration History* 1 (1997): 63-80.

Mance, Sir Osborne. *International Road Transport, Postal, Electricity and Miscellaneous Questions*. London: Oxford University Press, 1946.

Mastanduno, Michael. "Strategies of Economic Containment: U.S. Trade Relations with the Soviet Union." *World Politics* 37, no. 4 (1985): 503-531.

———. "The Management of Alliance Export Control Policy: American Leadership and the Politics of COCOM." In *Controlling East-West Trade and Technology Transfer: Power, Politics, and Policies*, edited by Gary K. Bertsch, 241-279. Duram: Duke University Press, 1988.

Matlary, Janne Haaland. *Energy Policy in the European Union*. London: Palgrave Macmillan, 1997.

Matos, Ana Cardoso de, Fátimal Mendes, Fernando Faria, and Luís Cruz. *A Electricidade em Portugal: Dos primórdios à 2a Guerra Mundial*. Lisbon: Museu de Electricidade, 2004.

Mattelart, Armand. *The Invention of Communication*. Minneapolis: University of Minnesota Press, 1996.

Mayntz, Renate, and Thomas P. Hughes, eds. *The Development of Large Technological Systems.* Frankfurt am Mainz: Campus Verlag, 1988.

McGlade, Jacqueline. "COCOM and the Containment of Western Trade and Relations." In *East-West Trade and the Cold War*, edited by Jari Eloranta and Jari Ojala, 47-63. Jyväskylä: University of Jyväskylä, 2005.

Millward, Robert. *Private and Public Enterprise in Europe: Energy, Telecommunications and Transport, 1830-1990.* Cambridge: Cambridge University Press, 2005.

Milward, Alan S. *The Reconstruction of Western Europe, 1945-'51.* Berkeley: University of California Press, 1984.

——. *War, Economy and Society: 1939-1945.* Berkeley: University of California Press, 1977.

Misa, Thomas J., and Johan Schot. "Inventing Europe: Technology and the Hidden Integration of Europe: Introduction." *History and Technology* 21, no. 1 (2005): 1-22.

Mitchell, B.R. *European Historical Statistics, 1750-1920.* New York: Columbia University Press, 1975.

Morgan, Philip. "The First World War and the Challenge to Democracy in Europe." In *Ideas of Europe since 1914: The Legacy of the First World War*, 69-88. New York: Palgrave, 2002.

Morsel, Henri. "Industrie électrique et défense, en France, lors des deux conflits mondiaux." *Bulletin d'histoire de l'électricité* 23 (1994): 7-18.

——. "Panorama de l'histoire de l'électricité en France dans la première moitié du XXe siècle." In *1880-1980. Un siècle d'électricité dans le monde: Actes du Premier colloque international d'histoire de l'électricité*, edited by Fabienne Cardot, 85-118. Paris: Presses Universitaires de France, 1987.

Myllyntaus, Timo. *Electrifying Finland : The Transfer of a New Technology into a Late Industrialising Economy.* London: ETLA, 1991.

Myrdal, Gunnar. "The Research Work of the Secretariat of the Economic Commission for Europe." In *25 Economic Essays in Honour of Erik Lindahl*, edited by Erik Lindahl, 267-293. Stockholm: Ekonomisk tidskrift, 1956.

——. "Twenty Years of the United Nations Economic Commission for Europe." *International organization* 22, no. 3 (1968): 617-628.

Nachmani, Amikam. "Civil War and Foreign Intervention in Greece: 1946-49." *Journal of Contemporary History* 25, no. 4 (1990): 489-522.

Nadau, T. "L'Électrification rurale." In *Histoire générale de l'électricité en France,* edited by Maurice Lévy-Leboyer and Henri Morsel, vol. 2, *l'Interconnexion et le marché, 1919-1946*, 1199-1232.. Paris: Fayard, 1994.

Nederveen Pieterse, Jan. "Fictions of Europe." *Race and Class* 32, no. 3 (1991): 3-10.

Nelson, Brian, David Roberts, and Walter Veit, eds. *The Idea of Europe: Problems of National and Transnational Identity.* Providence: Berg, 1992.

Nye, David E. *Electrifying America: Social Meanings of a New Technology, 1880-1940.* Cambridge: MIT Press, 1990.

Olesen, Thorsten B. "Choosing or Refuting Europe? The Nordic Countries and European Integration, 1945-2000." *Scandinavian Journal of History* 25 (2000): 147-168.

Oliven, Oskar. "Europas Großkraftlinien. Vorschlag eines europäischen Höchtspannungsnetzes." *Zeitschrift des Vereines Deutscher Ingenieure* 74, no. 25 (June 21, 1930): 875-879.

Padgett, Stephen. "Between Synthesis and Emulation: EU Policy Transfer in the Power Sector." *Journal of European Public Policy* 10, no. 2 (2003): 227-245.

——. "The Single European Energy Market: The Politics of Realization." *Journal of Common Market Studies* 30, no. 1 (1992): 53-75.

Pagden, Anthony, ed. *The Idea of Europe: From Antiquity to the European Union.* Cambridge University Press, 2001.

de Palacio, Loyola. "Challenges Towards a Unified European Energy Market" presented at the Roundtable on Energy, Nyenrode, The Netherlands, November 13, 2003.

Parrish, Scott D., and Mikhail M. Narinsky. "New Evidence on the Soviet Rejection of the Marshall Plan, 1947: Two Reports". Cold War International History Project working paper. Washington, D.C.: Woodrow Wilson International Center for Scholars, 1994.

Pasture, Michèle. "Francis Delaisi et l'Europe, 1925-1929-1931 (extraits)." In *L'Idée européenne dans l'entre-deux-guerres*, edited by Michel Dumoulin and Michel Stelandre, 43-49. Louvain-la-Neuve: Academia, 1992.

Pasture, Patrick. "The Interwar Origins of International Labour's European Commitment (1919-1934)." *Contemporary European History* 10, no. 2 (2001): 211-237.

Patel, Kiran Klaus. "Überlegungen zu einer transnationalen Geschichte." *Zeitschrift für Geschichtswissenschaft* 52, no. 7 (2004): 626-645.

Pegg, Carl H. *Evolution of the European Idea, 1914-1932*. Chapel Hill/London: University of North Carolina Press, 1983.

Pemberton, Jo-Anne. "New Worlds for Old: the League of Nations in the Age of Electricity." *Review of International Studies* 28 (2002): 311-336.

———. "Towards a New World Order: A Twentieth Century Story." *Review of International Studies* 27 (2001): 265-272.

Persoz, Henri, and Jean Remondeulaz. "Consolidating European Power." *IEEE Spectrum* 29, no. 10 (1992): 62-65.

———. "40 ans d'interconnexion internationale en Europe. Le rôle de l'UNIPEDE." In *Electricité et électrification dans le monde. Actes du deuxième colloque international d'histoire de l'électricité*, edited by Monique Trede, 293-303. Paris: Association pour l'histoire de l'électricité en France, 1992.

———. "Les grands réseaux modernes." In *Histoire générale de l'électricité en France*, edited by Henri Morsel, 3. *Une oeuvre nationale: L'Équipement, la croissance de la demande, le nucléaire (1946-1987)*, 556-576. Paris: Fayard, 1996.

Potter, Pitman B. "Note on the Distinction between Political and Technical Questions." *Political Science Quarterly* 50, no. 2 (June 1935): 264-271.

Pradier, Veronique. "L'Europe de Louis Loucheur: Le projet d'un homme d'affaires en politique." *Études et documents* V (1993): 293-306.

Prodi, Romano, and Alberto Clô. "Europe." *Daedalus* 104, no. 4 (1975): 91-114.

Radkau, Joachim. "Zum ewiger Wachstum verdammt? Jugend und Alter grosstechnischer Systeme." In *Technik ohne Grenzen*, edited by Ingo Braun and Bernward Joerges, 50-106. Frankfurt am Mainz: Surhkamp, 1994.

Ranieri, Liane. *Dannie Heineman, patron de la SOFINA: Un destin singulier, 1872-1962*. Brussels: Éditions Racine, 2005.

Rathkolb, Oliver, and Florian Freund, eds. *NS-Zwangsarbeit in der Elektrizitätswirtschaft der 'Ostmark' 1938-1945: Ennskraftwerke - Kaprun - Draukraftwerke - Ybbs-Persenbeug - Ernsthofen*. Vienna: Böhlau Verlag, 2002.

Rostow, W.W. *The Division of Europe after World War II: 1946*. Austin: University of Texas Press, 1981.

Rueckert, Steven L. "Transferring Electrical Power Between Utilities: Economics and Reliability Tie Energy Suppliers Together." *IEEE Potentials* 7, no. 4 (1988): 13-14.

Ruppert, L. *History of the International Electrotechnical Commission - L'histoire de la Commission Electrotechnique Internationale*. Geneva: Bureau Central de la Commission Electrotechnique Internationale, 1956.

Salter, J.A. *Allied Shipping Control: An Experiment in International Administration*. London: Clarendon Press, 1921.

Salvemini, Gaetano. "Economic Conditions in Italy, 1919-1922." *Journal of Modern History* 23, no. 1 (1951): 29-37.

Saminaden, Vivian. *Histoire du développement des réseaux interconnectés d'Europe*. Paris: Electricité de France, 1994.

Saunier, Pierre-Yves. "Learning by Doing: Notes about the Making of the 'Palgrave Dictionary of Transnational History'." *Journal of Modern European History* 6, no. 2 (2008): 159-179.

Schaper, B.W. "Albert Thomas: Dertig jaar sociaal reformisme." PhD diss., Leiden University, 1953.

Schipper, Frank, Vincent Lagendijk, and Irene Anastasiadou. "New Connections for an Old Continent: Rail, Road and Electricity in the League of Nations' Organisation for Communications and Transit." In *Europe Materializing? Transnational Infrastructures and the Project of Europe*, edited by Alexander Badenoch and Andreas Fickers. London: Palgrave (forthcoming).

Schipper, Frank. *Driving Europe: Building Europe on Roads in the Twentieth Century*. Amsterdam: Aksant, 2008.

Schirmann, Sylvian. "Introduction." In *Organisations internationales et architectures européennes 1929-1939. Actes du colloque de Metz 31 mai - 1er juin 2001. En hommage à Raymond Poidevin*, edited by Sylvian Schirmann. Metz: Centre de Recherche Histoire et Civilisation de l'Université de Metz , 2003.

Schivelbusch, Wolfgang. *Disenchanted Night: The Industrialization of Light in the Nineteenth Century*. Berkeley: University of California Press, 1995.

Schmidt, Susanne K. *Liberalisierung in Europa. Die Rolle der Europäischen Kommission*. Frankfurt: Campus Verlag, 1998.

Schönholzer, Ernst. "Ein elektrowirtschaftliches Programm für Europa." *Schweizerische Technische Zeitschrift* 23 (1930): 385-397.

Schot, J.W., H.W. Lintsen, and A. Rip, eds. *Techniek in Nederland in de Twintigste Eeuw*. Vol. 2. *Delfstoffen, Energie, Chemie*, Stichting Historie der Techniek, 2000.

Schot, Johan, and Vincent Lagendijk. "Technocratic Internationalism in the Interwar Years: Building Europe on Motorways and Electricity Networks." *Journal of Modern European History* 6, no. 2 (2008): 196-217.

Schot, Johan. "Transnational Infrastructures and European Integration." In *Europe Materializing? Transnational Infrastructures and the Project of Europe*, edited by Alexander Badenoch and Andreas Fickers. London: Palgrave, forthcoming.

———. "Transnational Infrastructures and the Rise of Contemporary Europe: Project proposal." Transnational Infrastructures of Europe Working Documents Series, no.1. Eindhoven: Eindhoven University of Technology, http://www.tie-project.nl/publications/pdf/Proposal.pdf.

Schröter, Harm. "A Typical Factor of German International Market Strategy: Agreements between the U.S. and German Electrotechnical Industries up to 1939." In *Multinational Enterprise in Historical Perspective*, edited by Alice Teichova, Maurice Lévy-Leboyer, and Helga Nussbaum, 160-170. New York: Cambridge University Press, 1986.

Schultz, Hans-Dietrich, and Wolfgang Natter. "Imagining Mitteleuropa: Conceptualisations of 'its' Space in and Outside German Geography." *European Review of History - Revue européenne d'histoire* 10, no. 2 (2003): 273-292.

Scott, James C. *Seeing Like a State: How Certain Schemes to Improve the Human Condition Have Failed*. New Haven: Yale University Press, 1998.

Segreto, Luciano. "Financing the Electric Industry Worldwide: Strategy and Structure of the Swiss Electric Holding Companies, 1895-1945." *Business and Economic History* 23, no. 1 (1994): 162-175.

———. "Stratégie et structure des sociétés financières suisses pour l'industrie électrique (1895-1945)." In *Allmächtige Zauberin unserer Zeit. Zur Geschichte der elektrischen Energie in der Schweiz*, edited by David Gugerli, 57-72. Zurich: Chronos Verlag, 1994.

——. "Stratégies militaires et intérêts économique dans l'industrie électrique italienne: Protection ou interconnexion des installations électriques, 1915-1945." *Bulletin d'histoire de l'électricité* 23 (1994): 63-82.

Seyeux, Claire. "Gestion du personnel: La réponse de Loire et Centre 1912-1932." In *Stratégies, gestion, management: les compagnies électriques et leurs patrons, 1895-1945: Actes du 12e colloque de l'Association pour l'histoire de l'électricié en France les 3, 4 et 5 février 1999*, edited by Dominique Barjot, Henri Morsel, Sophie Coeuré, and Coraline Clément, 377-392. Paris: Fondation Electricité de France, 2001.

Shore, Cris, and Annabel Black. "The European Communities and the Construction of Europe." *Anthropology Today* 8, no. 3 (1992): 10-11.

Sick, Klaus-Peter. "A Europe of Pluralist Internationalism: The Development of the French Theory of Interdependence from Emile Durkheim to the Circle Around Notre Temps (1890-1930)." *Journal of European Integration History* 8, no. 2 (2002): 45-68.

Siegel, G. *Die Elektrizitätsgesetzgebung der Kulturländer der Erde: Westeuropa.* Vol. 2. Berlin: VDI - Verlag, 1930.

——. *Die Elektrizitätsgesetzgebung der Kulturländer de Erde Deutschland.* Vol. 1. VDI - Verlag, 1930.

Smith, Anthony D. "National Identity and the Idea of European Unity." *International Affairs* 68, no. 1 (1992): 55-76.

Smuts, J.C. *The League of Nations: A Practical Suggestion.* London: Hodder and Stoughton, 1918.

Sörgel, Herman. *Atlantropa.* München: Piloty & Loehle , 1932.

Spiering, Menno, and Michael Wintle, eds. *Ideas of Europe since 1914: The Legacy of the First World War.* New York: Palgrave, 2002.

Stier, Bernhard. "Expansion, réforme de structure et interconnexion européenne: Développement et difficultés de l'électricité sous le nazisme, 1939-1945." In *Les entreprises du secteur de l'énergie sous l'Occupation*, edited by Denis Varashin, 269-290. Arras: Artois Presses Université, 2006.

——. *Staat und Strom. Die politische Steuerung des Elektrizitätssystems in Deutschland 1890-1950.* Mannheim: Verlag Regionalkultur, 1999.

Stivers, William. "The Incomplete Blockade: Soviet Zone Supply of West Berlin, 1948-49." *Diplomatic History* 21, no. 4 (1997): 569-602.

Théry, Franck. *Construire L'Europe dans les années vingt: L'action de l'Union paneuropéenne sur la scène franco-allemande, 1924-1932.* Geneva: Institut européen de l'Université de Genève, 1998.

Thue, Lars. "Electricity Rules: The Formation and Development of the Nordic Electricity Regimes." In *Nordic Energy Systems: Historical Perspectives and Current Issues*, edited by Arne Kaijser and Marika Hedin, 11-30. Chicago: Science History Publications USA, 1995.

Trachtenberg, Marc. *A Constructed Peace: The Making of the European Settlement, 1945-1963.* Princeton: Princeton University Press, 1999.

Trédé, Monique, ed. *Electricité et électrification dans le monde: Actes du deuxième colloque international d'histoire de l'électricité, organisé par l'Association pour l'histoire de l'électricité en France, Paris, 3-6 juillet 1990.* Association pour l'histoire de l'électricité en France, 1992.

UN Library Geneva. *The League of Nations in Retrospect: Proceedings of the Symposium.* Berlin: Walter de Gruyter, 1983.

Urwin, Derek W. *The Community of Europe.* London: Longman, 1991.

Varaschin, Denis. "Etats et électricité en Europe occidentale. Habilitation à diriger des recherches." Habilitation, Université Pierre-Mendes-France: Grenoble III , 1997.

Verbong, G., E.van der Vleuten, and M.J.J. Scheepers. *Long-Term Electricity Supply Systems Dynamics: A Historical Analysis.* Eindhoven: SUSTELNET, 2002.

Verbong, G.P.J., A.N. Hesselmans, and J.L. Schippers. "Crisis, oorlog en wederopbouw." In *Techniek in Nederland in de Twintigste Eeuw*, edited by J.W. Schot, H.W. Lintsen, A. Rip, and A.A. Albert de la Bruhèze, vol 2. *Delfstoffen, energie, chemie*, 190-201. Zutphen: Stichting Historie der Techniek/Walberg, 2000.

Verbong, G.P.J., L.van Empelen, and A.N. Hesselmans. "De ontwikkeling van het Nederlandse koppelnet tijdens de Tweede Wereldoorlog." *NEHA-Jaarboek* 12 (1998): 277-309.

Viel, Georges. "Etude d'un reseau 400.000 volts." *Revue generale de l'electricité*, no. 28 (1930): 729-744.

Van der Vleuten, Erik, and Arne Kaijser. "Networking Europe." *History and Technology* 21, no. 1 (2005): 23-54.

———. "Prologue and introduction: Transnational Networks and the Shaping of Contemporary Europe." In *Networking Europe: Transnational Infrastructures and the Shaping of Europe, 1850-2000*, edited by Erik van der Vleuten and Arne Kaijser, 1-24. Sagamore Beach: Science History Publications, 2006.

Van der Vleuten, Erik, and Rob Raven. "Lock-In and Change: Distributed Generation in Denmark in a Long-Term Perspective." *Energy Policy* 34, no. 18 (2006): 3739-3748.

Van der Vleuten, Erik, Irene Anastasiadou, Vincent Lagendijk, and Frank Schipper. "Europe's System Builders: The Contested Shaping of Transnational Road, Electricity and Rail Networks." *Contemporary European History* 16, no. 3 (2007): 321-348.

Van der Vleuten, Erik. "Electrifying Denmark: A Symmetrical History of Central and Decentral Electricity Supply until 1970." PhD diss., University of Aarhus, 1998.

———. "Introduction: Networking Technology, Networking Society, Networking Nature." *History and Technology* 20, no. 5 (2004): 195-203.

———. "Towards a Transnational History of Technology. Meanings, Promises, Pitfalls." *Technology and Culture* 49, no. 4 (2008).

———. "Understanding Network Societies: Two Decades of Large Technical System Studies." In *Networking Europe: Transnational Infrastructures and the Shaping of Europe, 1850-2000*, edited by Erik van der Vleuten and Arne Kaijser, 279-314. Sagamore Beach: Science History Publications, 2006.

Wæver, Ole. "Europe Since 1945: Crisis to Renewal." In *The History of the Idea of Europe*, edited by Kevin Wilson and Jan van der Dussen, 151-214. London: Routledge, 1993.

———. "Nordic Nostalgia: Northern Europe after the Cold War." *International Affairs* 68, no. 1 (1992): 77-102.

Walk, Joseph. *Kurzbiographien zur Geschichte der Juden, 1918-1945*. Munich: Saur, 1988.

Wallace III, William, and Russel J. Christesen. *Ebasco Services Incorporated: The Saga of Electric Power: Meeting the Challenge of Change*. New York: The Newcomen Society of the United States, 1986.

Walter-Busch, Emil. "Albert Thomas and Scientific Management in War and Peace, 1914-1932." *Journal of Management History* 12, no. 2 (2006): 212-231.

Walters, F.P. *A History of the League of Nations*. London: Oxford University Press, 1952.

Weber, Eugen Joseph. *Peasants into Frenchmen: The Modernization of Rural France, 1870-1914*. Stanford: Stanford University Press, 1976.

White, Hayden. "The Discourse of Europe and the Search for a European Identity." In *Europe and the Other and Europe as the Other*, edited by Bo Stråth, 67-86. Brussels: Peter Lang, 2000.

Wightman, David. "East-West Cooperation and the United Nations Economic Commission for Europe." *International Organization* 11, no. 1 (1957): 1-12.

Wightman, David. *Economic Co-Operation in Europe: A Study of the United Nations Economic Commission for Europe*. London: Stevens, 1956.

Williams, Warren W. "The Road to the Austrian State Treaty." *Journal of Cold War Studies* 2, no. 2 (2000): 97-107.

Wilson, Kevin, and Jan van der Dussen. *The History of the Idea of Europe*. London: Routledge, 1995.

Winand, Pascaline. *Eisenhower, Kennedy, and the United States of Europe*. New York: St. Martin's Press, 1993.

Wintle, Michael. "Cultural Identity in Europe: Shared Experience." In *Culture and Identity in Europe: Perceptions of Divergence and Unity in Past and Presence*, edited by Michael Wintle, 9-32. Aldershot: Avebury, 1996.

Zaidi, S. Waqar H. "The Janus-Face of Techno-Nationalism: Barnes Wallis and the 'Strength of England.'" *Technology and Culture* 29, no. 1: 62-88.

Zubok, Vladislav, and Constantine Pleshakov. *Inside the Kremlin's Cold War: From Stalin to Khrushchev*. Cambridge: Harvard University Press, 1996.

Summary

This book sets out to uncover the origins of the idea of a European electricity network. It explores historically the roots of a transnational European system, showing how engineers came to think in terms of 'Europe' already in the 1920s, and how these ideas continued to influence network-building in later decades. This thinking not only corresponded to economic and technical attributes of the system, as first described by Thomas Hughes.[1] This thesis claims that a European system was also legitimised by ideological motives, as a complement to – but not always complying with – economic and technical efficiency.

Covering the period between 1918 and 2001 the book provides a detailed analysis of ideas on, and the building of, a European electricity system. By doing so, this thesis makes two original contributions. First, based on extensive archival research, it makes a substantial contribution to the much-neglected history of international collaboration in Europe. Prevailing histories of electricity infrastructures mainly focus on national developments. Second, drawing on a wide variety of historiographical insights, it places this history in the broader historical context of the twentieth century, paying ample attention to the influence of both hot and cold wars, and interwar developments. By combining the specific history of this international collaboration with a more general political and economic history of the twentieth century, Lagendijk explains why a European solution emerged. The thesis primarily focuses on Western European developments and explains how this network took its specific shape through the building of different regional powerpools among national systems. In addition, the thesis presents a contribution to the emerging field of transnational history by focusing on the work and activities of international organisations, without neglecting the power and influence of nation-states.

The book starts by revealing how an international community of electricity entrepreneurs and electrical engineers had existed since the turn of the century. Yet at the same time, national legislations came to limit the extent of international network development and operation. Whereas the first objections to these limita-

---

1 Thomas P. Hughes, *Networks of power: Electrification in Western society, 1880-1930* (Baltimore: Johns Hopkins University Press, 1983).

tions were general, they became intertwined with the European movement over the course of the 1920s. While engineers proposed bold schemes for European electricity networks, politicians pursued the study of such projects within international organisations. Arguments for a European network cited not only technical and economic reasons of rationality and efficiency, but had idealistic and ideological undercurrents as well. Such a network, it was argued, would contribute to economic and political stability, stimulate renewed international investments, lead to economic rejuvenation of underdeveloped countries in Eastern Europe, and create a strong physical interdependence between countries.

These efforts did not see a European network materialise, however. The idea of organising electricity supply on a European level nevertheless was inscribed into the minds of engineers and policy-makers, also after WWII. Stressing solidarity, both Western European network operators and American Marshall Planners agreed that European collaboration in the field of electricity was essential to make more electricity available for economic recovery and growth, and to make more efficient use of existing and new capacity. Cooperation was shaped by gradually emerging interconnections between national networks. This took place in a framework of close personal relationships between electrical engineers in charge of their respective national systems. Within several international organisations – both technical and political-economic – the very same group of network operators was influential.

The U.S.-led NATO alliance also saw interconnected systems as contributing to Western Europe's defence strength in the light of the Cold War. In order to prevent the antagonistic Soviet bloc from benefitting from Western development, the export of electrical equipment as well as network connections were prevented as much as possible. Still, this exclusion of Central and Eastern Europe was contested. Schemes proposing electricity transmission across the Iron Curtain enjoyed little success before détente in the 1960s. After that, however, the troubled expansion of networks and capacity in Western Europe supported a rapprochement to the East in the 1970s and 1980s. Political and economic turmoil after 1989 in Central and Eastern Europe accelerated this process, leading to an interconnected system encompassing most Western and Eastern European countries by 1995.

Printed and bound by CPI Group (UK) Ltd, Croydon, CR0 4YY

16/04/2025

14658438-0001